Natasha Walter was born in 1967. She was educated at Cambridge and Harvard, and has worked and written for *Vogue*, the *Guardian* and the *TLS*. She currently writes for the *Observer*. She has recently edited a book of essays on feminism called *On the Move* which are published by Virago. She lives in London.

the new feminism

natasha walter

Virago

VIRAGO

Published by Virago Press 1999
Reprinted in 2006

First published by Little, Brown 1998

A CIP catalogue record for this book is available from the British Library

ISBN-13: 978-0-86049-639-4
ISBN-10: 0-86049-639-3

Typeset by M Rules in Goudy
Printed and bound in Great Britain by
Clays Ltd, St Ives plc

Virago Press
An imprint of
Little, Brown Book Group
Brettenham House
Lancaster Place
London WC2E 7EN

A Member of the Hachette Livre Group of Companies

www.virago.co.uk

For Mark

contents

acknowledgements

Thank you first of all to my parents, Ruth Walter and Nicolas Walter, whose support and encouragement have always sustained me. Thank you to all those who shared their opinions, knowledge and experience with me, particularly – but not exclusively – Ann Bowtell, Jacqueline Brathwaite, Susannah Brunert, Geraldine Caulfield, Ruth Cohen, Donna Covey, Sheila Doherty and the other women at the Greater Easterhouse Women's Centre, Fiona Driscoll, Kate Edwards, Barbara Follett, Carol Giblin, Janine di Giovanni, Linda Grant, Harriet Gugenheim, Leonie Hilliard and her colleagues at Suma, Annie Hockaday, Rose Hunter, Sadakat Kadri, Amor Jones, Philippa Kaufmann, Adah Kay, Oona King, Samantha King, Darian Leader, Professor Sue Lees, Lisa Longstaff, Gaille McCann, Laura McCreadie, Lucy Malein, Emma Must, Gabrielle Osrin, Allison Pearson, Sylvie Pierce, Brenda Procter, Angela Rumbold, Louisa Saunders, Deborah Saunt, Clare Short,

Hannana Siddiqui, Mhairi Stewart, Rebecca Thomas, Alison Thorne, Sue Tibballs, Bernadette Vallely, Helen Wilkinson. Many of you spent many hours patiently responding to my queries.

I would also like to thank pupils at Camden School for Girls, Epping Forest College, and Mulberry School; and staff at the Association of Women Solicitors, Families Need Fathers, Family Service Units, the Fawcett Society, the GMB Union, Lucas Industries, MORI, MSF Union, Newcastle Riverside Community Project, the National Group on Homeworking, Northern Foods, NCH Action for Children, Opportunity 2000, the Royal College of Nursing, the Transport and General Workers Union, the TUC, Women Against Rape and Women's Aid Federation. Thank you too to the staff of the British, Fawcett, LSE and London Libraries, and to Lynne Stokoe at the Office for National Statistics.

I have been lucky to benefit from the support of two great agents, Anne McDermid and Felicity Rubinstein, and two great editors, Philippa Harrison and Lennie Goodings. My gratitude also goes to the memory of Ruth Picardie, who inspired me on so many occasions. And thank you to Liz Jobey, Mark Lattimer and Robert Winder, who read and commented on drafts of this book.

chapter 1

what is the new feminism?

Has feminism had its day? It often seems as if a movement for women's rights must be a thing of the past. Everywhere you look, you see individual women who are freer and more powerful than women have ever been before. You see women driving sleek cars to work through urban traffic; you see women with dreadlocks arguing for the environment on the national news. You hear the confident tones of female politicians; you see the charismatic faces of young female actresses; you read about a 13-year-old girl who took a sex discrimination case to an industrial tribunal;[1] you see gaggles of young women downing pints in pubs; you see packs of young girls walking down streets with a swing in their stride. Women live alone, and pay their own bills; women live with men, and don't bother to get married; women do get married, but they don't promise to obey their husbands. Women decide not to have children, and spend more time dashing off to work; women decide to have children, and their partners hold their hands during childbirth.

Are we living in the kind of utopia about which women in the nineteenth century could only dream? Perhaps we are. There are almost as many women at work as men; and more women than men now say they would work even if they didn't have to.[2] We have seen women scaling all kinds of heights; we have seen a woman Prime Minister and a woman head of MI5, a woman Speaker of the House of Commons and a woman President of the Board of Trade. Some professions are beginning to admit more women than men; more than half of all newly qualified solicitors are women[3] and nearly half of junior doctors.[4]

These changes are having extraordinary effects on women, their culture and their desires. Young girls, especially, seem to be a new breed of women. Not only do they surpass boys in examinations at all levels, they have begun to speak a new language, and it is one of buoyant confidence. I remember talking to three girls aged 12, 13 and 14, and asking them who their heroines might be. The first chose the Spice Girls: 'They've done it, they've made it to the top,' she said admiringly. The second chose Margaret Thatcher: 'I respect her for getting there,' she said. And the third chose Queen Elizabeth I: 'She didn't let people boss her around.'

These women are beginning to move somewhere without any markers or goalposts. Although they have heroines, they are making up their lives as they go along. No one before them has ever lived the lives they lead. They are combining traditionally feminine and traditionally masculine work and clothes and attitudes. They are wearing a minidress one day and jeans and boots the next. When they grow up, they expect to be able to give birth one year and negotiate a pay rise the next. The raw, uncharted newness of these lives makes the old certainties of feminism look outdated. Does that mean that feminism has no part to play in women's lives today?

On the contrary. Feminism is still here, right at the centre of these new lives. Because beside women's freedom lies another truth: the truth of their continuing inequality. The constraints that operate upon women are still fierce, and those constraints can come as a terrible shock to those insouciant young women as they move out of school and into their adult lives.

It is difficult for women to confront the reality of their own inequality. Can such Victorian constraints still exist in the late twentieth century? Is their freedom really so uncertain? Does blatant inequality still exist although women have travelled so far and so fast? Tragically, it does. The average woman, with all her new dreams and beliefs, still has an independent income that is only half that of the average man.[5] Forty per cent of working women earn less than £150 a week, compared to ten per cent of men.[6] When a woman has children, she loses, typically, more than half of the money she would have made throughout her lifetime if she had not had children; but having children typically makes no difference to a man's lifetime income.[7] Ninety-four per cent of an estimated one million homeworkers are women, earning as little as 50 pence an hour for piecework in their own homes.[8] More women than men live on benefits, and a single woman on income support would not even have the means to feed her children the diet laid down in Victorian workhouses.[9] These extreme inequalities, so out of place in our brave new world where girls often seem more sure of themselves than boys, run throughout society. When we talk about women's power we are still talking about potential rather than reality. Ninety-three out of 100 university professors are men;[10] 96 out of 100 general surgeons;[11] 96 out of 100 company directors.[12]

Feminism has recently been associated more with a movement to change women's attitudes and society's culture than with these material inequalities. If feminism is to mean anything to women in this generation, this is an emphasis that must shift. In the seventies, feminism did win concrete battles, especially over equal pay and abortion rights. But it gradually became primarily associated with sexual politics and culture. One slogan encapsulated that: 'Pornography is the theory, and rape the practice,' Robin Morgan wrote in 1974.[13] She meant that women should not be satisfied with trying to root out concrete abuse and inequality; they should attack any cultural, social or sexual behaviour that they disliked. Other feminists continued this way of thinking. 'Fashion=control=violence against women,' women argued at a feminist conference in 1981.[14] These feminists encouraged women to believe that by attacking cultural manifestations of inequality one could radically change women's position in society.

That impetus is now reversing itself. We have seen that interrogating cultural and sexual behaviour has not led to a thoroughgoing change in the balance of power. Feminism has enunciated many, too many, critiques of dress and pornography, of poetry and film-making, of language and physical behaviour. It has sought to direct our personal lives on every level. And yet women have still not achieved fundamental equality; they are still poorer and less powerful than men. Rather than concentrating its energy on the ways women dress and talk and make love, feminism now must attack the material basis of economic and social and political inequality.

So the new feminism must unpick the tight link that feminism in the seventies made between our personal and political lives. The slogan 'the personal is the political' sprang up in the seventies in debates about abortion, sexual harassment, rape and the division of domestic labour, often to good, and even revolutionary effect. But identifying the personal and the political in too absolute and unyielding a way has led feminism to a dead end. This generation of feminists must free itself from the spectre of political correctness. If feminism is to build on all the new female confidence that exists in Britain, it must not be trammelled by a rigid ideology that alienates and divides women who are working for the same end: increased power and equality for women. Feminism is a social movement, like environmental or civil rights movements, that relies on a spreading consensus among diverse people. It is not a self-help or religious movement that relies on good behaviour from its disciples and correct attitudes at all times. We do not all have to dress the same, or have sex in the same ways, or vote for the same party. The old myth about feminists, that they all wear dungarees and are lesbians and socialists, must be buried for good.

This change is essential for this generation. Young women today are unlikely to want lectures from feminists about their private lives. They have learnt to question the precepts of their parents, their teachers, their politicians and their employers in their search for new identities. However young women dress, however they make love, however they flirt, they can be feminists. They do not want to learn a set of personal attitudes before being admitted into the club. The search for political equality today must go on alongside the acceptance of personal freedom.

This new freedom also leads us to argue that feminists do not have to be women. Feminism does not have to be something that arises only from personal experience of oppression. In working for an equal society, men must be women's allies, because unless they take on an equal part of the caring work women cannot hope to go on and on moving into employment and public life. Otherwise, our children may be left without proper parents, our sick without proper care, and our homes without any spirit of joy at all. Women need men to work with them in finding ways of preserving and sharing those domestic, small-scale activities that were once the sole preserve of women.

If you separate out the personal and the political you achieve two things. First, you give the social and political demands of feminism more edge. Freed from the straitjacket of political correctness, feminists can embrace any strategy that will help to achieve the goal of material equality for women. Pragmatism, not purity, will be the watchword.

And second, you will free up the personal realm. Feminism has over-determined our private lives and interpreted too many aspects of our cultural life as evidence of a simplistic battle, patriarchy versus women. When feminist academics began to theorise the very structure of language as oppressively patriarchal, or saw the very techniques of cinema as evidence of an oppressive male gaze, they did us no favours; they forgot all the subtleties of culture and art in their desire to map out an overarching pattern into which everything else had to fall. When feminist writers chose to trawl through every detail of their own sexual lives in the search for their power or lack of it, they forgot that personal life does not always march to a political drumbeat.

There is a new feminism rearing its head in Britain today. I'm not trying to invent it, but to describe it. You can see it in politics and journalism and television dramas and everyday life. You can see it among actresses and writers, schoolgirls and politicians, mothers and businesswomen. Everywhere you go, you see women flexing their muscles and demanding equality. In this book, I track the characteristics of this new feminism, and set out how it could develop. Above all, the new feminism is materialist. It concentrates on the material reality of inequality, and allows women to live their personal lives without the constraints of a rigid ideology.

Two further marks of the new feminism are worth mentioning at the very outset. First, this book is about Britain. That may seem obvious, but feminist debate has been so dominated by American ideas during the past decade that we sometimes risk forgetting that there is a homegrown tradition of feminism that is here to be celebrated and extended.

That is not to say that we shouldn't admire some of the works that have come our way from the United States over the last few years. Feminist writers such as Naomi Wolf, Camille Paglia and Susan Faludi have added vigour and excitement to our debates. But we should resist being in thrall to their ideas. British women do not need to feel that they are trailing in the wake of their sisters across the Atlantic. Recent American feminists have lauded the United States as the 'epicentre of the genderquake'[15]; but is American society able to give us pointers to a new negotiation between the sexes? With its cult of the Hollywood gun-toter and the Baywatch babe, its far higher rates of rape and murder, and its far higher rates of cosmetic surgery, the States often looks as if it is mired in an old-fashioned sexist culture that is dying out in Britain. British women deserve a revitalised British feminist debate. We have our own extraordinary history of protest, success and intellectual ferment. We are aware of our own problems, and we are now confronting an exciting situation of change and renewal.

Second, the new feminism looks to me as if it is already, and will be in the future, a celebratory and optimistic movement. Women in Britain can reclaim the history of feminism. We can remember that it is a uniquely happy story. The feminist revolution as it has developed so far has already brought women phenomenal advances in education and employment, contraception and sexual mores, economic and cultural freedom. Although we have not yet reached the end of the road, feminism can now allow itself a little celebration and a little laughter.

That laughter and celebration occurs in all sorts of different places. We saw it on the night of the Labour landslide in May 1997, when Clare Short MP hugged Gisela Stuart, the first woman MP to gain her seat in the first Labour gain of the night. Their happy faces lit up the newspapers the next morning. We see it in the smiles of the Spice Girls, and their feisty words. 'We're completely into girl power,' says Mel Brown. 'Our band is a projection of female power,' says Geri.[16] We see it in the laughing faces of a group of dinner ladies from Yorkshire, just after they won their case for equal pay for work of equal value against North Yorkshire County Council.[17] We see it in the swaggering laughter of Jennifer Saunders and Joanna Lumley in the television series *Absolutely Fabulous*, in which women dare to be as drunk and bawdy as any comic heroes. We hear it in the confident voice of the Speaker of the House of Commons, Betty Boothroyd, as she calls 'Order, order' across the floor of the House. We see it at work and at home, on television and on the streets around us.

It is worth remembering our successes as well as how far we still have to go. The feminist revolution has already touched all women in Britain; and all women can feel part of the feminist future.

In arguing that what we should ask of feminism now are concrete political, social and economic reforms I am not trying to say that those are necessarily the most important aspects of our lives. Although this book concentrates particularly on women's inequality at work, of course we all exceed and go beyond our working lives. Love and literature, music and art may well be more important. But perhaps feminism now has done its work for this generation in making us believe that love and literature can be transformed. We have Virginia Woolf and Doris Lessing and Adrienne Rich to read, we have new ideals of love to pursue. If we fail in those areas it isn't because we don't have feminist models of creativity and sexuality.

But look at what we lack. We lack equality, and everything that comes with that. We lack the commitments to parental leave and flexible working that would make men and women equal players in the workforce. We lack support for women facing grinding poverty, for women bringing up their children alone in miserable circumstances. We lack training and education for women in dead-end jobs. We lack legal support and refuge housing for women fleeing violence. We lack women's voices in the highest courts and debating chambers of the country. We must understand that feminism can give us these things now, if we really want them. This may sound like a shrunken agenda, but it is the right arena for the new feminism. As I have said, to believe that feminism's rightful place is in the cultural and personal arena both destroys our freest and subtlest reactions to art and love, as well as removing feminism's teeth as a strong political movement. But if we can achieve the preconditions for equality, our souls will be free, not framed in the reductive language of victim or oppressor.

chapter 2

the reality gap

Most women feel free, freer than their mothers did. Most women can choose what to wear, whom they will spend their lives with, where to work, what to read, when to have children. It comes as an incredible shock to these women when they are confronted with the solid, unquestionable facts of their inequality. Young women especially tend to look askance at reality, hardly able to take in the facts, hardly able to believe that these constraints still operate as we move into the twenty-first century. They assume that they will be the exception; or that if, by any chance, they take on second-class economic status, it will be down to their individual choice.

But as they grow up women tend to find that the disadvantages of femininity press ever more closely upon them.[1] Women who have children, particularly, find it almost impossible to deny those disadvantages. A woman who has children loses, on average, over half of the earnings she would have made over her lifetime if she had stayed childless. Successful women tend not to have children at all; only 30 per cent of senior women managers have children compared to 75 per cent of men.[2] What does that say about the constraints that still bind women? Women who find other obstacles in their path, like a low level of education or racial discrimination, discover that being a woman is an extra hindrance; women are more likely than men to live on benefits both when they are young and when they are old.

Even if you, female reader, feel that these inequalities have so far passed you by, that you are earning good money, fulfilling your potential both at home and at work and contributing your share to society, you will have experienced the knock-on effects of women's lack of material power. You will have watched television and found that as soon as the programme switches from drama to current affairs, women become unimportant, the spoken-about rather than the speakers: for every one woman who speaks on a news programme, four men do.[3] At times of real excitement, that number slips further. If you took an interest in the 1997 general election, you would have found yourself listening to a man, a man, a man, a man, a man, a man, a man, a man, a man, a man, a man, a man, a man, a man, a man, a man, a man, a man, a man, and then a woman; for every female politician heard on television news in that election, 19 male politicians spoke.[4] If you have children, you will usually find that the final decisions in their education are taken by a man: for every female headteacher of a secondary school, there are three male headteachers.[5] Women's voices are curiously absent from many of the most powerful places in the land.

You may well encounter a police officer or enter a lawcourt at some point in your life. Then you will find that you are six times more likely to be confronted by a male than a female police officer,[6] and that you are three times more likely to see a male barrister than a female one.[7] It is understandable if you find that this makes it harder for you to be taken seriously in your dealings with the criminal justice system. Again, all women are likely to go into hospital at some point in their lives. If you do so you will find that your consultant is more than four times as likely to be a man than a woman.[8] Again, it is understandable if that makes you feel your experience is somehow out of kilter with what your doctor knows. If you publish a book you may feel that you are in an influential position. But 80 per cent of directors in publishing are men,[9] and three men review books in national newspapers for every one woman.[10] Again, it is understandable if you therefore feel that your words are being screened by men, who may be out of tune with your experiences, before reaching your readers. This slow drip-drip of alienation may seem normal to you, or it may seem outrageous, but it will be everywhere, part of your experience of society in all its guises.

And this sense of absence will have impinged on you, to a greater or lesser degree. You will have understood that your face, as a female face, is not one that looks normal in the most powerful places in Britain. You may compensate with a greater determination and will to succeed, or you may be angered and alienated by the way that voices like yours are not heard wherever you go, or you may idealise the role of the outsider, and believe that it is somehow finer and more noble than the position of insiders. Even if you idealise it, you may still become angry if you discover that because women are still not expected to be wealthy or powerful, requests that you have made for money or influence have fallen on deaf ears. For instance, when one Glasgow-based female engineer was seeking finance for a management buy-out of her company, she had this experience, even though women are less likely to default on business loans than men.[11]

We needed £10,000 each. The other two men took the business plan to their bank managers and raised the money no problem. I really didn't think that I would have any problem either, you see I had £8,000 of my own personal savings – which were nothing to do with my husband – plus the house in my name not his. So I went to my bank manager, told him about the buy-out, showed him the business plan and asked him for the extra £2,000 that I needed, and he said no, he just turned me down flat. I was absolutely furious, I just couldn't believe it. So I said to him, if I had wanted the money for a car loan would he give it to me and he said, well, of course I would, it's just that we don't lend to women for business ventures.[12]

More women than you may think find that their sex stands in the way of their advancement. It is wonderful to see women scaling the peaks of all kinds of work; wonderful to see women in charge at the Department of Social Security, or MI5, to have seen a female Prime Minister or a female Speaker of the House of Commons. But many women in professional work also bear witness to another kind of truth. In one survey carried out by the Manufacturing, Science and Finance Union (MSF) in the engineering and aerospace industries, over three quarters of women said that it was easier for men to get promoted, and over a half believed that they had personally lost out on promotion purely because they were women.[13] These women are not imagining such blocks on their advancement: research carried out by the National Institute for Economic and Social Research shows that women at all levels of management stand a smaller chance of being promoted than their male colleagues.[14]

Many men feel that women should not be encouraged at work. Only a third of men surveyed by the Institute of Management agreed that women managers bring positive skills to the workplace, compared to 74 per cent of women, and one-third of the female managers said that they did not receive adequate respect from male superiors.[15] Headhunters for senior positions believe that ten per cent of their clients would reject a female candidate.[16] In another survey, more than one in five men said that they would, or do, find it difficult to work for a woman manager.[17] One study of 500 male and female managers found that the average salary for women was £13,500 while their male colleagues earned £18,000. The researcher, Dr Melamed of Central Lancashire University, concluded that some of the difference was down to differing experience and qualifications, but '60 per cent could only be explained by simple sex discrimination.'[18]

In some areas of work – particularly areas where traditional masculine behaviour is prized – such hostility flares into open aggression. A woman police officer tells a tribunal that her male colleagues told an arrested man to rape her;[19] another that she was forced to bend over while colleagues rubber-stamped the station name on her bottom;[20] another that she was held down by two officers while a colleague simulated sex with her;[21] a woman police officer in the army tells of her colleagues throwing CS gas pellets into her room;[22] a company director tells of being humiliated and handcuffed by a male stripper at work.[23] All these women's voices have been heard in the past couple of years; we can assume that for all those we hear there are many who remain silent. In the past few years, and not in connection with researching this book, a woman postal worker told me that she was advised not to apply to a certain London post office 'because they don't take women'; a woman solicitor told me about being pushed to the ground from a bar stool by her male colleagues; a woman journalist told me that she left her beloved job because of harassment by her boss; and yet none of these women ever made the discrimination they encountered public.

In her brash bestseller *Blonde Ambition*, the former City broker

Samantha Phillips explores the way that men in the City grind women down by a mixture of patronising fun and outright aggression. When her heroine, Charlotte Christie, is asked to give a speech at the firm's Christmas party, she is sprayed with aerosol foam, sugar and salt:

> Her eyes were tight shut, but she could hear her fellow diners shrieking with mirth, cackling hyenas, screeching owls, howling demons, and she knew that this was meant to be a joke, she was supposed to laugh . . . show herself a sport, one of the boys . . . she felt violated as if by a rape. A fury rose in her that was stronger than ambition, over-riding her native self-restraint. As the inundation ceased she was shaking with rage and shock, her dress glued to her body, a viscid ooze creeping down her thighs. She wanted to sob, to scream, to rend their bloated smirking faces with nails grown to claws.[24]

Let us not overstate the sense of alienation that women feel at work today. Even the benighted heroine of the passage above eventually wins out against her colleagues, and women in every area of work are challenging discrimination wherever they find it. Women are becoming more and more powerful, and in chapters 8 and 9 I explore that growing power. I don't believe that young women feel themselves to be victims; rather the contrary. There is a very important distinction between pointing out wrongs that must be righted and giving oneself the immutable status of a victim. Yet no one can deny that there is still a great dragging weight of inequality on the backs even of powerful women; a knowledge of injustice; an anger. If we can hold the reality of both facets of female experience in our minds – that women are becoming more powerful and yet that there is still a long way to go – we will overthrow the inequalities that still exist without uncertainty or backtracking. Is this two-sided truth too difficult to comprehend? For most women, it is vividly obvious that they are becoming more powerful – and yet they are still unequal.

Much feminist debate in recent years has centred on women with good careers and education, who are prevented from consolidating their power because of the glass ceiling that still stands between them and the top echelons of society. This is not, as some have chosen to see it, the whingeing of lucky girls. It is undeniable, however unpalatable in its unchanging starkness, that the glass ceiling still hangs above women's heads in Britain. In fact, it is worse in Britain than in many other countries. Until 1997, Britain's pitiful showing on the representation of women in the main legislature, the House of Commons, made this country forty-ninth in a world league of female representation, lagging not just way behind progressive countries such as Sweden, Norway and Finland, but also way behind – for instance – Eritrea, Turkmenistan, Uganda, Spain, Italy, Latvia, Mexico, Costa Rica, Poland, Estonia, Ireland, Belgium, Dominican Republic, Senegal, Tanzania, Bolivia, Columbia, Iraq, Australia, New Zealand, China and Switzerland.

Everywhere at the top of society, if you play the numbers game, the till rings empty. Although women make up half the students entering examinations for the Bar, only 60 of the 925 QCs are women and the numbers applying for silk have remained static and low, while just 1 out of the 34 Court of Appeal judges is a woman.[25] What is it like elsewhere? In all companies, just 4.5 per cent of directors are women – a small rise from 3.3 per cent in 1995.[26] In medicine, women make up 30 per cent of GPs, and only 18 per cent of hospital consultants,[27] while just 4 per cent of general surgeons are women.[28] In academia, although more women than men now enter universities as students, 93 per cent of university chairs are held by men.[29] In the media, the situation is no better. In advertising, women make up only 14 per cent of the members of boards of directors in all IPA advertising agencies.[30] Of the 63 top jobs on the quality broadsheets, 61 were taken by men in 1994.[31] In 1995, Women in Journalism found that 90 per cent of those writing editorials in broadsheets were men, as were 80 per cent of those in daily news conferences. In television, only 4 out of the 106 executive directorships on ITV boards across the country were taken by women; and 21 out of the 120 top executives at the BBC.[32] Let us not go on quoting figures to describe the absence of women in power, they are ubiquitous and well known.

To understand how far women still are from realising the dream of equality, we must look at a bigger picture. Women's inequality is not something that hurts only middle-class women. On the contrary, for women beyond the successful middle classes the weight of inequality presses even more heavily. The new feminism must hold this truth to the fore: although women's lives may differ greatly, and some women may escape from the pressures on their sex to a greater or lesser degree, the reality of inequality runs throughout all classes, throughout the whole of British society, from north to south, from council estates to plush clubs in St James's, from boardrooms to shopfloors.

At whatever level they enter working life, women are likely to find that their experience of work is affected by the fact of their sex. They find that although all kinds of work are theoretically open to them, certain areas are much more open than others. Although women who work in the professions are now used to working alongside men, many other women are not. Astoundingly, although men and women now go to the same schools, drink in the same bars, and report the same attachment to work, they do not tend to do the *same* work. In one recent survey, researchers found that about 15 per cent of workplaces have a workforce that is 85 per cent women, and 15 per cent of workplaces have a workforce that is 90 per cent men. In the same survey, it was found that a half of workplaces employ only women as clerical and administrative workers; nearly a half of workplaces employ only men in senior professional roles, and over a half of workplaces employ only men in management roles.[33] Such extraordinary statistics remind us how far work is still sexed; how much women's – and men's – choices in their working lives are still moulded by a weight of expectation and custom.

This split between men's work and women's work means that a woman who works in a traditionally masculine area will find herself in a peculiar position. It may not always be a negative position – she may enjoy the attention she commands, she may find that she easily attracts mentors and supporters among the men around her – but she will be aware that she is not quite normal, and that if the approval of her mentors and supporters is withdrawn, she may become vulnerable in a way that a normal-looking, accepted, ordinary man will not be. Despite the good intentions of employers who recruit women, they will often slip back into bad old habits: women tend to get pay rises when they move jobs, men get pay rises when they stay in jobs.[34]

Although this weight of custom still weighs heavily on women, there is nothing intrinsic about any work that fits it only for men or women. Indeed, jobs can change over the years and become masculine or feminine, for no obvious reason. After all, remember the chapters in D.H. Lawrence's *Sons and Lovers* when Paul Morel starts working in a stocking manufacturer. He is the secretary, working with another man in an office writing out orders and letters. The manual workers are women, sitting over their machines in another room and teasing the young boy when he comes up with the orders. The division between the masculine and the feminine realms is entrenched, we feel a frisson of dangerous sexuality as Paul crosses from his office to the shopfloor. Now, that situation is more likely to be reversed, and we are more likely to feel that the female secretary who crosses into the male-dominated shopfloor is crossing into a sexually charged area. Similarly, certain occupations that are seen as masculine here are not segregated in other countries: for instance, only 20 per cent of those working in information technology in Britain are women, but in Singapore 55 per cent are women.[35]

Wherever men and women are segregated at work, women's work tends to become a ghetto in which skills are downgraded and pay is lower and routes to promotion are fewer. More than anything it is pay that divides men and women rather than the actual tasks the job demands. When I asked home carers why they thought there were so few men in their line of work, they always answered: 'Because it pays so badly.'

The difference between men's work and women's work does not just give men and women different experiences in the workplace, it gives them unequal experiences. The statistics say it clearly. When they are in full-time work, women earn only 80 per cent of the male hourly wage.[36] Women working in manual trades do worse – they earn just 69 per cent of the money per hour that men in manual trades do.[37] But women are even more poorly rewarded than these figures would suggest, since 45 per cent of working women are working part-time, compared to fewer than 10 per cent of working men.[38] The hourly wages of part-timers remain at only 63 per cent of average male wages.[39] Part-time work can be an advantage to a woman, but it also hurts her financially: one in five part-time workers has no paid holidays, compared to one in twenty full-time workers, and one-third of all part-timers receive no sick pay.[40] And of course the short hours that women work result in far greater disparities of income than the comparison of hourly wages would suggest. The average woman receives £79 per week from wages and salaries; the average man receives £174.[41] It is not just in words, or pictures, or jokes that women see the truth of their inequality, but in the sad reality of their slim pay-packets.

Above all, the split between the masculine and feminine work-ing life is seen when a woman has children. One recent social research study tells us the tale of 'Mrs Typical'. Mrs Typical has two children, the first when she is 25 and the second when she is 28. Mrs Typical takes typical breaks from employment to care for her children, and then resumes employment at first on a part-time basis. She earns less than her male partner, because of her time out of work, because of her time in part-time work, and because of the lack of employment experience that keeps her in a less senior job even when she returns to full-time work. The researchers calculate that over Mrs Typical's lifetime, she loses 55 per cent, or more than half, of the earnings she would have made from the age of 25 onwards if she had not had children.[42] Of course, no woman wants to believe that she is 'Mrs Typical'. But the spectre of Mrs Typical is always in the background, pressing on an individual woman's life, making it stranger and harder for her to insist that her husband organises his working life differently, or that she deserves more respect from her employers.

Mrs Typical is not a real individual, but her experiences are echoed in the lives of millions of women. I met Ellen Jones[43] while I was researching this book. Her story must stand in for those of countless women, the women who are currently absent from the boards of companies, whose faces we do not see on the news and in Parliament, whose voices we do not hear in the offices of consul-tants and headteachers. Ellen Jones is a barrister, aged 34, and yes, she used to want to be a judge, but now she doesn't believe she'll do it. A man will probably step into her place in the corri-dors of power. 'I loved my work,' she says passionately, looking hard into the distance. 'It wasn't just stimulating. I really believed in what I was doing, and I loved feeling that I was doing good things and going on to the next good thing and that life was always going forwards.' Then Ellen had children. 'At first I thought my career would go on straightforwardly, but it was just such a struggle. I was going crazy. I felt that I was always in the wrong place. So I've cut my hours right down and give more time to my children. They're happier and I'm happier. But at work I'm an also-ran.'

It's not only women in successful, glamorous careers who find that family life can crash into their working life and smash it up. Anne Smith[44] is a 40-year-old cleaning supervisor in a school in Strathclyde. 'I started off working as a secretary for an oil company,' she tells me. 'I really enjoyed that. They trained me up and I planned to stay there and move up through the firm. But then the company moved and though I was offered a job in the new place, I couldn't move because of my husband's job. Then I worked in a shop but when I got pregnant they found they didn't need me any more.' Anne gave up paid work altogether for a while, and now works as a cleaner. She feels she has missed her opportunities. 'Cleaning . . . it's what you do at home anyway. I clean for older ladies in the morning, then I clean at the school, then I come home and clean here. There aren't any men in the cleaning jobs – it's something we're all used to so we don't mind it, but men find it degrading.'

In *Our Treacherous Hearts*, the British feminist Rosalind Coward speaks to a series of women who have realised they cannot hold on to the ideal of the masculine career if they want families. 'I've switched from being highly ambitious and getting an enormous buzz out of my work to being practically a full-time mother,' said one woman, a former production editor of a national newspaper.[45] She cried when her husband gave her her first housekeeping cheque. 'That hurt, not because I had no money, but because I had no independence.' Another woman, a university teacher who felt forced to go part-time, said: 'It was a real pull between the baby's needs and mine . . . I was very tired. I just wanted something easy . . . but I have no rights, get paid less and have none of the perks a regular job gives you.'[46]

Similarly, in her book *Professional Progress: Why Women Still Don't Have Wives* the writer Terri Apter spoke to many women who are professionally successful, but who look into the future with a terror men never feel. 'I can't come to a decision – I can't decide to have children or not to,' says one 27-year-old chemist. 'I reach out to the future, and I just see chaos.' A materials manager who was offered promotion and relocation and realised that she couldn't take it for the sake of her children, said, 'I kept so cool, so blank, and nodded, and said I'd think it over, but I was in a panic. I couldn't think, because deep down I knew I would reject this offer, and that turning down this opportunity would be the end of the upwards path that had been a big part of my life.'[47]

The writer Helen Simpson wrote a short story recently in which she brilliantly dramatised the rift between the nonchalant, charming power of the young woman and the life experienced by the older woman with children. In 'Lentils and Lilies',[48] the young Jade Beaumont reflects on the lovely vistas of life that are opening out in front of her. On a summer walk to her very first job interview, she sees herself 'moving like a panther into the long jewelled narrative which was her fate . . . There was the asterisk trail of a shooting star, on and on for years until it petered out at about 33 or 34, leaving her at some point of self-apotheosis'. But then, Jade meets a mother with two children, one of whom has a lentil stuck up her nose. 'She did not want to be implicated in the flabby womany-ness of the proceedings', but she follows the older woman into her house, and notes with disgust the listless, distracted air of the mother, the chaos of the home life. Simpson's lyrical touch makes something both poetic and real out of this eternal contrast between the young woman's dreams and the older woman's reality. It is not the loss of beauty

and sexuality that interests her, though that has been the traditional focus for male writers looking at women's ageing, but the
loss of power, identity and control experienced by women as they
retreat into the home.

The image that we have of women's inequality is too often a
complacent one. The statistics of injustice are muffled by our belief
that Mrs Typical is, in fact, doing quite nicely, relying on her husband for money to tide her over the lean years, or choosing to opt
out of participation in working life because she really wants to
withdraw into the home. Such an interpretation, naturally, ignores
the knock-on effects that inequality has on women's self-esteem,
independence and ability to find justice from public organisations.
Being coddled is no substitute for being equal. And let us not forget
that inequality can lead to stark disadvantage as well as relative
injustice. Let us remember, for instance, that although women are
working more than ever before, their work is not always a route to
economic independence.

Yes, women are working more. But they often work on the
fringes of the economy – in 'atypical' jobs. Atypical work means
part-time, temporary, seasonal employment; assisting relatives;
homeworking; and illegal employment. Yet for women, atypical is
typical, and low pay is normal pay. Let's hit the statistics again.
Only 5 per cent of men earn less than £100 per week, but 24 per
cent of women do.[49] Three quarters of all female part-time workers
earn less than £5.75 per hour.[50] Full-time or part-time, 31 per cent
of working women are paid less than £4 an hour, compared to 11
per cent of working men.[51]

Women are working more than they ever have before. But they
are not always earning enough to keep themselves or their families
out of poverty. One recent study showed that while 5 per cent of
families headed by a male breadwinner, where the woman did
not work, were poor, 30 per cent of families headed by a female

breadwinner, where the man did not work, were poor. And 40 per cent of families headed by a single woman were poor.[52]

Look at those statistics. Think behind the clunk of the numbers. Imagine what it means for a woman to work for a week and end up with less than £100, week after week after week; imagine what it means for her children, for her health, for her house, for her clothes, for her social life. Imagine what it feels like for such a woman if, say, her husband begins to beat her up and she knows she can't move out because she can't support herself. Imagine what it feels like for such a woman if her child gets a bad cough and her doctor tells her the child mustn't get damp or cold and must eat more fruit and vegetables. Imagine what it means when she looks in the mirror and realises that she's getting old, and that she's saved nothing for her old age and has nothing left to hope for.

I began this book intending to record the growing power and confidence of women in Britain. But I kept finding myself up against other stories: women who, despite their talents and desires, had not benefited from the genderquake. There are too many of them, too many women who are cut off from fulfilling their potential, for anyone to ignore. I met Leyla Zadad[53] in a Turkish community centre in north London. She is 21 and works 40 hours a week for £90, as a machinist in a garment factory. 'I work very hard,' she says, 'like a robot. The factory is dirty. There's no clean air. My head aches all day when I work.' The factory is illegal, unknown to health and safety inspectors. What would happen if she had an accident at work? 'The boss would forget me.' What would she do if she could do anything at all with her life? 'I would like safe work, clean work. Maybe with children.'

I talked to Gillian Brown[54] through the National Group on Homeworking. Gillian is 33 years old and has two young children. She tried to do homeworking in the evenings to earn some extra money. She was packing screws, at a penny a packet. 'I worked from nine p.m. for about four hours, and the repetitiveness made my arms ache really badly. I wasn't even making £1 an hour. The employers would say, you need to do so much, and you'd take the strain.' She lasted six months, and is now unemployed again.

Lynne Dobbie, the 16-year-old daughter of a woman I met in a women's centre in Glasgow, works in a restaurant. She earns £50 for a five-day week, working nine to five-thirty. 'Sometimes I am really knackered, and I do get annoyed. You have to set everything up, cook and serve everything. I will stick with it because I want to work, I want a career. I want a life that's really different from my mother's.'

Such women know the reality gap that lies behind the shining rhetoric that some feminists speak. And they know that if you look closely into the effects of sexual inequality in Britain, you come up against a hard, miserable word, an unfashionable word. Poverty. More women than men are poor. Women who are living on pitiful benefits of about £70 a week with no prospect of training or employment, have hardly benefited from the genderquake. Women who earn £2 or £3 an hour doing piecework at home or cleaning or working as prostitutes may be forgiven for thinking that feminism has not appreciably shifted their lives out of the Victorian age. Women are ten times more likely than men to have an independent income of less than £25 a week.[55] And they are more likely to rely on benefits than men are.

The statistics for people who receive income support are generally published in a form that hides the reality of women's greater poverty. If you contact the Department of Social Security you are simply told that 2,702,000 men receive income support, and 2,973,000 women do. Hardly any difference, one is therefore led to believe, between women and men. And yet if you look more closely at those recipients, it is possible to see that 1,077,000 of those men are single, but a massive 2,360,000 of the women are. And that suggests that the number of adult men living in a household reliant on income support is 3,315,000, whereas the number of women is 4,598,000.[56]

The number of women in poverty is growing all the time. Again, you only have to glance at the statistics to see the shocking reality of women's inequality. In 1979 the proportion of the population with incomes below half of the average income was 9 per cent; in 1994 it was 25 per cent.[57] In 1979 only 19 per cent of those were single people with children, in 1994 58 per cent of them were single people, usually women, with children. How poor are these women? The poorest 20 per cent of households in Britain have an average gross income of £79 a week; while the average for the country as a whole is £369.25.[58]

What does poverty mean for these women? Life on benefits at the end of the twentieth century is not an easy life. The vast increase in unemployment means that it can be a permanent situation, an entire life spent counting every penny, unable ever to buy unthinkingly a pound of cherries or a cinema ticket or a bottle of shampoo. Very few writers, very few artists, have tried to contemplate what kind of lives women on benefit lead. The novelist Livi Michael is one of the few. In her novels she has portrayed women on the edge, who are pushed into misery and death not because of emotional inadequacy, but because of lack of money. In her novel *Under a Thin Moon*, one of her protagonists, Laurie, a woman living on benefits, goes for a walk to an affluent area one night:

She walks past one set of ornate gates after another and pauses, peering through railings at massive lawns, and squares of light from great bay windows. There is so much beauty in the gardens, in the buildings themselves. Her fingers curl tightly round the railings. She wonders if the people who live there have ever seen the council estate where she lives . . . It is close by, but they have probably never even seen it.[59]

This sensation of invisibility, of having dropped off the edge of society, is one that too many women in Britain currently experience.

Apart from such alienation from ordinary life, women on benefits experience all kinds of problems that even the coarse nets of social surveys can pick up. They have a lower life expectancy: the poorest people in Britain live five years less than the richest.[60] These women are being denied years of life because of their social situation. It means misery: in one study of families on benefit, the adults were asked to fill up a 'malaise inventory' – 63 per cent of the women said they often felt miserable and depressed, compared to 46 per cent of men. It means not being able to meet basic needs and desires like that of food: nearly half of those questioned in the same survey said there had been times during the past year when they did not have enough money to buy food that the family wanted. And it means boredom, facing unimaginably narrow horizons. In the study of families on benefit, the researchers commented: 'The most striking finding was the very high proportion of time spent by all members of the family at home . . . They all spent over half of their week asleep or watching television.'[61]

In families that rely on benefit, there is evidence to suggest that women have a harder time in terms of the distribution of the small amount of income that there is. In one study of two-parent families on benefits in Tyneside in 1987, just 2 per cent of the women had been out for a meal in the last week, compared to 7 per cent of men; just 3 per cent of the women had been out for a drink compared to 18 per cent of men. Sixty-two per cent of the women had not been out for a drink in the last month, compared to 39 per cent of the men.[62] This uneven distribution of income is sometimes vividly illustrated by women's preference for living alone. Since men earn more than women, a family with a male partner will usually have a higher household income than the family of a lone woman. And yet many studies have found that a high proportion of lone mothers – between a quarter and a third – say that they feel better off on their own than as married women because they can have control over their resources, however limited those are.[63]

Anecdotal evidence suggests that women tend to deny themselves rather than let their families do without. Sandra Coles, a lone parent on benefit, told researchers in 1992, 'I've known me to have three lots of toast in one day: breakfast, lunch and dinner.' Anjum Abbas, another lone parent, said, 'Many times I've been without food myself, many times . . . and probably will have to do so in the future, goodness knows how many times.'[64] The study of two-parent families living on benefit found that of the wife, the husband and the children, 'women's clothing tended to be in the worst condition and children's clothing in the best'.[65]

The low level of employment among single parents is more striking in Britain than any other European country; in Britain 70 per cent of single parents depend on benefit, while in France only 37 per cent do and in Sweden only 33 per cent.[66] Women's unemployment is seen as a mild, unimportant social problem in contemporary Britain. Male unemployment, the unemployment of unskilled young men, is always seen as the greatest social evil of our time. Certainly, male unemployment can lead to the obvious, in-your-face results of crime and violence. But we must keep female unemployment on the agenda too. It is a terrible failure of imagination to think that just because unemployed women aren't swarming around beating up old ladies and stealing cars, they don't mind, or they don't suffer. They too can find that unemployment has unforeseen consequences. As one woman who was made redundant from a clothing factory in South Wales said: 'I have missed working. I've missed the company as much as the money . . . I do miss it, the girls and all. I still haven't really settled to it because my nerves have gone all wonky being in the house. It's all right when the children are here but when everybody goes I am back on my own all day.'[67] We know how desperate such women are to work; they take the very worst jobs, part-time, insecure, low paid work. And it's not because they don't value themselves. It's because they need the money.

Given the rising numbers of families headed by single women, women's poverty may not lead to women joyriding or drug-dealing, but it does lead to extreme deprivation of children. One children's charity recently released a study that suggested single mothers on benefit would not even have the money to feed their children the diet laid down in Victorian workhouses.[68] Such deprivation now threatens the health of millions of children. One in three children is now born into poverty, with their parents dependent on benefit or the equivalent in low wages. Those children have poor nutrition, show poor growth rates and at the age of six they have IQ deficiencies of between 5 and 20 points below their advantaged peers.[69] Poor children entering school are 4 cm shorter, and weigh less than their peers. Can we bear to see the results of women's inequality visited so harshly on the children of Britain?

Women bringing up children in such poverty are not fools, they can see how much their children are being hurt from not getting good food and stimulation. They don't walk out on their families nearly as much as men do, their sense of responsiblity runs too deep. Maureen Smith[70] is bringing up her son alone in a flat in Devon on £77.95 benefit a week. Her fixed outgoings, including debt repayments, are over £65 a week, which leaves her just £12 to feed herself and her boy. She said, 'I might go two days without a main meal – I just eat, like, a sandwich at lunch-time and supper if we have enough bread. I might have one banana a week. That's the only fruit. Sometimes when he has said to me he's hungry, I just feel very desperate and alone . . . and a bit of a failure, really.'[71] Many women, women who earn good wages and live in affluent areas, will never know such solitude and despair. But it is up to all of us to understand how inequality affects women's lives throughout Britain, and that inequality can only be combated if we make a concerted effort to stand up for one another.

I met Jacqueline Brathwaite, a 34-year-old Afro-Caribbean woman with a nine-year-old daughter, in south London one spring afternoon. She has been living on benefits for 17 years, but she never imagined life would turn out that way. 'My mother worked all her life. I always thought I'd work. But there aren't any jobs around that would cover my rent and childcare and everything.' She knows how poverty has damaged her life and that of her daughter. She tells me in a sonorous monotone what life is like for them.

'I only manage without buying any clothes, without going out anywhere. I would so dearly love to take her to the cinema. I would love to get on a bus and take her out anywhere. It's hard for her not to be able to have what her friends have. Right now she'd like a bicycle, but it's too expensive. She has to stay in with me – the estate is very dangerous, and I haven't got the money to go elsewhere. Of course she gets stroppy. It's very hard for her to understand.'

Jacqueline is lonely as well as poor. 'I don't keep company with people on the estate,' she tells me sadly. 'We are isolated. When she was a baby, I'd go in, shut the door, and I wouldn't talk to anyone else for a week at a time.' You can't help but wonder what effect this deprived, inactive life is having on her daughter. 'I feel we're not eating adequately,' she tells me. 'I'd like to buy the freshest, quality food. But I'm reduced to tinned stuff. It's not very good for her. But so long as she has a full belly and can go to bed without feeling hungry, that's what matters. What scares me is when the benefit is delayed, and we can't eat.' Despite her harsh life, Jacqueline still wants her daughter to do better. She helps her with her schoolwork, and hopes that one day she'll work. 'Even if it's only street-cleaning. I hope she'll find something.'

Inequality is not easy for women. It may delay their promotions; it may destroy their working lives altogether; it may keep them dependent on low wages; it may keep them beside abusive men; it may condemn them to lives of humdrum misery. Often, we have to strain to make out this grim reality. But it is time that we looked at it, full in the face, and understood that despite all the battles feminism has already won, feminism still has a part to play in Britain today. We want women to take their place in the world, to be able to play a part in the corridors of power alongside the men, to earn decent wages for their work, and to bring up children with dignity. Although women have come a long way, we still have a goal on the horizon: nothing more, and nothing less, than equality.

out of the ghetto

When people ask where the British women's movement is today, they are not looking for something that has ceased to exist, but they are looking at something that has changed. Once upon a time there was a Women's Liberation Movement, defined at annual conferences of groups and individuals. Women knew they could join it, or stay apart from it. This organisation spelt out demands, that women could agree with, or reject. It had definite figureheads that women could identify with, or not. By being so clearly defined, the women's movement in the seventies had both strengths and weaknesses: the strength that exists in identifiable activity and solidarity, but the weakness of being seen as an isolated group. The movement seemed to be containable. For most people, feminists were different, they were outsiders.

Today, the women's movement may have fragmented and splintered, but splinters of it are lodged in the hearts and minds of the majority of women in this country. The women's movement lives on, sometimes in organisations such as professional networks or campaigning movements or community groups. But often it just lives on in the everyday life and attitudes of women and men. Feminism now does not work from the outside – the Women's Liberation Movement – to the inside – the rest of society. No, today it works from the inside, throwing up feminist breakthroughs in different and diverse places – the Labour Party, *Vogue* magazine, Sara Thornton's appeal hearing, one woman's home, another's place of work, a conversation overheard on a bus or the lyrics of a pop song.[1]

This sense of being on the inside, at the centre, is what distinguishes feminism now from the feminism of every other age. We can take one telling image to remind ourselves that feminists today are not just to be found in small and powerless groups: the photograph that was published in national newspapers on 5 May 1997, of Clare Short and Harriet Harman meeting in front of 10 Downing Street and embracing as they congratulated one another on their Cabinet appointments. These two women have always been passionate and committed feminists. Clare Short is well known for her campaign to ban page three pictures in newspapers and for spearheading the Campaign Against Pornography, while Harriet Harman is well known for arguing that women need flexible working practices and better childcare if they are to compete equally with men in the workplace. To see these two women hugging each other in the very centre of British power shows us that feminists today are to be found everywhere, from the classroom to the Cabinet, from the home to government.

This is a revolutionary change. In the nineteenth century, feminists were working on the fringes of society. They were necessarily outsiders, because as women they were excluded from all areas of public debate – Parliament, universities, newspapers – and they were even banished to the fringes of private, domestic society by being mythologised as dangerous, deviant and anti-family. Nineteenth-century feminists stood noisily outside the corridors of power, banging on the doors for admission.

In the sixties and seventies, when feminism caught fire again, feminists still tended to be on the fringes of mainstream society. Partly, they were forced to be there: because university courses undervalued women's history, feminists set up women's studies courses; because few journalists cared to cover women's issues seriously, they set up feminist periodicals and women's pages in newspapers; because publishers were so bad at employing and publishing women, they set up women's publishing houses. But they also chose to develop theories that emphasised women's difference and separateness. 'I think we have to begin by trying to form again a kinship circle that is simply a circle of women and children,' wrote one feminist in the seventies.[2]

But for today's generation of young women, the outsider mentality – whether enforced or voluntary – has little resonance. Women assume that women's history should be included in core history courses; they assume that mainstream publishers should publish all kinds of books by and about women; they assume that so-called women's issues have a place in the editorials and straight news pages of newspapers; they assume that politicians should respond to women's concerns. Now, the changes we are looking for must happen within the context of paid work or Parliament or prime-time television, not in some separate space. So we have seen the breakdown of one feminist tradition and a new, less embattled ideal spring up to take its place. Among the women I interviewed for this book, I often heard about that sense of change. Clare Short MP said: 'I think we've moved from having a few women's groups here and there, and a few famous writers, to a position where feminism is in the mainstream, among women of all ages and backgrounds.'[3] Amor Jones, the Equal Opportunities Research

Officer at the MSF Union, said: 'Feminism is an accepted part of society now. It lives in people's minds rather than in a tangible movement.'[4] Peggy Alexander, who runs the National Group on Homeworking in Leeds, said: 'I think the women's movement is just as strong – if anything it's getting stronger. Ordinary women are getting up and saying, "I'm not having that", even if they don't associate it with feminism.'[5]

Many women who call themselves feminists find that their beliefs inform their behaviour at work and at home without pressing them into any kind of activism. And many women who say that they are not feminists nevertheless act exactly like feminists, to further the cause of equality either in everyday life or in organisations and protests. That makes the movement nebulous. It is easy, in these conditions, for the strength of feminism in Britain to be downplayed. Polly Toynbee wrote rather despairingly in the *Independent* in 1995[6] that 'The cause has not died, only the fire.'

But she is wrong. The fire is still burning – if anything it is getting stronger. In a recent poll carried out by MORI,[7] 71 per cent of women of all ages felt positively about feminism, but while only 66 per cent of women over 55 were positive, a striking 85 per cent of women under 25 were. In a recent reader-response survey carried out by the *Guardian*, 58 per cent of respondents called themselves feminists, and the self-proclaimed feminists were more likely to be under than over 35.[8] Meanwhile, an NOP survey found that 63 per cent of women would call themselves feminist some of the time.[9] Wouldn't any political party or movement kill for such overwhelming support? After all, if 58 per cent of all British people called themselves socialists and 85 per cent of young people felt positively about socialism, the Labour Party would never have to campaign again. And aren't the growing numbers of feminists and those sympathetic to feminism among young women proof that the fire is not dying?

It is true, however, that far more women feel positively about feminism or say they are in favour of women's equality than will call themselves feminists. And this is because feminism does have a particular image that can be alienating to young women: it is associated with man-hating and with a rather sullen kind of political correctness or puritanism. Feminists are perceived as obsessed with sexual politics, body image, language and pornography rather than with pragmatic strategies to take women nearer to equality. The movement is seen as intolerant, strident and sloganeering. Its characteristic attitude is understood to be angry rather than optimistic, whingeing rather than buoyant, negative rather than positive. This feminist is seen as an outsider, not an insider.

Some of these attitudes have been true of some feminist writing, meetings and actions. And even women who believe that this is solely an artificial myth created by detractors to weaken feminism often feel ambivalent about associating themselves too directly with it by standing up publicly for feminism. This ambivalence is particularly caused by one facet of the myth: the feminist is imagined as an unattractive physical type, desexed and fiercely rejecting traditional feminine behaviour. As the girls in one school I visited put it succinctly, each adding an adjective in a kind of chorus: 'She's a fat hairy angry lesbian.'

This has always been a striking problem about feminism. The myth about the unwomanly nature of the feminist has hidden, and still hides, women's ease with feminist ideas even from themselves. Once, feminists were seen to be wanton and lustful, then they were seen to be ugly and frustrated. Women were told that Mary Wollstonecraft, the great feminist whose book, A *Vindication of the Rights of Woman*, was published in 1792, was oversexed. After her husband William Godwin published his candid memoirs of her, journalists called it a book of 'whoredoms', 'brothel feats of wantonness', and indexed the book under 'Prostitution: see Mary Wollstonecraft'.[10] Women who were open feminists in the early nineteenth century were pushed to the very fringes of acceptable society, on account of their so-called loose sexuality. Understandably, other women were nervous about joining them there; it is surprising that so many did.

Following that, the women of the Suffragette movement were pilloried for their unfeminine appearance and hostility to heterosexuality, exactly as the women of the women's peace movement were nearly a century later. In cartoons and posters, Suffragettes were depicted in bizarrely monstrous ways, horribly disproportioned, hugely fat or tall, with enormous teeth and tiny eyes, screaming mouths and distorted faces. 'One never sees any pretty women among those who clamour for their rights,' wrote one commentator in 1907.[11] The *Daily Mirror* in 1914 headlined one page, 'The Suffragette Face: new type evolved by militancy', above a montage of Suffragettes caught in unflattering poses.[12] This attempt to deal with the unsettling rise of female independence by making it physically ridiculous ran from popular culture to contemporary literature. H. G. Wells wrote a striking portrait of an ugly, frustrated Suffragette in his popular book, *Ann Veronica*:

> She opened out into a long, confused, emphatic discourse on the position of women . . . As she talked she made weak little gestures with her hands, and she thrust her face forward from her bent shoulders . . . Ann Veronica watched her face, vaguely sympathising with her, vaguely disliking her physical insufficiency . . . She did not understand the note of hostility to men that ran through it all, the bitter vindictiveness that lit Miss Miniver's cheeks and eyes.[13]

We note here that physical 'insufficiency', being 'weak' and 'bent', is tied up with wanting the vote, and that being 'bitter' and 'hostile' towards men is already seen as part of the demand for equality.

The peace movement of the eighties was parodied by a similar caricature. Even the *Guardian* emphasised that the women at Greenham Common were 'punks, some have shaved heads, and others make no secret of the fact that they are lesbians. They make no attempt to behave as middle-class housewives.'[14]

Traditionalists still use these laden, leaden judgements to try to make us believe that a 'feminist' is a particular kind of woman, and in order to make other women uneasy about identifying with her. The more successful feminism becomes, the more desperate is the desire of the traditionalist to make feminists look unwomanly, undesired and undesirable. Using feminists' appearance as evidence of their lack of femininity is central to that project, especially now that feminist ideas have become so widely and easily accepted. When the *Sun* uses the most granite-faced and hard-edged picture of Clare Short that it can find to run by its stories of how she would like to ban page three pictures, it is clearly still trying the old trick. Rather than engage with her arguments it will resort to trying to alienate women from identifying with someone who is apparently so unfeminine.

Even women who are aware of this conspiracy that attempts to make a normal movement look abnormal are nervous about being so exposed. Women who have understood feminist analysis of the beauty myth and the feminine mystique are not always ready to ditch all claims to femininity themselves. Emma Must, a leading activist in the new environmental movement and a conscious feminist, says: 'Feminism did free me from certain worries about my own body. It made me realise what a con the pressure to be thin and feminine was. But at the same time perhaps one of the reasons why I didn't become active as a feminist was because I didn't want to be entirely identified with that feminist stereotype.'[15]

We should no longer allow this image of feminism, as something abnormal and unfeminine, to hide from us the vibrant, mainstream nature of feminism today. Feminism will always argue that women should not feel pressured to conform to traditional femininity or heterosexuality. But we should not allow this tenet to be used against us. The new feminism is a political movement that any woman or man can support; traditionally feminine women and heterosexuals are as much part of that movement as anyone else. In the history that we are looking to reclaim, we can remember not just our crop-headed, bloomered foremothers but also the elegance of Rebecca West and the deliberate physical charm of Vera Brittain, two great feminists from the early part of the twentieth century. We can remember that the daughter of Elizabeth Cady Stanton, the great American feminist, wrote to Christabel Pankhurst, Emmeline's daughter, that: 'Emmeline Pankhurst was very beautiful. She looked like the model of Burne-Jones' pictures – slender, willowy, with the exquisite features of one of the saints of the great impressionist.'[16] And in our current tradition we can look at the dressy chic of the British politician Barbara Follett or the unselfconscious femininity of the American writer Naomi Wolf as well as the dungareed refuseniks of the Greenham movement. We should never be taken in by the idea that feminism does not, has not always, encompassed traditional femininity as well as a deliberate breaking of feminine codes of appearance.

We should also be aware of the too-easy link that is made between socialism and feminism. For many feminists, that link is not a problem. But for many others, it is another aspect of the popular image of feminism that alienates women who are committed to equality for women, but who have not taken on the socialist package of how that should be achieved, and are understandably wary about being read as a certain kind of political animal. Feminism and socialism are two quite separate choices, and we can imagine and work towards a feminism that crosses political boundaries. A popular truism exists that Conservative women don't really like feminism, and that Conservative women would like to see wives back in the home. But a MORI poll has shown that support for feminism is much the same among Conservative and Labour voters. Previously unpublished statistics show that among female Conservative voters, 21 per cent thought that feminism had been good for women but not for men; among Labour women, that figure was 24 per cent. Among Conservative voters, 51 per cent thought feminism had been good for both women and men; while among Labour voters, only 47 per cent agreed.[17]

This support for feminism and the changes it has brought is clearly a solid reality among Conservative women, but it remains almost invisible. Individual women who are both Conservative and feminist feel isolated and misrepresented by a culture that denies the compatibility of the two creeds. Are the two incompatible? Angela Rumbold, a former government minister, has said: 'I am a feminist and a real Conservative.'[18] Another Conservative MP, Teresa Gorman, describes the House of Commons as 'a factory for boring men' and says, 'We need more women in the Commons . . . to constrain the excesses of male behaviour.'[19] She has spoken out against judges who fail to take sexual violence against women seriously[20] and against her party's shift towards a traditionalist approach to families.[21] As Edwina Currie has said plaintively, when she looked through literature on women's issues, 'Nobody seemed to be speaking for me, or for people like me. Most of the writing about women's issues in the last 20 years has come from the left. Feminism in both Europe and in the USA has been corralled by people with whom . . . I could not agree on any other issue.'[22] And as Employment Secretary, in 1993, the Conservative MP Gillian Shephard drew attention to the 'shock statistics'[23] of women's low achievement at work and is regularly called a 'sensible feminist'. Fiona Driscoll, the current chair of the 300 Group, whose aim is to get more women into Parliament, is a strong Conservative supporter. 'Feminism is associated with the loony left,' she says sadly.[24] But she still calls herself a feminist.

Feminism is about equality for women, nothing more nor less. The socialist and the conservative can hold to that ideal with equal passion, although they will differ about how it is to be achieved. So a socialist may argue for a minimum wage, quotas for female parliamentary candidates, and more state support for single mothers. But a conservative may believe that a deregulated economy will give women more opportunities in the long run, or that quotas are a sticking plaster remedy that tends to patronise women, or that state support for a woman simply replaces one kind of dependence – that on a man – with dependence on the state, and cannot help her to achieve her full potential.

It is, after all, notable that the first woman MP to take her seat, Nancy Astor, was a Conservative, and that the only female Prime Minister has been a Conservative. And until recently, the Conservative Party has also captured more female votes. So although feminism may have been associated most clearly in the public mind with left-wing causes, with left-wing councils, with union activism and peace campaigns, in fact feminism cuts across all political boundaries.

The idea that feminism still exists in some kind of ghetto has never been so completely out of step with the desires and perceptions of most women and men. How can the journalist Richard Littlejohn write in the *Daily Mail* that 'to most modern women, the feminist movement has become an archaic, embarrassing irrelevance', when his own paper's survey revealed that 71 per cent of women felt positively about it? How can Polly Toynbee write in the *Independent* that 'it [the women's movement] always did alienate most ordinary women', when another survey among students showed that only 5 per cent were 'not at all' sympathetic to feminism?[25]

In fact, the ideas of feminism were never in a ghetto, although many critics would like us to believe that they were out of touch or out of step with the beliefs of most women. Feminism began and has remained thoroughly embedded in the grass roots; and the desires of ordinary women for education, votes, better childcare facilities, equal pay, contraception, abortion and a fairer division of domestic labour, have been heard through the voices of feminists and the strength of feminist organisations. Feminism is one of the few profound intellectual shifts that have occurred in books written for a general audience, published by mainstream publishers, and sitting on the shelves of ordinary people. Feminists from Emmeline Pankhurst to Germaine Greer are household names. The catchwords of seventies feminism – sexism, male chauvinist pig – are everywhere understood. The penetration of feminism into everyday thought is equivalent to the penetration of Freudian psychoanalysis; it is a taken-for-granted touchstone in the minds of the general public. Although during the eighties the discipline of women's studies began to feed on itself and produce, in line with most cultural and literary studies departments, a deluge of print that was only marginally, if at all, relevant or comprehensible to a wider audience, that must not be allowed to obscure the way in which feminism has penetrated debate at all levels. We cannot now imagine living without its intellectual breakthroughs.

For instance, in one 1996 issue of the *Daily Mail*, the newspaper with the largest proportion of female readers in Britain, one feature was headlined 'Feminism has been a disaster for women'. And yet on other pages all the breakthroughs of feminism were celebrated. The front page was given over to mourning the death of Fleur Lombard, the first female firefighter to die on duty: 'Fleur lived for the job. She was brilliant' and 'The best firefighter I have ever seen', ran the quotations from her colleagues. Further on, a large article railed against the Foreign Office for not appointing a woman, Dame Pauline Neville-Jones, ambassador to Paris: 'Her rise has been blocked by the very male world of the Foreign Office.' So the changes feminism has wrought are celebrated and pushed forwards, while the name of feminism is still derided.[26]

Perhaps it doesn't matter, given this outright support for women's equality, whether young women are calling themselves feminists or not. I wondered that at one school I visited – a vast sixth form college on the outskirts of east London. The young girls there were certainly aware of all the demands of feminism; they disliked images of women in advertising, they felt men should do more childcare, they wanted to work and support themselves. When I asked them, 'Do you think women are equal?' they called out, with one voice, 'No!', and when I asked them, 'Are you in favour of women's equality?' there was another unanimous 'Yes!', but when I asked, 'Do you call yourselves feminists?' there was only one lone 'Yes!' Yet in their awareness of discrimination and of increasing potential these girls were passionate and intelligent feminists – without the name. Feminism is in the very air they breathe. All wanted to seek economic status and independence; all of them believed that men could be as good at caring as women are. And they happily launched into discussions about whether the point of feminism now was to make women more like men or men more like women, showing a real knowledge of debates of the past. Feminism is part of their lives, their hopes, their dreams. Compared to that success, what is a label?

This taken-for-granted status of feminism is its strength – and, of course, its weakness. It means that we are often in danger of forgetting all the unfinished business that feminism can help us to solve, and it means that our sense of outrage and injustice about the continuing oppression of women can feel like old hat. 'Didn't they

say all that 20, 30, 100, 150 years ago?' women might say, despairingly, when reading feminist polemic of this generation.

Yet despite the taken-for-granted nature of most central feminist
ideas, there is still an urgent project confronting this generation of
young women. They may no longer want to spend hours and
months heatedly debating the nuances of the sex war, they may not
want to spend acres of print on ever-more subtle definitions of feminism. But they do want straightforward material equality and they
intend to achieve it.

In that project this generation of young women can, contrary to
many media myths, count on overwhelming, almost unanimous
support from one another. Not only do 71 per cent of all women
feel positively about feminism, but when asked whether they agreed
or disagreed with the statement: 'A husband should earn and a
wife should stay at home', a staggering 92 per cent of women under
25 disagreed, and 89 per cent of those aged 25 to 35. That is the
measure of feminism's success in this generation.[27]

What's more, something that looks very like a women's movement does still exist in Britain. It is not a mass movement that
marches to one drumbeat, but a large collection of single-issue
organisations that press for feminist aims in many different accents.
Because each organisation is involved in its own struggle, it is
unnecessary for them to define themselves as part of a single, unified 'Women's Liberation Movement'. But these organisations
testify to a living feminism in Britain, one that gives the lie to the
pessimistic pronouncements of most commentators. These organisations work in different ways that reflect their different goals:
some hold parties with champagne and canapés, others hold
demonstrations with banners, others hold drop-in sessions; some
lobby government for changes in the legal system, others are trying
to get into government, others are just trying to make life better for
the women on their street. Some work with women who

experience violence, such as Refuge, Women's Aid Federation, Women Against Rape and Justice for Women. Some provide a voice for professional women aiming to crack the glass ceiling, such as Women in Journalism, the City Women's Network, Women in Management, the Association of Women Solicitors and Women in Medicine. Some are composed of women in political and public life, such as the 300 Group or the Labour Women's Network. Some foreground women's experience based on their race, such as Southall Black Sisters and Akina Mama wa Afrika, or based on their experience of childbearing, such as the Abortion Law Reform Association, National Childbirth Trust and the Maternity Alliance or their experience of specific health problems, such as the Hysterectomy Support Network and the Anorexia and Bulimia Nervosa Association.

Given the sheer range, the number, the breadth of such organisations, there is no unified culture that characterises the women's movement in Britain. If you wanted to find out what kind of woman gets involved in this movement, I would have to take you to some very different places. First, let's visit the small, frayed office of Southall Black Sisters, where Hannana Siddiqui, a young Asian woman in a loose sweater and trousers, is sending a fax while talking on the telephone and motioning me to a chair. The bookshelves of the little room are lined with Shulamith Firestone and Andrea Dworkin, but the organisation is not a fringe group of radical women. They provide straightforward, much-needed services mainly to Asian women suffering domestic violence. Those services include finding shelter for them, advising them on benefit and employment possibilities, counselling them, and helping them to fight their legal battles. Hannana says to me: 'There was an article in the *Guardian* saying that the women's movement in Britain no longer exists. I thought, but here we are. We may not be as big as we'd like, there may not be as many of us as we'd like, but here

we are, and the fruits of our work are so obvious. We have prevented death, we have prevented abuse, we have politicised
women. What do they mean, the women's movement no longer
exists?'

The second place is rather different; it is the vast, echoing tea-
room of the Institute of Directors in Pall Mall. Alison Thorne,
arrayed in big jewellery and shoulder-padded turquoise jacket,
orders tea from obsequious male waiters. She is the head of the City
Women's Network, a networking organisation made up of women
managers, which aims to raise the confidence and clout of senior
businesswomen: 'The network helps women to put themselves forward, to get into public life. Women need to bring other women
on, and to feel that they have every right to be powerful.'

It seems to me that if I brought Hannana Siddiqui and Alison
Thorne together they wouldn't have much to say to one another.
No one would be able to think up a manifesto that both women
would sign up to, nor would they be able to run a conference that
both women would feel easy attending. And yet they are working
for the same end: equality for the sexes; power and self-respect for
women.

If you're not convinced, come to two more places. The first is a
training day on the economy, run by the 300 Group, which campaigns to get more women into Parliament and public life. Fiona
Driscoll, the chair, says that she loves 'being in a room with all
these women who will be running the country in 20 years time'.
One woman who aims to use the training day as a springboard into
politics is the cool and elegant Carole Cohen, who wants to be a
Conservative MP. She 'joined to support other women', and has
since realised her own passion for politics.

The second is a community centre in west Newcastle based in a
bleak and windswept square, where two young women, Judith
Stephens and Debbie Riley, both of whom are bringing up children

on benefits, have set up a baby equipment loan scheme. For mini-mal charges, they can lend out prams and high-chairs and buggies to the women in their local community. 'They're all on really low incomes, so it's great for them,' they explain. And what's in it for them? 'It's good to make some kind of difference. We've been there so we know how hard it is when you're struggling like that.'

Having spoken to women like these and many others involved in yet other organisations, it seems to me that most commentators who argue about the death of the women's movement have simply never scratched the surface of the movement that does exist. It may not be a unified, centralised movement, but it is strong, con-stantly growing in one place and falling back in another, building on its successes, springing up from real political and economic and emotional needs. Different parts of the movement may each have their own little moment to influence politics or the public. We have seen many of those moments recently. When Sara Thornton lodged a successful appeal against her conviction for killing her violent husband, she was supported by the organisation Justice for Women, which brought her case on to the legal and media agenda. When the scare about the presence of phthalates in babies' milk surfaced, it was the National Childbirth Trust that took the micro-phone on the national news, arguing that women should be trusted with information about their children's health. When the Family Law Bill was going through Parliament in 1995 and 1996, the Women's Aid Federation lobbied successfully to make sure that mediation was not imposed on women seeking divorces from vio-lent men. When a bill to give local authorities the powers to reduce waste went through Parliament in 1997, it was brought because of the lobbying and research of the Women's Environmental Network. When the law was changed to make rape in marriage a crime in 1992, it was as a result of a long campaign by organisations like Women Against Rape and Legal Action for Women.

And apart from all these myriad organisations small and large, in every other area of society, women keep a real feminism active within their daily lives. If you listen to what individual women are saying, it quickly becomes very clear that women who call themselves feminist may be left-wing or right-wing, middle class or working class, and those who don't call themselves feminist may yet hold absolute feminist beliefs. In the presence of such conflicting definitions, no wonder the mainstream, majority nature of feminism in Britain is often underplayed.

Emma Must is a leading environmental campaigner at 28 years old. She spearheaded the protests on Twyford Down, and calls herself a feminist. She takes part in occasional women-only demonstrations, and does not divorce her feminism from her environmentalism, but, she says, 'I really dislike the idea that some feminists have put about, that women are naturally more peaceful than men. I think that is a complete red herring.'[28]

Anne Blaine, a single mother who is active in the network Gingerbread, the organisation for lone parents, says: 'I don't know if I would call myself a feminist – though I think women don't get a fair deal. I think it's really central that men get more into childcare.'[29]

Ann Bowtell, who is now one of the most senior woman in the civil service, Permanent Secretary at the Department of Social Security, is very wary about describing herself as a feminist and yet very conscious of the ways that women's lives are changing and the obstacles that they still might face. 'I believe in equality of opportunity for women. I wouldn't call myself a feminist, but my whole life has been lived on that basis. I get fairly impatient about what seem to be the frills, like whether people should hold doors open. I've always been too busy getting on and doing it, while other people were fiddling around talking about it.'[30]

Sylvie Pierce, chief executive of the London Borough of Tower

Hamlets, calls herself a feminist and believes that the primary barrier to women's continued advancement is still the discrimination they face. She longs to change that, and she believes that her experiences as a woman have moulded her dedication to her work, 'Perhaps because I've been on the other side of the counter, I have a passion never to treat other people as I was treated. Women are the greatest users of the welfare state and so perhaps they are better at delivering the services.'[31]

Rebecca Thomas, a 33-year-old director at Framlington Investment Management, says, 'I wouldn't call myself a feminist because I associate it with whingeing and railing rather than getting things done. But I am passionately in favour of equal opportunities. There does need to be legislation to help those who find there are barriers put up in front of them. I want to help other women. It's really important that women don't just rely on men, but develop their own potential.'[32]

Geraldine Caulfield, a 27-year-old production manager at a Northern Foods company in Shropshire, does call herself a feminist: 'Women now are saying to themselves, "I have to go out and get it, it won't be handed to me," so they're working out their careers very early on. As these career-minded women get into more senior jobs, I think things will change, you'll see more flexible working, more crèches and so on. I'd call myself a feminist, although I never make an issue of being a woman. I've made it in a man's world and that makes me feel strong.'[33]

What do these voices tell us? That although some women call themselves feminists and some do not, almost all women, almost without exception, want to move closer to equality. There seemed to me, as I talked to women throughout Britain, to be very little difference between those women who call themselves feminists, and those who avoid the label. A majority of women have taken on the insights and visions of feminism, and are working for that vision in their everyday lives.

The reluctance that many women feel in saying that they are feminists is understandable; they feel alienated from the label because they feel it puts them in some sort of a ghetto, that it defines them as an activist or a socialist or a lesbian or somebody who is humourless or dowdy or celibate. A woman should be able to say 'I am a feminist' without feeling that she is implying any of these other positions. It should be a statement of allegiance to women's equality that a Conservative prime minister or a million-aire or a happily married woman or a prostitute could say, alongside any other woman.

And we must reclaim the history of feminism – not as the history of an embattled minority, but as the story of a mainstream, major-ity movement. It's a great story, a happy, triumphant story. Feminism is a unique philosophical and political movement that has transformed women's lives, that has brought about the greatest and most peaceful social revolution that has ever been seen. And yet it is constantly trivialised.

For instance, many historians shrug off the achievements of fem-inists in winning the vote for women. They argue that women's contribution to the economy during the First World War made it expedient for politicians to give women a more central place in pol-itics and society. No doubt women's increased economic activity was a factor in the politicians' decision to grant them suffrage. But the fact that this shift in women's work could be harnessed to their political advantage shows the mainstream penetration of feminist argument and the influence of feminist political activity. Wars and changes in women's employment had occurred before, but never before had feminist arguments about women's right to political equality been heard so strongly and for so long. The movement for women's suffrage was a mass movement of women from all classes and all political affiliations, who worked in a broad range of campaigns throughout the latter half of the nineteenth century, and won, against enormous odds. Rather than simply accepting a tale of the inevitability of men seeing the light, we should tell and retell this positive story about women's ability to revolutionise the political establishment. When it is told, it inspires women. As Geri of the Spice Girls once said, 'I didn't really know that much history, but I knew about the Suffragettes. They fought. It wasn't that long ago. They died to get a vote. The women's vote. You remember that and you think, fucking hell.'[34]

We also need to reclaim the history of the way that feminists, and feminist arguments, changed women's lives in Britain through their influence on the creation of the welfare state. The gradual humanisation of the role of the state, that turned it from a small organisation that simply passed laws and waged wars to a mass employer that organised health care and social insurance, for the whole population, was a change that was spearheaded by women.[35] This change in attitude to public welfare coincided with the entry of women into the political establishment and the influence on government of organisations such as the Women's Co-operative Guild and the Women's Labour League. Feminists then congratulated themselves on the fact that women's suffrage brought about such a revolution in attitude and legislation;[36] but their consciousness of triumph has been hidden by the passing years.

Similarly, women's contemporary freedom is often put down to scientific or economic accident.[37] Particularly, the development of the contraceptive pill is credited with springing women from traditional feminine behaviour and confinement to the home. Clearly, contraception helped women to become more independent. But why do women in the developing world not use reliable contraception even when it is made available to them? As evidence shows us, women's education is a necessary precondition to women taking the decision to limit their families. If nineteenth-century feminists had not broken open the doors of schools and universities for young women, and opened their minds to the possibility of female independence and self-worth, the contraceptive pill alone would have had much less effect on women's lives.

Again, we are often told that women's increasing role in the workplace is an economic accident, caused by the shift from manufacturing to service industries, by a growth in part-time work, or by fiscal policies that encourage both wife and husband to seek work. These economic changes are important, but it is also true that for the first time, under the influence of feminist ideas of equality and power, women see paid work as integral to their lives and seek to exploit their foothold in the labour force. There is no reason that men should not have moved as easily from hegemony in manufacturing to hegemony in service work, as they once moved from agricultural to manufacturing work. It is no accident, but women's conscious tenacity in not giving up, and even extending, their presence in the workplace, that has resulted in women's growing economic strength.

It is a serious historical error, and a mystifying one, that we are often reluctant to pay tribute to the intellectual and political force of feminism. Feminism is not just the movement that enabled us to tick men off if they leered at us, it is the movement that brought us the vote; the welfare state; the legal right to equal pay; legal protection from harassment, rape and abuse; rational dress; contraception and abortion rights; and new patterns of work. Without feminism, women would still be unable to own property or be educated or control their fertility. Men's sudden generosity did not lead them to share economic, scientific and political advances with women. Women's own efforts to gain equality, voiced through two centuries of feminist argument, brought them these advances. If we understand the extraordinary achievements of feminist women in the past, we will be all the more able to view the future with optimism, with the knowledge that it can be shaped as we desire.

But if we believe that the women's movement does not exist, has achieved nothing, has betrayed women, is nothing but a tiny faction or even a delusion, then all the millions and millions of feminists in the country tend to feel atomised, isolated and unsupported. As things stand, they fail to pull at full strength, because they don't realise how many other women are in the boat with them. It seemed clear to me, as I went from meetings with women from the Association of Women Solicitors to a female solicitor who had never joined it but clearly espoused feminist beliefs in her work, or from an Asian women's group to a highly successful school dominated by Asian girls, that although one of them might be part of an identifiable women's movement and one might not, they all existed on the same, very effective, but strangely silenced continuum. A feminist continuum, that is still spearheading social change in our society.

Women are not encouraged to believe in this movement, even though it blooms in the work and attitudes of a majority of women in this country. They are not encouraged to be proud of their successes. Instead they are asked to believe that anything feminist is irrelevant to the needs of ordinary women, and belongs to some tiny, ghettoised, loony-lefty group. Nothing could be further from the truth.

We need to reclaim this fragmented, diverse, tolerant feminism for ourselves. We need to be aware of the campaigns and organisations that exist, we need to be aware how many other women and men share our views on equality and discrimination. Then we will recognise the true strength and potential of feminism. Currently, it comes as quite a shock to realise that 85 per cent of young women feel positively about feminism, or that 92 per cent of young women disagree with the statement 'a husband should earn and a wife should stay at home'. We have allowed a smokescreen to come between ourselves and our feminist movement.

If we realise this huge support for feminism, we will make more pressing demands on our employers, our partners and our politicians. We need not allow ourselves to be atomised and dispersed. This feminism is composed of a million points of light, and we can celebrate many little advances without asking any of them to be the whole answer. But one by one, as each little light spreads, we will realise that a new dawn is shining full into the faces of every one of us.

chapter 4

the new feminism is less personal and more political

There's a Good Girl, Marianne Grabrucker's description of trying to bring up her daughter in a non-sexist way, shines a light on one facet of female development:

> One of the boys takes a little figure made of sugar away from Anneli, which our hostess had just given her. Anneli yells and wants to grab it back off him; she almost succeeds but he's too quick and sticks it in his mouth. Anneli screams with rage. The boys' parents are standing next to the children, watching; they tell Anneli to be a bit more careful and a bit quicker next time. Not a word to the boy who has snatched the thing from her, no admonition to him not to do it again. Once again it's the girl who is told to alter her behaviour. Even in cases where the boy has used force and is in the wrong the girl is expected to prevent this happening again by adapting her behaviour.[1]

Oddly, in much feminist debate over the past 20 years, we have seen a repetition of this pattern. What began as a movement for pursuing equality – for taking the sugar away from the boys – has gradually turned into a self-improvement movement, in which women are continually persuaded to concentrate on their own behaviour.

Women have always been aware of the need to use their own experiences as a starting point for feminism. A sense of injustice, a sense of claustrophobia, a sense of anger: such emotions were the springboard for many political journeys. But feminist writers and activists in the nineteenth and early twentieth centuries always took their insights outwards, even if they had been gained from looking within. Virginia Woolf's great book, *A Room of One's Own*, is exemplary in this regard. Although she begins with her own particular experiences, detailed with poetic brilliance – her experiences of being refused entry to a university library, of eating lunch with male academics, or doodling in the British Museum – these experiences are turned into an economic, not a poetic exhortation. Women must have financial independence if they are to write. 'You may object that in all this I have made too much of the importance of material things,' she says finally, but: 'Intellectual freedom depends on material things.'[2]

Similarly, the writings of women seeking the vote in the nineteenth century were founded on a sense of fierce personal anger at being excluded from political debate. But the movement that arose out of personal anger became a political alliance of hundreds of thousands of women, middle class and working class, left and right, militant and non-militant. Christabel Pankhurst wrote: 'The spirit of the movement was wonderful. It was joyous and grave at the same time . . . There was a touch of the impersonal in the movement that made for its strength and dignity.'[3]

The second wave of feminism, the voices raised in the sixties and seventies, made this link between the personal and the political more intense. They showed how personal life was constructed in the image of wider inequalities of power, and they showed how political life could never be divorced from private values.

The link that feminists made between the personal and the political shattered the complacency of the traditional masculine viewpoint. The knowledge that one can no longer say 'man' and mean 'human' is both a small and a revolutionary change. Women have questioned the universality of almost every traditional theory, and the earlier certainties of politics, of psychology, of social policy, of literary criticism, have been shaken as a result. Feminists revealed to us how politicians were guilty of ignoring the weight of their economic decisions on unpaid women or of their foreign policy decisions on civilian women. Feminists revealed to us that Freud's theories relied on his ability to relegate women's own tales of childhood abuse as he cast reality as fantasy. Feminists revealed to us that when male critics are told that a work is by a woman, they judge it more harshly than when they are told it is by a man. For every so-called impersonal theory, they revealed the importance of admitting its dependence on personal prejudice. This made the masculine viewpoint seem partial at best, and encouraged women to believe in the value of their own judgements.

Feminists determinedly brought aspects of private and domestic life into the public arena; they openly discussed and campaigned against sexual and domestic violence and they delivered the right to legal abortion. As they transformed political life, so feminists also transformed personal life; they encouraged women to dress and speak more freely at home and at work. Through feminism women gained courage in throwing off the personal constraints of traditional femininity. This fusion of private and political issues can never now be put aside. It has transformed our lives. Above all, it has been our weapon for freedom. Young women can now explore a range of different ways to behave; aggressive and articulate behaviour is rewarded as well as passive or quiet behaviour. Women now have countless naughty, large and noisy heroines to emulate as well as the good, small and quiet heroines of the last century.

This link between the personal and the political has become accepted to such an extent that it is hard for women of this generation to understand what society was like before feminism's second wave. If a woman who is raped finds that her story is not believed; if a woman finds that she is expected to do all the domestic work while her husband slips down to the pub; if a female worker is consistently paid less than her male peers for the same work; or if she encounters sexual pressure in return for promotion, these women can snap the single instance of personal discrimination into a wider framework. They can realise how it feeds off and into wider inequalities of power, and they can feel justified in confronting those involved. Lisa Stone[4], who is now 53, was sexually harassed in her first job more than 30 years ago. But she didn't have the framework to make that into a public issue, and it went unreported. 'If you didn't have words like sexist or sexual harassment, it was hard to find an explanation of what was going on. Because there was no framework for me to express my anger – I couldn't hit him or shout at him because he was my boss – I just got guilty and miserable, and I left. It's only now, with hindsight, that I can explain to myself and other people why I felt so demeaned.' Now, the idea of sexual harassment is something that everyone from schoolgirls to politicians are aware of, and it can be treated as an abuse of power rather than simply a messy personal experience.

But this new weight given to women's private experiences also made for a shift of direction in feminist culture. As the private sphere became more and more important, the endpoint of the feminist revolution was often seen to be not changing the balance of power in society, but purifying women themselves – or pulling themselves to pieces in the attempt.

The Female Eunuch, Germaine Greer's classic contribution to the literature of liberation, shows the start of this shift of direction. The revolution that Greer envisages will be achieved by women in the privacy of their own homes. Her argument is therefore addressed primarily to women, exhorting them to change their own behaviour. 'The married woman must . . . analyse her buying habits, her day-to-day evasions and dishonesties, her sufferings, and her real feelings towards her children.' Women 'must refuse to marry', 'ought to get over the prejudice attaching to second-hand clothes', 'could make their own perfumes', must 'stop loving the victor in violent encounters'.[5]

Up to a point this desire to change female behaviour makes sense. Wars will only cease when soldiers refuse to fight, and, as Dorothy Dinnerstein observed in 1976, 'without substantial female compliance, male rule would at this point be a pushover'.[6] And the shift in emphasis clearly answered a desire from the grass roots. Eileen Malos, who was at the first national Women's Liberation Conference in 1970, said: 'The most strongly expressed wish was for a total transformation of society from the bottom up, not only a change in economic and political organisation, but in the organisation of the family and personal relationships.'[7]

But this shift was not only enlightening. It also made for a more and more claustrophobic sphere of debate and activity; feminism gradually began to be associated only with fine-tuning women's personal lives, and particularly women's sexuality. In 1978, at the last national conference of the women's movement, the 'right to define our sexuality' was adopted as *the* overriding demand of the feminist movement.[8] This desire to define one's own sexuality became not about finding ways to resist violence and coercion – if and when they were encountered – by, say, strengthening women's economic and legal power; but simply about changing one's own behaviour on a merely personal level. To become celibate or lesbian was often the touted solution to women's problems. At the end of the 1970s, one radical feminist group in Britain published their message that 'giving up fucking for a feminist is about taking your politics seriously',[9] and many women were made to feel alienated from the women's movement because of such ideals. As the feminist writer Lynne Segal has said: 'I think that many of us did feel undermined and confused, if not guilty, by the accusation that we were too "male-identified" and "soft on men". It was as though feminists should be able to eliminate all the contradictions of a political struggle for the "purity" of our cause.'[10] This was not, any more, a political movement, but a psychological steam-room, in which women were invited to sit and cleanse themselves. And if this was not the truth about the women's movement, it was certainly the way it was seen by most of its enemies and some of its friends. 'What is crucial is that women begin disengaging from male-defined response patterns,' said the Radicalesbians in their influential paper, 'The Woman-Identified Woman', in 1972. '*In the privacy of our own psyches*, we must cut those cords to the core . . . if we are male-identified in our heads, we cannot realise our autonomy as human beings [my italics].'[11]

The second wave women's movement had at first been primarily concerned with righting economic and social disadvantages. It had delivered legislation on equal pay and sex discrimination in employment, and women's groups in the seventies were involved with labour disputes, political campaigns, and local agitations for better health care and transport and housing, in which self-confessed feminists could join hands with other women. But it eventually seemed to collapse under the weight of its insistence on the importance of women's personal experiences. One article that

I remember reading in *Spare Rib* as an idealistic 19-year-old struck a particular chill to my heart. It was little enough in itself: the testimony of a woman in the Merseyside *Women's Paper* collective, about why the paper had folded. The article throbbed with an overriding obsession with the women's own emotions, angry as they were that the women's movement had not brought them personal happiness: 'we have become depressed, demoralised and worn out,' ran the editorial in their final paper; 'we have found the climate in the women's movement hostile and intimidatory.' In the absence of any clear vision of what they wanted to achieve, it appeared that the women had slipped into believing that the women's movement had to be their substitute mother or psychotherapist. One statement, above all, stuck in my mind: 'When I first got involved with the Women's Movement,' the interviewee said, 'it made me feel better about myself. Now, it makes me feel worse.'[12] This article alienated me profoundly. It suggested that the women's movement should be a crutch for vulnerable women rather than a channel through which women could build on their achievements. It seemed to me that neither I nor any woman I respected would be proud to identify with such a movement.

Many recent books have supported this inward gaze. *Our Treacherous Hearts: Why Women Let Men Get their Way, The Cinderella Complex: Women's Hidden Fear of Independence*, and other titles suggest a feminism that began to concentrate more and more on women's own complicity in inequality rather than the external barriers that they face. The latter book suggests that feminism is more properly a self-help than a political movement. In this self-help movement women must learn to blame themselves for their own lack of power, and try to find psychological explanations for their disadvantages and psychological strategies for overcoming their 'Cinderella complex'. 'Personal, psychological dependency – the deep wish to be taken care of by others – is the chief force holding women down today,'[13] the author writes, and 'We will not begin to experience real change in our lives, real emancipation, until we begin the process of working through the anxieties that prevent us from feeling competent and whole.'[14]

What effect has this tendency to concentrate on women's private lives had? The mindset of the women's movement has become a shell that we must crack. Feminism has overpersonalised the political and overpoliticised the personal, and in the process has lost sight of its two great, longstanding goals: political equality and personal freedom. It is tough working for concrete political goals when one is forced to listen to individual judgements and psychological arguments at every point. Similarly, it is hard to feel free in one's private life when every personal and cultural gesture is weighed down with political freight. Although the fusion of the personal and the political was once our weapon for freedom, it has now become a cage. Can we imagine a new separation of the personal and the political?

As far as the overpersonalisation of the political goes, many feminists began to believe that anything that dealt with women's personal lives was part of the feminist struggle and worthy of immense respect. In 1972, Michelene Wandor wrote in *Spare Rib* that 'no irritation or discontent should be ignored, however small,' in trying to change women's lives.[15]

This image we have of the women's movement as being self-obsessed and apolitical is a damaging one. It seems to reinforce women's helplessness rather than resist it. In her recent novel *Promised Lands*, Jane Rogers takes her heroine to a consciousness-raising group in the seventies: 'They talk as if women were weak and helpless; they talk about needing support and counselling; they talk about emotions they can't control. One speaks of bursting into tears repeatedly for no reason, the others murmur in sympathy. They are like self-indulgent children.' The woman goes home and tells her partner, with heavy irony, 'They are taking political action, the women . . . They look up their own private parts.'[16] Although we know that the narrator is being too harsh, and Rogers makes it clear that this heroine has her own problems of lack of empathy with other people, there is a kernel of recognisable truth in this description. Although women certainly felt empowered by building safe spaces where they could talk about their own emotions and build more positive relationships with their own bodies, this clearly cannot be the only goal for feminism.

Over the last few years in Britain, much feminism has been trapped in a spiral of personal obsessions. At the What Women Want Festival on the South Bank in London in summer 1995, the inspiring cross-fertilisation of personal and political issues seemed to have degenerated into the merely personal. Dubbed a celebration of womankind, the festival offered aromatherapy, tantric sex workshops, music, art, Body Shop products and a talk by the astrologer on the *Sunday Times* magazine. The Women's Communication Centre organised a survey which simply asked women to fill up cards saying what they wanted. When I interviewed Bernadette Vallely of the Women's Communication Centre about the survey she was very excited about the range of responses: 'It's everything from "I want curtains like her at number seven", to "I want larger bra-sizes in the shops" to "I want to be safe on the street".' When I suggested that such a range, in the absence of any transforming analysis, might be difficult to turn into political demands, she shrugged off the idea. She would show them to the Prime Minister, and then he would feel the full force of women's desires.

It has become hard to resist such ideas, because it is often assumed that women's personal experience of oppression is the only bedrock of their feminism. This is called 'identity politics', the idea that your political ideas arise directly out of your own experiences, and that as your identity differs from another woman, so will your feminism. The growth of identity politics split middle-class and working-class women, women and men, heterosexual and lesbian women, white women and black women, able-bodied and disabled women, into an ever-more disparate series of political positions. One researcher even deliberately set up three groups of women, one of black and white women, one of Jews and Gentiles and one of lesbian and heterosexual women, in order to observe that 'in every group, past experience with oppression and domination distorted the participants' . . . identification with people in common political situations who did not share their history.'[17] But maybe the problem was that she was looking for identification with other women, rather than simply shared activity.

This trend towards identity politics has made it very difficult to sustain serious arguments about what themes or strategies now make sense to many women; everything is reduced to small, personal debates. The British media have happily taken up this trend, and run with it. The media like to reduce debates to personalities, who are easily praised or vilified. So, the resignation of *Cosmopolitan*'s editor Marcelle d'Argy-Smith comes to stand in for an argument about the difficulties that career women face; a slanging match between the feminist writers Germaine Greer and Suzanne Moore comes to stand in for an argument about the future of feminism; being for or against Paula Yates in her divorce stands in for a debate about why we expect such different standards from men and women as partners and parents; scare stories about one abusive childminder can stand in for parents' worries about the lack of regulated childcare.

This unrigorous concentration on women's private lives can become a mere continuation of how women are traditionally expected to behave – fixated on the domestic, on sexual matters, on their bodies, on their romantic relationships. The inwardness that has dogged the women's movement for the past decade or so is, maybe, especially attractive to women because of their socialised habits. Perhaps it comes more easily to women, trained as they are to keep to private spaces and domestic dialogue, to debate their own complicity in unequal conditions rather than look for ways to change those conditions.

Even the most committed and dynamic contemporary feminists now tend to concentrate on the psychological rather than the political sphere. Many of them believe that women's failure to achieve real equality, especially in the higher echelons of society, is down to the fact that women are not sufficiently eager for worldly power, and that they need to develop new and more ambitious attitudes. This seems superficially convincing, given that there are no longer any concrete barriers to keep them out, and yet women are signally failing to take their places in the most powerful arenas.

It is true that in many areas of work women seem to be oddly slow at coming forward to take on greater power, even when they are qualified to do so. For instance, although Parliament has been open to men and women for 75 years, only about a fifth of those on the list of possible parliamentary candidates for the Conservative Party are women.[18] Feminists who confront the need for more equality in the corridors of power often argue that we have to work on women's personal attitudes to overcome the barriers that still exist. The American feminist Naomi Wolf, in her search for political and economic equality, also lays out an agenda for psychological transformation in her book *Fire with Fire*. 'We must look at the very last obstacles in our path: feminine fears about using power,' she says. 'The female psyche still harbours great ambivalence about claiming power'; 'The notion that fears about using power stand in women's way just as concretely as do external obstacles was brought home to me by my own experience'; 'In my experiences discussing these matters, younger women were the most hesitant about touching power.' Her strategies for reaching equality therefore include psychological strategies. She advises us to 'claim our dark side', to 'remember and take possession of the girlhood will to power' and to 'create private pantheons of women, real or mythical, who braved dissent, created controversy, showed leadership and wielded power.'[19]

This idea of personal transformation is often picked up by British businesswomen. Fiona Driscoll, the chair of the 300 Group and managing director of a PR company, wants women to boost each other's sense of power. 'Women's networks need to grow,' she said to me. 'Men have been helping each other for years, and women need to learn from them.'[20] Alison Thorne, the head of the City Women's Network, also believes that women can be their own worst enemy. 'They still have an "impostor syndrome",' she complained over tea in a St James's club, 'even if they are overqualified they're afraid they'll fail. Men would never think that. Women need to display the trappings of success, they need a decent suit, a car, jewellery. Previous feminists didn't bother with all that.'[21] Jean McIntosh, the chief executive of Women in Management, agrees: 'Even if women have amazing qualifications, too often they just can't sell themselves, they don't have the body language and the confidence. Men talk themselves into a higher job than their abilities suggest, but women do the opposite. We have to change that.'[22]

This emphasis on a new attitude to power is seductive, but it can drift into the simple exhortations of self-help books. 'Developing a female style of power is the answer', runs the advice in one such book, *The Influential Woman*. 'You have to turn inwards, and confront deep-seated attitudes towards power which may be holding you back from acquiring or using it.'[23] Kate White, the author of *Why Good Girls Don't Get Ahead But Gutsy Girls Do*,[24] aims to encourage women to be gutsier by instructing them on what to wear ('If you need clout, wear high heels'); how to sit; how to hold someone's gaze; how to enter a room as if you own it; how to ask for a raise, a company car, or a promotion.

Although such encouragement can be inspiring, we do have to ask whether the most pressing agenda for feminism today is to change women's own attitudes. Women who are now defining a new feminism in Britain have lived their entire lives in the light shed by the feisty and articulate feminists of the sixties and seventies. They have grown up while a woman was running the country and women were participating in civil disobedience at Greenham Common. They have already changed their attitudes to power and femininity. They have changed the way they talk, the way they see their careers, the way they dress and the way they work. As I explore in more detail in Chapter 8, these young feminists have already turned what was once a utopian socialist dream into a story of bourgeois success.

This means that women in Britain have a healthy sense of scepticism that 'the trappings of success' are all they need to change their fortunes. Many social and political structures still militate against the flight of free will, and often we need to look at a wider map than the one showing the path of our own desires. The personal and the political are not identical, and we cannot deal with political problems purely by an effort of individual will. Power, after all, is not an epithet that can be affixed to women if they have the right attitudes, and indulge in enough power-dressing, power-lunches and power-breakfasts. It is a concrete attribute.

We may also feel suspicious of a brand of feminism that seems to narrow down the wide notion of equality once associated with feminism. 'Power-feminism' may be bright and glossy, but is it just about jobs for the girls? It sometimes seems to lack a heart, to have lost its commitment to equality for all women. The disadvantages that women face are not just in boardrooms and parliaments, but throughout society, and no notion of power will mean much to women now unless it taps into this wider impatience with inequality.

Recent feminist debate has therefore been wrong to concentrate so heavily on women's personal attitudes. Indeed, this highly personal viewpoint may weigh upon women. By insisting that they remould their attitudes in line with a particular ideal, some feminists encourage women to indulge in more personal guilt, not less, and this steers them in the wrong direction. I have often heard women who are making choices in their working lives blame all the obstacles and problems they encounter on their own failure to seize power, so increasing their sense of guilt and helplessness. At the same time, they will judge men's failures in terms of external, excusable factors, taking guilt away from men and making their lives easier.

For instance, Jane Allen,[25] a successful 32-year-old woman, was offered a promotion at the publisher where she worked. She turned it down because she was happy in her present job, happier than she had ever been before. She had worked once before in the area of the proffered job, and hated it. But when she talked to me about it, she judged herself in terms of personal fault. 'I'm just not eager for power, am I?' she said. 'It's true, what they say about women.' I had to point out to her that a man had been offered that job only six months before, and also turned it down because he didn't think it would leave him any time for the writing he wanted to do. He had not then wallowed in a sense of personal failure.

Similarly, a male senior publisher I know went through a bad patch at work. His partner had just had a baby, and his company had gone through a difficult merger. He resigned his prestigious job, and went down to about one third of his previous income by freelancing from home. And yet no one in his circle of friends blamed his resignation on his inability to combine work and home, or on his dislike of power, both of which would certainly have been cited if he had been female. They blamed it on personal differences between him and his boss, or his desire to 'be independent'. The fact that once he was at home he spent about half his time with his child was seen as a passing phase, rather than the working out of a primitive necessity, as it would have been with a woman. The easy judgements we make about men and women, that women are not hungry for power and that men are, often make a bad fit with our own experiences.

A recent MORI poll found that when women were asked why they thought women didn't succeed as well as men at work, the only two answers that drew much agreement were the disadvantages of having children, which was chosen by 60 per cent, and discrimination by men, which was chosen by 33 per cent.[26] And a survey undertaken by the Institute of Management found that female managers cited 'the existence of the men's club network' as the greatest barrier to women in management, followed by other tangible barriers such as lack of childcare.[27] Neither survey rated women's own lack of confidence as an important factor.

Similarly, when research has been done into how organisations can increase the number of women holding power, changing women's personal attitudes has been exposed as a dead end. Rather, what seems to result in change is a commitment from senior executives to equality, combined with training and definite goals for equality. When Opportunity 2000 investigated why British companies lagged far behind the rest of Europe in the numbers of women in powerful positions, they found that one of the possible reasons was that equal opportunities training in Britain was focused too narrowly on women, 'with little effort to amend the content or style of training more generally . . . There was little concept of shared ownership, and the development of women was perceived to be at the expense of men and, by inference, not in the best interests of the company.'[28]

This implies that we must shift our attention away from narrowly trying to change women's own attitudes and ambitions, and look to changing the lie of the land in which they move. Those who choose to concentrate on women's personal attitudes often do so as a way of refusing to do anything more to try to level the field. For instance, the Conservative Party's inability to back affirmative action for female candidates leads them to attack women themselves for not coming forwards. Dame Angela Rumbold once told me: 'The main thing we have to do now is to encourage women to feel that politics is for them.' But such talk has not led to any rise in the numbers of Conservative women elected to Parliament.

As this generation of women has come so far, we can look a little further than women's personal attitudes to ask why women are not taking up an equal amount of space in the corridors of power. After all, concentrating on personal empowerment can feel invigorating, but often leads only to placing more burdens upon women looking for material changes: are we speaking the wrong language? Are we not dressing for success? These questions often lead women to blame themselves for a lack of advancement even when the blame may better be put elsewhere.

And they can be patronising to women who are often working against great odds in attempting to secure greater equality. When I was talking to young women earning £50 a week for a full-time job, who nevertheless insisted that they wanted a career, or to women living on benefit who still wanted to help mothers around them by running a child-equipment loan scheme, it would have been pretty insulting for me to suggest that they needed to sharpen up their attitudes. Their own attitudes were not in question; bigger issues were at stake.

So let's move on from the idea that women are not taking on power because they don't really want it. Our problems may be less inside our own heads, and more in the world around us. Young women now are easier about power than any other generation, and they have role models and cultural images that reinforce their pursuit of it. But how do they change the systems they find around them, that still militate against women's greater advancement? If we want to crack the powerlessness of women in this generation, we must look not just at how women can change themselves, but also at how women can change the places in which they live and work.

Aside from the psychological and inward drive of recent feminist debate, there is quite another aspect to feminism. It is heartening to remember those women who took part in the very public, political struggles of first and second wave feminism as organisers and leaders. They learnt to push their private fears and differences into the background. Susan B. Anthony, an American feminist who was an effective public organiser, admitted in 1860, 'It is a terrible martyrdom for me to speak.' Similarly British Suffragettes, trained since birth to be quiet and ladylike, endured heckling and violence and prison to enter the public arena. The seventies were not just about cutting cords 'in the privacy of our own psyches', but also about ordinary political battles for equal pay, equal education and equal opportunities. We need to reclaim the history of the second wave women's movement, and remember that it was not just about our bodies and ourselves, but also about the world around us.

And times are changing again. Female journalists such as Suzanne Moore, Polly Toynbee, Nicci Gerrard, Linda Grant, Yvonne Roberts and others formulate a pragmatic feminism every day in our newspapers. And many recent books have emphasised the necessity for taking our personal experiences outwards again. In *Fire With Fire*, Naomi Wolf does not only stick with the need to teach women to like power, she also suggests what they might want to do with it: from getting more women promoted in business to building shelters for abused women.[29]

In a recent book about motherhood, the journalist Maureen Freely takes us through all her complicated experiences of being a mother with different men and in different countries. She dryly shows how impossible she found it to put the personal exhortations of feminists into practice, in the absence of concrete back-up such as better childcare and flexible working practices. And her ending strikes a low-key, practical note that is almost shocking in the modesty of its demand, simply 'to redesign school hours so that they mesh with work hours . . . There would be enough hours in the day if the work day and the domestic day were changed.'[30]

The same low-key chords are now constantly heard from women in unions, journalism, thinktanks and businesses as they press for changes in laws, social security provision and working practices to benefit women. The sudden increase in the number of women MPs, from one in ten MPs to one in six, has meant that feminism has begun to affect government policy – or at least government rhetoric – in terms of childcare policy and helping single mothers to move off benefit. And feminist organisations, as I outlined in the previous chapter, continue to agitate for political, social and legal changes to women's lives in an upfront, committed style.

Such women are reminding us of feminism's political edge, and its pressing agenda to give all women greater equality. As Barbara Follett MP, founder of Emily's List UK, said: 'Feminism has reached a point, as the struggle for black civil rights did, where consciousness-raising is not enough. We want to engage with the real world.'[31]

The personal-is-the-political theme has also tended to overpoliticise our personal lives. Originally, the link was a weapon for freedom. It enabled women to remove constraints upon their behaviour such as their lack of control over their fertility, sexual harassment, restrictive dress codes and the insistent exclusion of women from certain areas of debate. It allowed women to demystify the ideal of femininity – not to destroy it entirely, but to make it one of a series of ideals that women would grapple with as they grew up. Why is it, then, when I spoke to young girls around the country, they seemed quite certain that feminists, far from increasing women's personal freedom, want to propagate a rigid framework of personal behaviour?

When I visited schools in Britain, I found that young women would break into great debates about how they didn't mind being called 'love' and so they couldn't be a feminist, or how they liked fashion magazines and feminists would get rid of all that; or why they personally weren't very career-orientated and therefore couldn't be feminists. Other women, conversely, asserted that they hated the earth-mother myth and therefore couldn't be feminists. Against these waves of false – and completely contradictory – assumptions, it was difficult for me to assert that feminism was about equality in the real world rather than righteousness in the mind, about choice rather than a straitjacket for women.

This is a dangerous suggestion: that the feminist's commitment to linking personal and political issues means that she will politicise and overinterpret personal behaviour. Rather than seeking social equality, such a feminist will care too much about bras and depilation and language, and get bogged down in debates over sexual politics to the exclusion of everything else. Such a feminist must get angry over every door opened for her and muttering of 'love' or 'dear'. And such a feminist will concentrate too exclusively on the mote that is in her fellow-feminist's eye.

It is regrettably true that feminists' preoccupation with women's behaviour has often overtaken their commitment to tolerance and personal freedom. For instance, Helena Kennedy QC must be an

almost exemplary feminist. She has used her talents and her successes as a barrister on behalf of other women. As well as pursuing
her own career, she has spoken up about the ways that women are
badly treated in court, whether as witnesses, defendants, or victims
of crime. In her book *Eve Was Framed*, she has written about the
ways in which the justice system is systematically biased against
women. But once, when she offered herself as a volunteer adviser to
a group involved with the issue of rape, she found: 'My services
were turned down because it was known that I defended men on
rape charges and would not accept a rule against defending in such
cases.'[32]

Naomi Wolf's books, *The Beauty Myth*, *Fire With Fire* and
Promiscuities, have brought feminism to a new audience in Britain
and the United States. One of the greatest injustices to which she
draws attention is the way that women are judged not just for their
talents but their looks. But when she was published in Britain, she
faced a barrage of criticism from female journalists, all dedicated to
examining the side-issue of her own good looks. She is too pretty,
they decided, to employ these unimpeachable feminist arguments.
As one journalist put it: 'Something that bothered many readers,
including myself, was that while Wolf was exhorting her readers not
to waste their lives worrying about living up to the heavily marketed ideals of beauty and slenderness, her own heavily marketed
book featured a photograph of the author looking beautiful and
slender.'[33] This use of a woman's physical attributes to question
her arguments is only an extension of a traditional viewpoint, in
reverse. While the Suffragettes were said to be too ugly to fight,
Naomi Wolf is said to be too pretty to fight.

Barbara Follett is yet another woman who has tried to advance
women's equality. She set up the British Emily's List, which directs
cash to those women standing for parliamentary selection who are
most in need. But female commentators in the press decided that

Follett could not be taken seriously, because she herself was rich, and was therefore patronising such women. One journalist said that the very name Emily's List induces 'bewildered questions about whether it's something that appears in *Tatler*, or, among those who know what it is, a curling of the nostril suggestive of impending nausea . . . most discomfort with the organisation continues to focus on its smug, rich-but-right-on atmosphere'.[34]

These are only three cases among myriad similar examples. In every one, we note that women are not encouraged to work for women's equality, unless they fit into the uniform of the ideal feminist. The actual advantages that might accrue to women if their suggestions were heard or their actions were successful are drowned out under attacks on their possible motives. These women are asked to remodel their own behaviour, and until they do that journalists and women's groups will not give their ideas proper oxygen, but will concentrate on their personal attributes. Helena Kennedy must become more radical, Naomi Wolf must become plainer and Barbara Follett poorer, before each one will be allowed to intervene through influence, or debate, or money, to help the cause of women.

Why is this? It is because the idea that the personal is the political has been misinterpreted, and used to deny the central importance of women's personal freedom as they search for political equality. Why do we fail to consider the ends that these women might help us to attain, and instead become excessively hung up on the means that they use and the lives that they lead? Why can we not concentrate on trying to better the lot of all women, rather than concentrating our fire on trying to create one ideal feminist – a shifting, changeable figure, who is impossibly radical in her beliefs, dowdy in her looks and unimpeachable in her lifestyle? Surely this constant heaping of personal scorn and guilt on to women is simply a mirror of the way women have traditionally been treated by men if they sought a public profile; we assume that their private lives are on the line rather than respecting their public actions.

The links that feminists have drawn between the personal and the political mean that they believe they can tell other women how to behave with impunity. Yet this distracts us from the real battles and arguments that these women may be fighting for, and it alienates other women from joining in feminist debates. This is one primary question that the new feminism must pose: isn't it time for us to free ourselves from the weight of personal guilt that even feminists have tried to put upon women, and look for ways to change the world rather than ourselves alone?

There is a mainstream new feminism which is impatient with such personal carping. In many areas – especially the area of female sexuality – feminists have begun to cast off this tendency towards puritanism and political correctness. Compared to the seventies and eighties, in which many feminists seriously believed that if you had a boyfriend you were letting the side down, we are moving into freer times. Now, if you ask the question: Can a woman have a boyfriend and be a feminist? most women would hoot with laughter. Of course she can. But what about some thornier questions: Can a woman dress like a mannequin and be a feminist? Can she have rape fantasies and be a feminist? Can she have a white wedding and be a feminist? Can she buy pornography and be a feminist? Can she be a prostitute and a feminist? Can she be a Conservative voter and a feminist? Can she be a millionaire and a feminist?

I would say yes to all these questions, and to a lot more besides. The new feminism can look for solidarity without putting pressure on women to dress in the same way or speak the same language or dream the same dreams. There are many shades of feminism, a whole spectrum of ideas alongside a simple commitment. The commitment is straightforward: equal rights and opportunities for women. Given that freedom, a woman may certainly choose roles that enhance gender difference. People have deep-rooted allegiances, fantasies and dreams that a radical feminist may find irritating in her desire to create a better world. But feminism is not a religious movement. To gain its ends it need not ask for inner sanctification.

In this generation, women have begun to feel empowered by the range of behaviour that is now acceptable; a range that, let us not forget, feminism has achieved for us. I feel happy that I can take on feminine and masculine roles; that I can be gentle or shy without feeling I am compromising my power; that I can be assertive and ambitious and rational without diluting my femininity; that I can wear what I like and be friends with whom I like. This is not my personal schizophrenia. Everywhere in the Western world women are waking up to the range of behaviour that is now acceptable for them. And any feminism that attempts to restore control, to send us down one path, is now doomed to failure.

There was a trend in seventies and eighties feminism to look within oneself and ask, 'Am I a feminist? What does that make me?' rather than looking without and asking, 'What discrimination do I encounter? Can feminism help?' But young women now are much less happy about the idea of being directed on the right way to behave. Although the link between the personal and the political has been vital in the past, a certain separation of the two realms is now essential. Now that the rigid shell of traditional femininity has been broken, there must be areas of our lives that are free from political interference. For the sake of sanity and humour, of artistic nuance or intelligent irony, we need spaces to explore our dreams and desires without fearing that the thought police will come knocking on the window.

When Virginia Woolf sat down to write, she said she had to throw off the spectre of traditional femininity, which she called 'the

Angel of the House', which prevented her writing honestly. But perhaps women today, trying to write or think or paint, have to throw off the pressure of certain feminist themes. These are, above all, that women's imaginations are driven by their knowledge of oppression, and that their worlds are defined by their bodies and sexuality. Female novelists, with some notable exceptions, still constantly seem to be driven back into contemplating incredibly passive and sexual lives. And female visual artists, again with notable exceptions, continually take their own flesh and physical experiences as their inspiration.

If we are to create a culture where women artists are as diverse as male artists, we have to be sure that they are seen, and that they see themselves, as being as free as men. We don't want them to be hedged by fear that they should not betray other women by being too fierce or too crazy – or indeed too romantic or too traditional. They should always be seen as individuals, not representatives of their sex. So we have to be sure that, rather than becoming obsessed by the nuances of women's private and sexual lives, we simply set up the conditions for equality that will give artists real freedom. That involves making sure that there are as many women as men as gatekeepers in the cultural industry, as prizegivers or publishers, owning galleries or film production companies, buying or criticising art and books, so women artists are not hedged into particular, separate spaces. That involves making sure that equality takes hold even at home, so that no woman artist will ever say again, as the novelist Candia McWilliam did, 'With the birth of each child you lose two novels.'[35] And if female artists are to have the freedom they deserve, women need real economic equality. Virginia Woolf knew it. What women need is not so much a critique of the pen as phallus and a feminine model of creation, but a room of their own and an independent income. Then their imaginations will roam freely.

The problem with concentrating on the cultural results of oppression rather than the primary need for equality is that it asks us to confer a political value on phenomena – patterns of speaking, ways of dressing, methods of representation – that have no inherent political value. And yet once the political value has been conferred, it is very difficult to shrug off. For instance, when I was first interviewing professional women for this book, I simplistically asked them whether they found it difficult getting up the courage to speak at meetings and holding men's attention. I wanted to hear stories about the difficulties they had in speaking up because I believed that women had to learn to speak up to show strength; I had learnt from all those so-called scientific studies that proved that women spoke much less in meetings and at dinner parties, in the classroom and the office. One very successful young architect told me, 'Oh, if they're not listening to me I go completely silent. In fact, I sit right back from the table and cross my arms and look very grand and dissociated. After a while they go quiet and ask me what I think.' I was struck to realise that because she had power, her silence spoke; just as when we do not have power, even our speech can go unheard. As Gloria Steinem once said:

Male silence (or silence from a member of any dominant group) is not necessarily the same as listening. It might mean a rejection of the speaker, a refusal to become vulnerable through self-revelation, or a decision that this conversation is not worthwhile. Similarly, talking by the subordinate group is not necessarily an evidence of power. Its motive may be a Scheherazade-like need to intrigue and thus survive, or simply to explain and justify one's actions.[36]

Indeed, men's silence has often been taken as evidence of power – in the tradition of strong, silent male heroes in nineteenth-century literature, for instance – and women's speech has often been taken as evidence of powerlessness, in all the talkative, déclassé anti-heroines like Miss Bates in Jane Austen's *Emma* or Flora Finching in Charles Dickens's *Little Dorrit*.

In that case, we need much less concentration on cultural manifestations of power, and much more on shifting those co-ordinates that really define power in our society; access to money and paid work and public status. It is simply wishful thinking on the part of past feminists to think that we could radically change the balance of power by changing the way women speak, or dress, or make love. It is true that the more power women have the less they will do those things in ways to please men alone, but the reverse is not true, that if we simply change the way we speak and dress we will effectively change the balance of power.

When we criticise personal behaviour such as language, fashion or sexual mores, we should remember that many aspects of culture that feminists have required to bear a political weight, have no direct link to oppression. Although things that this society sees as typically feminine have been taken by feminists as demeaning, the fault lies not in the cultural tropes, but in their valuation. We need to shift the co-ordinates of social inequality that lie behind such valuation. After all, if men in seventeenth-century Britain could wear embroidered stockings and high heels and pose for portraits with one foot turned out to emphasise their pretty legs; or if boys in fifth century Athens were the prime object of the artist's gaze for sexy sculptures and vase paintings, it is clear that we should be wary of assuming that any of these cultural attributes – women's silence, women's fashion, women's objectification before the artist – are the areas where feminism needs to concentrate its revolutionary fervour, since these attributes can shift from men to women and yet women's material inequality remains the same. It is interesting to understand how aspects of personal behaviour have become linked to our inequality, but we should not mistake this link for a cause.

Similarly, we may find that even when we achieve material equality some of the cultural phenomena that feminists have often found alienating are still going strong. Many girls may still paint their faces and wear short skirts; many boys may still talk loudly and buy pornography. But these, as well as other, subtler and odder, elements of personal behaviour need not be seen as blocks to equality. Once women have power, their behaviour will not be seen as a sign of vulnerability even when it differs from men's behaviour.

Over the last two decades, feminism has produced a whole series of strategies to use in our private lives. It has produced hundreds of subtle critiques of pornography, fashion, film, beauty, language, literature. It has made us feel highly sensitised and angry in many areas of individual life. It has not always been so successful in producing strategies to use in our public life. And it has not provided us with enough ammunition to change the actual balance of power in Britain. We are burdened with knowledge. We must make sure that we can also act.

We should not forget the real, pragmatic struggles that still have to be fought. Too many women, of whatever class, have not yet benefited from the cultural breakthroughs of feminism. They are constrained by very ordinary bars – lack of money, low levels of education, lack of childcare – from taking on any but a very rigid role in society.

So we have to redefine the old slogan, the personal is the political, to make it much less personal, less inward-looking, less guilt-inducing. There are goals now that we know women want. We know we want better access to power, we know we want young women to be able to fulfil their new ambitions, we know we want to be paid the same as men doing the same jobs, we know we don't want women to live their entire lives in poverty, we know we want women who suffer abuse and violence to find justice. We don't have to interrogate ourselves and one another to discover if our motives in fighting injustice are pure. We can just get on with seeking equality, whoever we are.

chapter 5

let boys wear pink

Feminists down the ages have argued that the oppression of women is played out on their bodies, their clothes, their style of adornment. To politicise dress has been one of the enduring projects of the women's movement. In 1792 Mary Wollstonecraft told us bitterly that women, 'confined in cages like the feathered race . . . have nothing to do but to plume themselves, and stalk with mock majesty from perch to perch'.[1] In 1911 Olive Schreiner wrote: 'An intense love of dress and meretricious external adornment is almost invariably the concomitant and outcome of parasitism.'[2] 'The purpose of the fashions to which she is enslaved is not to reveal her as an independent individual, but rather to offer her as prey to male desires; thus society is not seeking to further her projects but to thwart them,' Simone de Beauvoir wrote in 1949.[3] And we find their words echoed with tragic repetition by Naomi Wolf, less than a decade ago, nearly two centuries after

Mary Wollstonecraft: 'We are in the midst of a violent backlash to feminism that uses images of female beauty as a political weapon against women's advancement.'[4]

Given that so many women believe their appearance and dress have been used against them, it isn't surprising that they have played out their commitment to equality on that level. The promotion of rational dress was a major part of the nineteenth-century women's movement, whose adherents favoured loose, flowing clothes or sensible bloomers as opposed to the stays and petticoats of conventional feminine clothes. In the thirties, the liberal feminist Winifred Holtby wrote that 'cropped hair and serviceable shoes [are] waging a defensive war against this powerful movement to reclothe the female form in swathing trails and frills and flounces to emphasise the difference between men and women'.[5] And in the seventies the desire to attack inequality on the level of feminine appearance took on a huge new impetus. There were the feminists who crowned a sheep beauty queen and set up a trash-can of bras and curlers and make-up. There were feminists who scorned depilation and dresses, dyed hair or make-up. 'Fashion=control=violence against women', one woman spelt out at a feminist conference held in London in 1981.[6]

Is this constant cry of the women's movement still to be heard? Or has this generation seen a unique turning point in feminism, a revolutionary change in the ways that feminists approach the thorny question of dress? Can we still be absolutely sure that, as De Beauvoir put it: 'What is decorated is what is offered'?[7]

The simplest analysis tries to impress on us that, first, we still live in a society where the sexes are unequal and, second, that women's bodies are still given far more sexual and decorative attention than men's bodies. Yet the link between the two facts is hardly unquestionable. To the bewilderment of many commentators, it seems that the strings that once tied women's decoration to women's lack of power have been cut. We can no longer be certain that the one leads to the other, or feeds off the other, or invariably involves the other.

The best exponents of the idea that 'what is decorated is what is offered' have always linked their analysis to the economic inequality that underlay the beauty myth. Charlotte Brontë gives us an early reminder of how demeaning it is for women to feel that they are dressed by men and for men. Yet when Jane Eyre goes shopping with Rochester, it is not the silks that demean her, but his ability to buy things that she cannot afford.

> The more he bought me, the more my cheek burned with a sense of annoyance and degradation. . . . 'It would, indeed, be a relief,' I thought, 'if I had ever so small an independency; I never can bear being dressed like a doll by Mr Rochester' . . . he smiled, and I thought his smile was such as a sultan might, in a blissful and fond moment, bestow on a slave.[8]

What she longs for is not simplicity of dress, but what that stands for, her independence, and her 'independency' – her financial security. Her sober clothes are a symbol of the fact that she does not court the position of a doll or a slave.

Yet when economic inequality is kicked away, does decoration itself degrade women? Is it innately demeaning for women to dress in bright colours and paint their faces? When men indulge their narcissism in ceremonial dress – the curling wigs of judges, the bright livery of the Horse Guards, the purple dresses of bishops, the stiff shirts of empire-builders at dinner – their peculiar costumes are seen as badges of power. Unless our costume actually stops us doing something – as the crinolines of nineteenth-century fashion slowed women down – we should not attribute some mysterious, individual life to it. Narcissism by the ruling group will always be seen as powerful, narcissism by subordinates as demeaning.

And as long as women are unequal, whether they are encouraged to be narcissistic or encouraged not to be, they are in an equally demeaning position. In many Muslim and orthodox Jewish communities, women's self-decoration is seen as sinful, and women are coerced into covering their hair and their bodies. For them, trying to seize power is not symbolised by throwing lipstick into a trash-can, but by flaunting their painted faces. In Afghanistan in 1996, women demonstrating against the Taliban militia who had just taken power 'threw off their traditional burkas to don lipstick, rouge, nail varnish and high heels in an act of defiance against Taliban'. They did this, though they knew that previous expressions of defiance against the Taliban 'had been rare and ruthlessly suppressed'.[9]

The further we get along the road towards equality, the easier feminists should feel about the decisions of individual women to wear traditionally elegant clothes or to spend time waxing their legs or painting their nails. In the past, feminine clothes were often restricting, and clearly tied into a culture that encouraged women to stay in the domestic sphere. But times have changed. Feminists themselves have changed our culture; we can begin to acknowledge and celebrate the freedoms that have already been achieved. What feminists are now seeking to change are not the symbols of past oppression, but the duller, too-often forgotten elements of women's continuing social and economic inequality. In this final march towards equality, the puritanism that was expressed by so many earlier feminists is a hindrance rather than a help.

Puritanism alienates women because it does not reflect the real, often wickedly enjoyable relationship they have with their clothes and their bodies. Feminists frequently write as if women's relation to their bodies is invariably tortured and full of self-loathing. But this is not the only, or even the main truth about that relation. If you watch women in shops, holding dresses up to their bodies and dreaming into the mirrors; if you watch them reading fashion magazines, flicking idly through the pages until, with an indrawn breath, they laugh out, 'Look at that! Look at that blue, that's the blue I want . . .'; if you watch women fashion designers at work, delighting in their craft, or women photographers, adoring the light on the skin of the beautiful women they work with, you know that there is a real, fresh, happy sensuality about women's feeling for self-decoration that can never be expunged.

Is this interest in their bodies and their clothes really forced on women by a masculine conspiracy? Or is it something that many women embrace whatever the outside pressures are on them? Remember the words of Anne Frank, who had been in hiding and outside the reach of her peer group since puberty, when she looked at naked women's bodies at the age of 14: 'Every time I see a female nude, such as the Venus in my art history book, I go into ecstasy. Sometimes I find them so exquisite I have to struggle to hold back my tears.'[10]

My mother is a feminist who dislikes make-up, heeled shoes, bras, depilation and expensive clothes. But as soon as I saw copies of *Vogue* and began to wander around West End shops with my friends at weekends, I fell in love with that sensual culture. When my friends and I wore gold eyeshadow to maths lessons in a girls' school, we were hardly ceding to a masculine conspiracy. There were no boys to respond to our artifice; we were telling each other that we were young and flamboyant and wanted pleasure as well as good grades.

The attempt to try to divest women of such pleasures has too often been used against the equality movement, used to impute a small-minded puritanism to feminism. 'Are you a feminist? You don't dress like one,' is a meaningless comment I have often encountered. 'Do you have a special outfit to write this book in?' a senior editor at the newspaper where I worked asked me.

But women run health clubs and glossy magazines, cosmetic and fashion businesses. If the pressure to be beautiful were simply a male conspiracy, it would have run out of steam long ago. When I think back over a lifetime of contact with the beauty culture – whether it was insisting that my mother plait my hair and tie it up with dinky ribbons at the age of five; or dressing up with my sister to go to teenage parties, carefully and lovingly doing each other's eyeliner and hair; or visiting salons where women young and old, white and black, preen in front of mirrors and engage their hairdressers or manicurists in fascinated conversation; or indeed working at a glossy magazine, where the hothouse, obsessive atmosphere produced complex cultural readings of a single pair of shoes – I adore the funny, female, comfortable atmosphere that rises back at me. An atmosphere that cossets the body, certainly, but doesn't degrade women or imprison them.

Against the feminist tradition I quoted from at the start of this chapter, there is another, hidden feminist tradition that delights in women's relations to clothes and their bodies, and underlines the sense of security and closeness to other women that such delight can provide. If celebrated and extended, this delight in all kinds of clothes and bodies would be more effective than a puritan response in destroying narrow social ideals of beauty and slenderness.

For instance, in one short story the feminist Rebecca West describes a tiny moment of recognition passing between two women meeting for the first time:

She smiled straight at me to show she meant well by me. I knew that this was because, as I had observed from the way she had run her eyes over my clothes when we had first been introduced, she liked the soft, bright primrose-leaf green of my silk jumper. She thought it was nice of me to choose such a jolly colour and nice of me to bring the result of my choice along to her, she preferred me for that reason to my more soberly dressed companions, she liked to give as proof of it this special smile.[11]

Here, the narrator's elegance and pointedly bright clothes are shown to enhance female-to-female relationships. The fact that the other woman smiles 'straight' at her and reacts to her jumper in ways that West characterises by breezy, unselfconscious words like 'nice' and 'jolly' emphasises to us what an easy, upbeat reaction clothes can induce in women.

In one of her novels, *The Diaries of Jane Somers*, Doris Lessing speaks from the point of view of a woman who works at a women's magazine, and who loves her clothes – her handmade linen suits and silk shirts, her muted colours and careful grooming. At the magazine, she and the other women pass expertise about clothes back and forth and are carefully appreciative of each other's chosen styles. Even when the narrator sees women with a completely different sense of style, she still reacts with the kind of breezy, unselfconscious delight that we saw in the passage above:

> Punk is *style*, I admire it, properly done. There's a girl at the corner, she's a pleasure, we exchange smiles as she even peacocks about a little for my benefit, miming a fashion model there on the pavement, often not only for me, but for her mates who are also punks, but not so elegant. She can look like a cat, little black ears carved out of her golden hair, black arms (gloves from a stall?), a suggestion of gallant tiger around the shoulders . . . It must take her hours.[12]

We note the admiration of equal to equal, the interested way in which the narrator wonders where accessories come from and how long the girl takes to get ready. And this peacocking is directed more at women than at men; this girl swaggers around 'for me' and 'for her mates'.

Similarly, in her first novel, *The Cast Iron Shore*, published in 1996, Linda Grant gives us a striking portrait of a female Communist activist who is in love with clothes and shopping. Subtly, Grant traces the lineaments of both desires – the desire to act for equality, and the desire to adorn one's body. Notably, they are not seen as opposing desires. This woman's femininity gives her a solidarity with her fellow female activists that more puritan women would have lacked. On a strike of secretarial staff, she notes:

> I got to know those secretaries very well: Marcia and Laurel and Lynette and Fay and Hannah and Inge and Mary. I had friends. I had whisper and gossip and camaraderie. I swapped recipes. I came over at weekends and styled their hair. I laughed with them . . . They were women and they did what women do . . . How will you ever convert a woman from an interest in fashion magazines and movie stars? Why would you want to?[13]

Here again, we see a feminist writer who explores self-decoration, not to mock and criticise it, but to show the pleasures and the mutual respect it gives to women.

Classic feminist analysis has argued against this tradition. It has argued that women are undermined by this traditional relationship to fashion and beauty rituals, that women are encouraged to hate themselves when they are confronted by ideals of beauty, that such ideals lead to self-loathing, even self-starvation. This analysis is clearly only partial as an explanation of eating disorders; it does not explain, for instance, why eating disorders seem to be hereditary, or why young women themselves often talk about anorexia nervosa as a more complicated psychiatric problem. Are we not guilty of patronising women when we attempt to put all their psychological problems down to Kate Moss and Gucci rather than acknowledging, as we do when we look at, say, the rise in suicide among young men, that young people experience many emotional, sexual and social pressures as they grow up? Certainly, some women and men do feel undermined by the glamorous standards around them. But how will we resist this? By presenting the influence of fashion as purely evil and women as children who need to be protected from it, or by arguing that at its best fashion can be a game or a pleasure, freely picked up or discarded by independent, freethinking women?

We can see that women's feelings about their clothes and bodies are easier now than at any time in the recent past. Women do not squash their feet into pointed-toe stiletto shoes; indeed, when such shoes appeared on the catwalks in spring 1995, the shoe-shops that ordered them lost money hand over fist. Women do not follow the dictates of Paris, they do not wear corsets or hobble-skirts or petticoats. Women are clearly easier about taking on or rejecting the images around them than they once were. In such a culture, feminists should be wary of simply insisting that women are oppressed by the imagery around them. Some may be oppressed, others may be revelling in it, others may be creating it, others yet may be ignoring it.

For instance, in Britain now, greatest equality has been achieved by young, professional, working women. And those women who have seen the greatest upsurge in their individual and collective power seem to be the easiest and most positive about retaining a culture of physical adornment. Fiona Driscoll, self-confessed feminist, chief executive of a PR company and chair of the 300 Group, was the image of the perfect, pulled-together executive when we met, in a chic plum-coloured skirt suit, glitzy earrings and hairband.

'We talk about work and clothes,' she said of her closest female friends. I found Sylvie Pierce, another self-confessed feminist and chief executive of the London Borough of Tower Hamlets, an unexpectedly feminine presence, with her long silver earrings, floating silk scarf, and jet necklaces. 'All that endless debate about what women should wear is essentially just loading more guilt on to women,' she said dismissively. 'I think young women now are much better at not falling for that puritan ethic.' Rebecca Thomas, 33-year-old director of Framlington Investment Management, stood out in the City wine bar where we talked in her frivolous pastel suit and long, untidy dark hair. 'I won't get my hair cut,' she said. 'And I will dress to please myself.' Donna Covey, the 34-year-old national women's officer at the GMB Union, was strikingly elegant in a silk suit when we met. She feels her appearance is directed at women rather than men. 'The men in the union think I dress up too much, but women expect women to be well turned out. They listen to me more if I am.' Clearly, once women do not have to rely on the goodwill of a Mr Rochester for their lovely clothes, they can feel much easier about enjoying them.

Even as we approach the equal, freer society we long for we cannot naively expect that women's bodies and clothes will suddenly become innocent of all messages, free of all pressures. Indeed, for some of the women to whom I spoke the image they wanted to rebel against, in order to keep their own individuality, was not the sexy, feminine image of the traditional woman, but the sober-suited image of the typical lawyer or executive or the deliberately dowdy image of the radical. Interestingly, this desire not to cede to conventional images was often centred on women's hair. Susan Smith, a 29-year-old barrister with waist-length curly hair, echoed Rebecca Thomas when she told me: 'I won't get my hair cut. It may not look very lawyer-like, but it is me.'[14] Gabrielle Osrin, a 29-year-old television producer, said: 'There is a hair uniform – a bob, mainly – that

I won't fall for. I like to keep my hair rather long and wild.' And Donna Covey, at the GMB Union, said she wouldn't stop dyeing her hair: 'I hate that Shirley Williams image, that to be a Labour woman you had to have really bad hair.'

This shows how much the norms are changing. We cannot just say that society puts pressure on women to be feminine and sexy. It also puts pressure on them to be managerial and sober, on occasion. And it puts pressure on them to be dowdy sometimes, and casual and sporty at other times. How we respond to such pressures – whether we want to resist them, or exploit them – cannot be simplified by talking of fashion as a simple conspiracy that patriarchy exerts on women.

As I interviewed women in various occupations for this book, I was constantly reminded of that. If I chose to wear a smart shift dress to talk to a woman at a glossy magazine, and then a trouser-suit to talk to a businesswoman, and then jeans to talk to an environmental campaigner, was I doing something as simple as capitulating to pressures on me as a woman? No, I was shifting my appearance, as I shifted my questions, slightly into their worlds, which involved slipping through more complicated nuances than a simple feminine/masculine divide would involve. There was the former's knowledge of fashion, who would appreciate my nicely cut summer dress; there was the success and efficiency of another, who might appreciate me looking dressed as if I meant to do business; there was the anti-consumer bias of another, who might open up less if I looked as if I preferred shopping to talking about the environment. The ways in which women dress often come close to the ways men dress, and the choices that women make today often speak less of their sex than of their occupation, or their class, or their politics.

Fashion, which has changed in response to the changing cultural and sexual world, can no longer be seen as a monolith of oppression. Particular moments of irony and self-critique – from punk, which was anti-fashion and anti-beauty made desirable, to grunge – have washed away the simple conception of fashion as a movement that only reinforces traditional femininity. On the contrary, fashion movements like punk and grunge intersected with the feminist impetus to find a rational way of dressing and women's increasing social power to create the freedom we now take for granted. In her book *Sexing the Millennium*, Linda Grant quotes feminist punk Lucy Whitman saying: 'Punk had a big effect on feminist fashion because at the beginning of it all, most feminists were still wearing dungarees and the idea of dressing up in any way was frowned on. I remember going to women's events and other women looking at me askance because of my punky appearance and yet within a year nearly everyone was looking like I did. Punk gave us the chance to reject conventional feminine attire but have fun with our appearance at the same time.'[15]

And let us remember that the world of fashion is peopled not just by six-foot gazelles. Many powerful women in that world do not conform to those ideals. There are designers like Donna Karan, a generously built woman who uses older women and large women in her marketing campaigns; or Vivienne Westwood, a woman whose in-your-face, peacock style free her from conventional femininity, but who has stamped her influence all over contemporary fashion. There are fashion journalists like Suzy Menkes of the *International Herald Tribune*, who sticks to the same purple and black clothes and inimitable, unfashionable hairstyle year in, year out; or Glenda Bailey, the editor of American *Marie Claire*, whose down-to-earth clothes and manner seem to owe little to the fashion world. These women show us the way forward in fashion; they remind us that fashion need not be associated just with skinny models, it can be seen as a skilled and enjoyable occupation, and a good spectator sport.

And ordinary women are now much more in control of fashion

codes, able to use or reject 'conventional feminine attire' without feeling like dupes or revolutionaries. Reflecting their growing power in the workplace and in society, women now have an easy uniform whenever they don't want to be bothered with fashion. For the first time in many centuries, women's clothes are beginning to look very like men's, neither fashionable nor unfashionable, but a-fashionable. Even when the corset is 'in' or the jacket is 'out', women can carry on regardless in their chosen uniform. That may be a mufti uniform – leggings, sweater, flat shoes – or it may be a working uniform. When we look at working women, from Helen Mirren in *Prime Suspect*, to Anna Ford on the television news, to Harriet Harman in the House of Commons, we see the same crisp working uniform, a knee-length skirt suit or straight leg trouser-suit, the jacket tailored, the colours muted. It speaks less of sex and youth than money and power; less of glamour and seasonal dictates than efficiency and durability. And it makes these latter qualities as unexceptional and as accepted in a woman as in a man.

The sudden ubiquity of this understated form of power-dressing, that has so changed the look of big department stores and high-street chains, is a sign of the growing confidence of women and the pragmatism of their approach to their own appearance. As their uniform becomes as unnoticeable as the male uniform, professional women find attention directed less and less at how they look and more and more at what they say and do.

As this continues, the traditional feminist desire to desexualise women's bodies looks unnecessary and miserable. Many feminists today feel that the battle over appearance is an old one, and not worth the angst it once engendered. Louisa Saunders was the editor of a feminist magazine called *Everywoman* in the early nineties. She laughed when she described to me how the rest of the media tried to pigeonhole her. 'They are always ringing up about the Wonderbra advertisements. I try to tell them, we're just not bothered by the Wonderbra advertisements. They're funny, they're tongue-in-cheek, and you know, it's quite difficult to advertise a bra without showing a woman wearing it. But then I'll still see the next day, "Feminists hate the Wonderbra advertisements because they say they demean women", or "Women's groups all over the country have condemned these advertisements". Why do they feel the need to say such things about us?'

Rather than trying to resist this by rejecting all images of and delight in beauty as tainted by male fantasies, we should now ally our growing power to the culture of decoration. Women's culture is already doing this both in Britain and America. *Vogue* runs features on sportswomen and their body care, *Everywoman* asked feminists how their clothes reflect their personality. Magazines like *Cosmopolitan* and *Marie Claire* and *She* insistently sell to an upbeat, feminist reader, and 'clothes to work in', 'clothes to relax in', sit happily by clothes to pull men. Many women want the beautiful colours and shapes of fashion, the frivolous fun of shopping and magazines, even if they also want equality; just as men want the mindless fun of football fandom even if they don't want the thuggish masculinity that it once entailed.

One reason, I know, that although I called myself a feminist in my teens and early twenties but found myself completely alienated from the movement was my own love of decoration and fashion. A couple of older women who had an uncompromising sense of themselves and their ambitions helped to convince me that feminism should recognise and embrace those urges in women rather than seeking to stigmatise them. The first of those women was the foreign correspondent Martha Gellhorn. I interviewed her in her flat in Knightsbridge in 1991. At the age of 82, she found it painful to walk because of arthritis, but she was still eager to look back on her free-travelling, free-spirited youth. As we drifted through various subjects, I asked if she hadn't found it difficult travelling alone as a young woman. She said that she had revelled in her own attractiveness, and the attention that it had brought her. She only missed that as she got older. Reading her books, I felt her humour and pride brought to bear on her own appearance. When she went for an interview for her first job in America at the age of 25, 'I wore the only clothes I had, a Schiaparelli suit in nubbly brown tweed fastened up to its Chinese collar with large brown leather clips, and Schiap's version of an Anzac hat . . . I could not afford to buy clothes in the ordinary way, and dressed myself in *soldes* . . . Also I painted my face like Parisian ladies, lots of eyeshadow, mascara and lipstick, which was not at all the style for American ladies then.'[16] And yet that giggly spirit of self-decoration hardly detracted from Gellhorn's independence. Given that she covered wars from the Spanish Civil War to the present day with extraordinary authority and compassion, she is still the great heroine for female war reporters in Britain today.

The second was Doris Lessing. In her autobiography, *Under My Skin*, she writes passionately about how she loved her body as an adolescent girl:

> In a corner of the bush near the big land, I stood with my rifle loose in my hand, and suddenly saw my legs as if for the first time, and thought, They are beautiful. Brown slim well-shaped legs. I pulled up my dress and looked at myself as far up as my panties and was filled with pride of body. There is no exultation like it, the moment when a girl knows that *this* is her body, *these* her fine smooth shapely limbs.[17]

When I interviewed Lessing I asked her whether she thought that there was any contradiction between her sensual delight in femininity, and her feminism; but she argued that that so-called dichotomy had all been a red herring for women. 'Simone de

Beauvoir didn't like being a woman, you see. She talks with real dislike and disgust about her body. Well, I don't think that's typical, do you? I think most women thoroughly enjoy being a woman.'

Indeed, many women who resist demeaning stereotyping of their bodies most successfully do so not through withdrawal from decorative physical culture but by openly enjoying their bodies on their own terms. There are women like Dawn French, who was happy to pose nude for *Esquire* despite being larger than a waif, or Vanessa Feltz, another woman on a large scale, who loves glamorous accoutrements and huge, crazy dresses. In this, white women may also have much to learn from black British culture, which seems to be more upfront about celebrating women's sexual allure alongside their power, and not getting bogged down in waif-like images.

Many young women today, who have become accustomed to seeing women as powerful, who move easily around society unhampered by corsets or excessive beauty routines, simply can't understand an ideology that requires them to throw out what now seems most fun and flamboyant about female culture.

In creating this new sense of freedom, we have learnt from certain potent icons. Those of course include Madonna, who used her swagger and costume-changes to demonstrate not her powerlessness but her sexual and financial independence. She played directly into the joy women take in their own bodies and sexuality, without screening it through the approval of men. And so she reinvented the significance of dyed blonde hair, dark lipstick, padded bras, polka-dot bikinis or fishnet tights. Her images were so loaded with female-to-female laughter and irony that few men found it entirely easy to respond; women, however, especially young women, went wild. In this way she reminded us of a vital truth, that women have often used fashion not to enhance their docility and femininity, but to advertise their untamed and undocile nature.

In Britain, where fashion has always been a more streetwise, vernacular art than in either Europe or the United States, women are particularly aware of this tradition. When flappers in the twenties put on make-up in public and shortened their skirts, they were not seen to be ceding to social pressures, but to be flouting them. In the late seventies, Siouxsie Sioux and punk girls all over Britain used safety-pins, vivid hair-dyes and deliberately unnatural make-up to signal their freedoms. This kind of flamboyance, the way that women use fashion to overturn expectations of good feminine behaviour, has always been part of fashion, and feminists can celebrate it rather than denigrate it.

Today, young women can link fashion with power rather than powerlessness. The rhetoric of young female singers like the Spice Girls, who associate their bright clothes with girlpower, has resonated with a new generation of young girls. And the cult of the supermodel is not necessarily just degrading. When girls dream of being supermodels, are they dreaming of being sexually available dolls? Or are they excited by the theatre and swagger of the catwalk, the ability of the model to travel by Concorde and play with fast cars and film stars? Is the identification with a victim or a winner? As one *Vogue* editor said: 'Contemporary agents recognise 'the killer thing' that girls need in order to make it. Striving for glamour presupposes a certain ruthlessness on all sides.'[18] She emphasised that models' careers can resurface in Hollywood or agenting, proving their own complicity and power in their business. The model Sara Stockbridge stressed the hedonism of the career when she once said of her experience of the catwalk, 'I used to forget I was showing them clothes. There's all these people watching you and it's like you're waving at them and showing your arse.'[19]

What's more, the women that young girls imitate in their clothes are not, often, slender supermodels dressed by grand designers, but more feisty heroines who have chosen their own styles. Sarah Cracknell, the distinctively dressed singer who fronted Saint

Etienne once said, 'I saw six little versions of myself at a gig in Cardiff, standing on a row of chairs, watching me.'[20] Like little boys in football shirts, such girls signal their adherence to an easygoing, sociable culture, not a divisive and isolating one.

The parallels between fashion and sport are certainly illuminating. After all, when men watch other men who may be much better looking and much fitter than they are kick a ball around, it is seen as good healthy fun. When women watch other women who may be better looking than they are wearing beautiful clothes, it is seen as sad. When I asked some girls aged 12 to 14 whether they felt the pressures of fashion weighed very heavily on girls, they told me it didn't, it was much worse for boys. I expressed surprise. 'My brother has to have every new football strip for his team,' one girl told me. 'My brother is so worried about whether he's going to the right games or supporting the right team or wearing the right trainers, it's pathetic,' another told me. Such pressures would be shrugged off by most commentators, because boys' obsessions are accepted, even when they lead to anxiety and peer pressure. But girls' obsessions are not accepted, even when they lead to pleasure.

Given the ways that fashion can work for us as well as against us, and be used to express women's changing lives, their place in the business world or their sense of fun and freedom, we can be suspicious of feminism's erstwhile claim to free us of the whirligig of fashion, and deliver a value-free zone for our bodies and clothes. There is, after all, a 'look' that says seventies feminism, just as clearly as there is a look that says fifties housewife or twenties flapper. You can see it, for instance, in the photograph of the Boston Women's Collective that fronts the seventies edition of the health handbook *Our Bodies Ourselves*: long hair, no bras, batik wraparound skirts. There was also a look that said eighties feminism – dungarees and short hair and bright earrings. How can we trust feminism's traditional promise to release us from the demands of fashion when it seems to trap us into such a precise range of sartorial responses?

And, essentially, we can question whether women today need to be delivered from the pressures of a mysterious beauty conspiracy. Some women are miserable about not measuring up to social expectations of beauty. But many, perhaps most, women are already comfortable with themselves. In a survey carried out by *Good Housekeeping* and Clinique, women said they enjoyed greater confidence as they aged and only one in six associated beauty with youth. Four out of five rejected the possibility of cosmetic surgery and said they were happy when they looked in the mirror.[21] The fact that so many women do not feel overwhelmed by the pressure of a male conspiracy of beauty upon them shows how wide the continuum of physical culture now is.

In one survey of male rather than female attitudes to beauty, three-quarters of men reported that they were dissatisfied with the shape of their bodies, 13 per cent said they would contemplate cosmetic surgery, 50 per cent feared growing old and only 4 per cent said that they thought they were attractive.[22] The two surveys are not directly comparable, since they were carried out using very different methods, but they do suggest that the beauty myth weighs on men as well as on women. If 80 per cent of women are happy when they look in the mirror yet only 4 per cent of men think they are attractive, we should not be too quick to argue that only women feel cast down by the pressures of beautiful ideals. Research in the United States has suggested that good-looking people earn 12 per cent more than their plain colleagues; but interestingly the difference was larger for men than for women.[23]

Certainly, men now tend to reveal their own desire for decoration and admiration. In his bestselling books about the SAS, famous hard man Andy McNab cannot resist treating his fellow-soldiers as tasty meat: 'Andy Baxter took his shirt off and revealed that besides film-star good looks he had a superb physique. He should have been on the cover of *Playgirl*.'[24] Men too hanker after youth and slenderness, as more and more men in public life are recognising. The transformation of Nigel Lawson from a tubby giant to a leaner, more lined version was watched with fascination and delight by other middle-aged men. Alan Clark notes with despair, in his diaries, his own accelerated loss of youth and looks once he becomes a minister. 'I realise how much I have aged in the last twelve months . . . Men are OK from thirty to forty-five . . . After that it's an increasing struggle because of jowl and neck lines, even if the waist can be restrained.'[25] It was Robin Cook, not a female politician, who the press decided was 'too ugly' to lead the Labour Party.

It is surely possible to see that men share both the weight of the beauty myth and the potential for revelling in it. Recent culture has been unique in seeing the culture of self-decoration as something that could be confined to women. Think of the languid male beauties of the Nigerian Woodaabe tribe, beloved of television documentaries, who spend hours making up their faces and competing in beauty contests judged by women; think of Louis XIV in his dinky red heels; think of Charles II in his perfumed wig. As women and men become more equal in their shares of social and economic power, perhaps men will feel free to acknowledge these desires again.

So let's not demand from women that they become clones of the least imaginative male dressers. Rather than insisting that women should disguise themselves in dungarees and flat shoes, many men and women are dreaming of the opposite, that men and women could share a more vivid and sensual culture of decoration. Over the past few years, male uniforms have loosened up – there has been an encroachment of colour, oddly casual cutting and different fabrics even into the greyest offices. But they still have a long way to go. Perhaps when women's power has grown to the point where women and men are equal, men will feel able to share in the decorative culture that is currently confined to women. The urge to adorn oneself is not only artificially encouraged in young girls, it is artificially driven out of young boys. I remember recently walking along a Devon beach, on a hot sunny day, with my three-year-old nephew. He had already admired my toenails, which were painted a striking shade of ice-blue. We stopped to admire the sandcastles that had been built by an articulate, confident girl of about six or seven. As she was pointing out to him the flags and the moats he was struck by her pearly pink toenails. 'Look,' he said, delightedly. 'Hers are pink and yours are blue. Hers are nicer.' We all laughed. 'Would you like pink nails?' I asked, and he grinned, but the girl broke in immediately. 'You can't have yours painted. That's weird.' The smile left his face. It wasn't for him, so he would look elsewhere for his pleasures.

Despite all the changes we have seen in feminine culture, masculine culture still seems to be fixed in old traditions. Take the case of Paul Kara, who lost his case against Hackney council when he was disciplined for wearing a skirt to work. Although he quite reasonably argued that women were allowed to wear traditional men's clothing, and his wife commented, 'A hundred years ago it was very unusual for women to wear trousers,' he lost his sex discrimination case.[26] All the commentators seemed to think that he was mad to act as he did. But there is surely no good reason why a man should not wear a skirt and find his power unimpeached, and it seems extraordinary that at the end of the twentieth century men are still lacking those freedoms. Indeed, just as we once saw women in trousers castigated and hounded for their masculinity, so now we see the same in reverse. David Thomas, author of *Not Guilty: In Defence of the Modern Man* believes that all men would love to wear women's clothes: 'It's a feeling that there's a realm which is denied them, which they suppress very, very hard, but which they quite envy.'[27]

Marianne Grabrucker, observing the dull rows of navy boys' socks next to the bright pastel ones destined for the little girls, writes:

> As long as boys are not able to dress in the same bright colours as girls, to adorn themselves as girls do, and this not only at home but also when they go out, then the pleasures of selection will, for women, continue to remain a duty. A woman remains chained to her feminine beauty. But I don't think we should abandon it; we need *more* beauty and have to extend it to include boys and men. Let boys start wearing pink at last.[28]

Even if one believes – as I do – that feminine and masculine attitudes to dress will always be rather different, this vision is still a vivid and vital one. Perhaps Mary Wollstonecraft and Olive Schreiner and Simone de Beauvoir believed that power and decoration were antitheses because they only had one model of power, a masculine model. Now, rather than going down the puritan route of enforced masculinisation, we can ask men to feminise themselves, we can encourage our sons to play with the dressing-up box, we can positively reinforce men's beauty routines, we can signal our desire for the camp and swagger that is often seen in male culture to come to the fore. Now that we see how possible, how attractive, female power is, perhaps mothers won't feel that a boy who likes to play with make-up, dresses or traditionally feminine ways of moving is ceding his potential strength.

The reason why feminists have previously found it so difficult to accept women's love of physical culture is a good one. It is because in a society where men held all the money, the power and the opportunities, any aspect of culture that was confined to women began to feel degrading. So all the activities that result from nar-cissism began to look like the toys that women were given to distract themselves with as the men got on with running the world. But we need not see our drives as a zero-sum game, either power or fashion, either running a board-meeting or putting on lipstick, either being active in a community or going shopping. Can't we work to remove the underlying structure of inequality, rather than become obsessive about its symptoms? One of those symptoms has been, since the nineteenth century, a division between the men who do and the women who decorate; but with women's growing power, that division will be broken.

After all, if we are being realistic, we shall not encourage the women who rely on the goodwill and money of richer men to throw out their push-up bras and heels merely by dragging them to con-sciousness-raising sessions. But if they know that they themselves are a better and more reliable source of independence and income than the men around them, we shall know that their accou-trements are a sign of fun and delight rather than oppression and degradation.

The agenda for new feminists is not to enforce a rigid code of rejection on women. No, the agenda must be to remove the real inequalities that underpin sexual difference, to remove the inequal-ities of pay and life choices and freedom of movement. Then the delight we take in our own bodies and the attractiveness we feel in ourselves and others will not be something that is directed by an unfair distribution of power. Social and economic changes must come first. The movement for equal pay, for shared childcare, for equal opportunities will free us up in our private lives too. The catwalk will then cease to be a symbol of our subordination, and become a path to simple delight.

chapter 6

sex without an order of battle

One theme, above all, dominates the contemporary view of feminism. This is that feminists believe that love between men and women is rather dodgy, since it encourages women to give up their own power and fall into the hands of the enemy. Like many of the aspects of feminism that one might now want to discount, feminists themselves have, on occasion, encouraged this view. 'Love is the pivot of women's oppression,' declared Shulamith Firestone in 1970.[1] 'Incestuous rape is becoming a central paradigm for intercourse in our time,' agreed Andrea Dworkin.[2] 'We can't talk of sex as anything but a joke or a battleground,' women declared at the first national Women's Liberation conference in Britain in 1970.[3]

A joke or a battleground. Never, in the history of Western culture, has the mystery of sexual love been so downgraded, so demystified. How did feminism become associated with such a reductive view of sexuality? And will women now forge a new feminism that will be free from this embittered view of romance?

This hostile view of heterosexuality began from deep roots. It began from women's desire to enunciate at last their own experiences of sexuality, told from their own point of view and in their own words. Throughout the latter half of the twentieth century, one of the most vital impulses of feminism has been to reveal the truth, the reality of women's physical life, a reality which feminists believed had been shrouded by masculine assumptions, by the veil of romance and the taboo of delicacy. This was a revolutionary development. When Simone de Beauvoir said in 1949, 'It's not easy to play the idol, the fairy, the faraway princess, when one feels a bloody cloth between one's legs,'4 she began a debate which raged through Western society. Female writers from Gertrude Stein to Anais Nin to Kate Chopin had attempted to write about women's erotic life before, but during the sixties a sudden explosion of frankness occurred.

Various female writers, some of them the best of their generation, pushed on this ideal of a new articulacy. Doris Lessing and Antonia Byatt, Mary McCarthy and Sylvia Plath, Anne Sexton and Angela Carter all wrote the stories that had never before been written, about women's menstruation and masturbation, their orgasms and their lack of orgasms.

In 1963, the year that – as Philip Larkin told us – sexual intercourse began, two novels vitally changed the way women spoke about their sexuality. In Mary McCarthy's novel *The Group* a woman loses her virginity.

He pinched each of her full breasts lightly and told her to relax, in just the tone Dr Perry used when he was going to give her a treatment for her sciatica . . . the second climax, which she now recognised from the first one, though it was different, left her jumpy and disconnected, it was something less thrilling and more like being tickled relentlessly or having to go to the bathroom.[5]

And in Sylvia Plath's *The Bell Jar* another woman does likewise: 'I lay, rapt and naked, on Irwin's rough blanket, waiting for the miraculous charge to make itself felt. But all I felt was a startlingly hard pain.'[6] Such writers were keen to unpick the long tradition of romance, which they clearly felt had hidden women's discomfort and pain. They wanted women to see their first sexual experiences not as miraculous, but as no more thrilling or mysterious than going 'to the bathroom' or a 'startlingly hard pain'. This gave women a new and more honest context from which they could begin to talk more freely about their own sexual lives.

In this context, perhaps the debate about female orgasm was *the* quintessential feminist argument of its generation. Where was the orgasm, in the vagina or in the clitoris? How should a woman attain it, through reliance on men or through independent clitoral stimulation? While the American feminist Anne Koedt declared, against the psychoanalysts and doctors who had insisted on the opposite for generations, 'the vagina is not a highly sensitive area and is not constructed to achieve orgasm',[7] Germaine Greer wanted women to include penile intercourse in their love-making, but to 'embrace and stimulate the penis instead of taking it'.[8] It was not so much that the female orgasm was being discussed that was important; male doctors and psychoanalysts had done that for decades. It was that women were discussing it, and that through popular books and, especially, women's magazines the discussion became a very public and mainstream debate.

So a new, positive value was given to women speaking about their sexuality. We can assume from cultural and anecdotal evidence that this changed people's behaviour in their bedrooms, as women gained the courage to insist that sex should engage their desires and provide their pleasures without being thwarted by fear that they might be acting in an unsuitable, unromantic way. The ability to throw off the gag of traditional femininity also brought women advances in the social and political sphere. It brought women advances in health care, as they spoke out about what they wanted from doctors and treatments. Their demands for rights over their own fertility were heard, and were successful. And above all, this new articulacy began to give women the courage to stand up to violence and coercion. Feminists organised mass speak-outs on rape and abuse. They gave women the courage to confront assailants in court, and, rather than asking other women who had been harassed or abused or battered or raped to hide their knowledge in shame and silence, they encouraged them to speak about their experiences and provided support services and care for those who did.

Feminist women as patients and therapists changed psychiatric practice. Not only did women begin to speak more clearly and loudly about their experiences of abuse, their words were given a new weight. They were listened to and their complaints were acted upon. Feminist women as survivors of violence and as counsellors, policewomen, journalists and lawyers changed the way that the abuse of women was spoken about in many different spheres. From being a kind of joke in the police force and the law it has become an issue which demands police time, media coverage and new legislation. That cultural revolution has relied on women's articulacy. This was an area where men could not and would not speak for women.

The importance of women's articulacy about sexuality goes on. Even now, women survivors of sexual violence dare to cede their own right to anonymity and silence in order to draw attention to injustice. Young prostitutes go on record with female journalists to speak of the abuse they suffer at the hands of their pimps. A woman who was brutally raped as a virgin by two men, Jill Saward, appears on *Newsnight* and gives interviews in newspapers and publishes a book in order to express her frustration with existing legal practice. A woman who was cross-examined by her own rapist in court appears on the front page of a newspaper to argue that what happened to her should not happen again. All women have benefited from this rise in articulacy, which was spearheaded by feminists and then taken into the lives of hundreds of thousands of ordinary women.

This dizzying explosion in women's speech has not always been hostile towards heterosexuality. It has articulated every experience, through love and desire as well as anger and hostility. Yet the theme that has often been given most attention by recent feminists is the theme of hostility. The rejection of heterosexual romance came to dominate certain feminist arguments. One spokeswoman of seventies feminism said, 'Lesbianism is the key to liberation and only women who cut their ties to male privilege can be trusted to remain serious in the struggle against male dominance.'[9] Or, as one woman at the first national Women Against Violence Against Women conference, which was attended by 1,000 women in 1981 summed up: 'Generally at this conference there was an assumption that pressures to be heterosexual were bad . . . and lesbian relationships [were] better for women.'[10] Other women felt pummelled or confused by this insistence. As Sylvie Pierce, chief executive of the London Borough of Tower Hamlets, said, 'It was quite an oppression, the idea that you had to choose between men and the women's movement'.[11]

Yet, bizarrely, this fierce rejection of heterosexual romance arose at just the time that women were beginning to mould cultural patterns of heterosexuality in their own image, were able to control their fertility and beginning to change attitudes of the legal system to rape and abuse. At the very time when many women were beginning to feel more confident and truly liberated, many feminists were warning them away from feeling too comfortable about sex; instead, they insisted that male and female attitudes to sexuality were so different that women's experience would always be moulded by abuse. According to Andrea Dworkin, the American feminist who would like to ban all pornography, the penis as 'a symbol of terror' is more significant than the gun, the knife, the bomb or the fist.[12]

And yet she wrote those words just as women were beginning to photograph nude males, or buy soft pornography magazines which featured extra-large penises for women's delectation, or write books which began, for instance, with a long, mocking description of the penises one woman had known. As Tama Janowitz began a book of short stories in 1987:

I had to deal with penises of every imaginable shape and size. Some large, others quite shriveled and pendulous of testicle. Some blue-veined and reeking of Stilton, some miserly. Some crabbed, enchanted, dusted with pearls like the great minarets of the Taj Mahal, jesting penises, ringed as the tail of a racoon, fervent, crested, impossible to live with, marigold-scented.[13]

This joking, partly disgusted and partly loving description of men's genitals is a close and confident reckoning of their physical reality. It does not see the penis as a symbol of terror; on the contrary, it shows how the strangeness of men's bodies can be fearlessly explored through the intimacy of frank language.

Yet too much feminist literature looked as if it were deliberately trying to prevent dialogue between men and women, rather than building on this easier and more articulate relationship that women were creating with men's bodies. When Catharine MacKinnon wrote in 1994: 'You learn that language does not belong to you, that you cannot use it to say what you know, that knowledge is not what you learn from your life, that information is not made out of your experience,'[14] she was choosing to ignore the great feminist revolution that had encouraged articulacy in women, and given their words weight and meaning. She was telling those women who felt newly empowered by their ability to discuss and write about sexuality that they were deluded, that nothing was changing.

The most obvious manifestation of this extremely hostile view of heterosexuality was in the anti-pornography movement. While Clare Short MP simply tried to move naked women out of newspapers with her attempt to reform the Indecent Displays Act in 1986, other feminists launched an attack on all pornography, in any guise. Pornography was seen as 'a dangerous form of propaganda that deliberately incites men to carry out acts of violence against women'.[15] This impetus eventually reached much more than what was usually called pornography. All treatments of sexuality in culture were forced to reveal the imprint of sexism: fairy tales, fiction high and low, erotica, cinema, photography, sculpture. For some feminists, any hint of sexuality in culture was proof of sexism.

Take one example: feminist criticism of fairy tales. It became commonplace to read that, say, 'Red Riding Hood is a parable of rape',[16] and that women were irresistibly moulded by such fairy tales, that they formed a one-way traffic into our minds: 'We have not formed that ancient world, it has formed us,' wrote Andrea Dworkin. 'We ingested it as children whole, had its values and consciousness imprinted on our minds as cultural absolutes long before we were in fact men and women.'[17] This picture of heterosexual culture sees women only as victims. But let us examine this one example. A tale like Red Riding Hood does indeed seem to invite interpretation as a sexist, violent parable. Red Riding Hood is, after all, a vulnerable little girl who is attacked by a wolf in a bed and then saved by a hunter, a good man. She is helpless in the face of male violence and male authority, and young girls are asked to identify with her vulnerability.

But if we look again at the tradition of Little Red Riding Hood, we find that the rape parable has always been questioned – by women's own words. There is an independent oral tradition of the tale, which survived long after the 'rape parable' of the classic version was written down, in which Red Riding Hood gets away by fast talking. She pretends she needs to shit just as the wolf is about to pounce: '"Oh Granny," says Red Riding Hood, "I've got to go badly. Let me go outside." "Do it in the bed, my child!" "Oh no, Granny, I want to go outside." "All right, but make it quick."' Red Riding Hood makes a quick escape, so the wolf 'jumped out of bed and saw that the little girl had escaped. He followed her but arrived at her house just at the moment she entered.'[18] We also have women's own modern rewritings of the tale that do not deny the attraction of wild male sexuality, but set it beside an equally fierce and articulate female sexuality. In 'The Company of Wolves', Angela Carter wrote: 'She saw how his jaw began to slaver and the room was full of the clamour of the forest's Liebestod but the wise child never flinched, even when he answered: All the better to eat you with. The girl burst out laughing; she knew she was nobody's meat.'[19]

This articulate, powerful tradition is the one that feminists now need to build on. If we insist on seeing heterosexual culture as alien, and insist on rejecting it, we lose the great power that women have often felt in that world. In fairy tales, as in erotic novels and art and photography, the resistance to patriarchy is often played out as well as its supports found. Unless feminists acknowledge the confidence and pride women have often felt within heterosexual culture they run the risk of placing women as victims even when they are not, and so reducing women's potential power. Especially now that women are finding their own social and artistic histories, and constructing their own stories of sexuality and ensuring that these are heard, we need no longer insist on a version of hetero-sexual culture that sites women as victims.[20]

When feminists in the seventies and eighties turned away from the power and confidence that women were building up in their sexual lives to concentrate on fear and rejection, this was not the first time that feminism had chosen an extreme view of sexuality that seemed at odds with broader changes in society. It is often forgotten now that Suffragette banners in 1913 carried the slogan, 'Votes for Women, Purity for Men'.[21] Celibacy, not contraception, was the feminist line on sexual liberation during the nineteenth and early twentieth centuries. While contraception would only increase women's subordination to masculine desires, nineteenth century feminists argued, celibacy could free them altogether. The feminist reaction to prostitution in the nineteenth century was rather like some feminist reactions to pornography in the twentieth century, an alarmist cocktail of horror and fury, with little interest in finding pragmatic ways to reduce women's abuse. And yet this fiercely asexual attitude was quite at odds with the more broadly sympathetic image of the 'New Woman', which also arose in the early twentieth century, and which suggested women could enjoy sexuality on their own, freewheeling terms.

This gap between feminist rhetoric and real shifts in sexual culture is apparent now too. While some feminists have been drumming up more and more fear, other women have moved on. It is impossible to site the woman as victim in the sexual battleground on every occasion. Contemporary society fields many sexual personae for women to admire, heroines that women themselves have constructed, and none of them are victims.

We have seen the bawd reappear. An older, witty woman who laughs at men as well as delighting in sexual pleasure, this woman is not at the threshold of sexual experience, but in her wise-cracking prime. The rise of frank women's magazines and television programmes and novels have released the bawd from the kitchen and made her a more public figure. Patsy Stone (Joanna Lumley) in *Absolutely Fabulous* is an egregious example of the bawdy woman; and she is cited again and again as women's favourite television character. Writer and chat-show host Vanessa Feltz treads a similar path, as she writes feature articles on what she feels about her vulva and how often she has oral sex, in a rather knowing, mocking style. Jo Brand is an even more bawdy comic who tells us she doesn't really like thin men because 'if you swing on top of them . . . they break. You may as well stuff the whole man up.'

The promiscuous lady is also around. She is a woman who sleeps with dozens of men, but does it in a way that enhances her fastidious, controlled demeanour rather than falling into the usual cultural trap of promiscuity, the image of the uncontrolled nymphomaniac. Andie MacDowell in *Four Weddings and a Funeral* crystallised that image as she sat, perfectly groomed and unembarrassed, counting up her 33 lovers to the delight and anguish of Hugh Grant.

The idealistic celibate is making a comeback too. Alicia Silverstone in the film *Clueless* played a gorgeous, popular 16-year-old who was a virgin and proud of it. Far from being a victim of her inexperience, she knew she wanted to choose a man at least as carefully as she chose her beloved Alaïa dresses. Helen Simpson, the British writer, treats the same image lovingly in one of her short stories, with a heroine who proudly rejects the 'who fancied whom' attitudes around her. 'She was determined to reinvent the business of love for herself. Her attitude was the determined opposite of pragmatic. It took some nerve. She was the Lydia Languish of her set.'[22]

Then there is the Lawrentian woman; the woman who, like D. H. Lawrence's heroes, trusts the messages of her blood and flesh more than the messages of conventional morality. The young

British novelist Julie Myerson, in her first novel *Sleepwalking*, describes a pregnant woman having a passionate affair: 'There's no particular gentleness, no reticence, neither of us stints: we are deprived people in a deprived landscape . . . My need is a childish thing, and I fulfil it without thinking, like a child.'[23] This woman takes what she needs from the affair – sensual affirmation of her self and her body – and then returns to her husband with an enhanced sense of her independence.

There is also the pornographic heroine, reworked from the woman's point of view. In 1975 Susan Brownmiller wrote disparagingly that, 'There can be no equality in porn, no female equivalent, no turning of the tables . . . Pornography, like rape, is a male invention, designed to dehumanise women.'[24] But many writers have recently disproved such a warning. There is Maureen Freely in her fantasy novel *Under the Vulcania*,[25] Alina Reyes in her pornographic novella *The Butcher*,[26] or Madonna in her photo-book *Sex* (all published in the nineties), and many lesser writers in the new brands of erotic novellas. Such writers revel in the commonplaces of pornography: the repetitive sex scenes in which no one ever gets tired or hurt or emotionally involved; the pneumatic perfection of young bodies, male and female; the terse thump of obscene language. They rejoice in making men surrender to them. 'He says, "I'm gonna come, baby, I can't hold it any longer!" I love that helpless sound in his voice,' writes Madonna. 'I tell him not to close his eyes when he comes. I want to look in them. I want to see the moment of surrender when he loses control.'[27]

We have also seen the rise of the glitzy, fun-loving lesbian – the 'lipstick lesbian'. The journalist Julie Burchill gives us the laughter embedded in this persona, as she writes for a mainstream audience about the joys of having a bottle of Bolly and a 25-year-old girl on her knee. There was little or no adverse reaction to the lesbian subplots in various television series in the last couple of years:

Emmerdale and *Brookside* and *A Village Affair*. These may have been glamorised or trivialised for their particular audiences, but they were warm-hearted and energetic and at peak viewing time. Chic, crafted images of lesbianism abound, from a famous *Vanity Fair* cover which showed Cindy Crawford shaving k d lang to the pop group Fem 2 Fem describing on television how a woman can give a woman an orgasm. Images of embracing models decorate magazines (some of whom, like Amber Valetta and Shalom Harlow, suggest they might be acting on the lesbian continuum in real life: 'No air kisses for us, we're into full on-mouth'[28]). *Dyke TV*, a 1995 series on Channel 4, enhanced this hedonistic spirit in its programmes on lipstick lesbians, lesbian clubs and lesbian actresses.

This articulacy has changed the accepted pattern of heterosexual energy. Now that women are able to own up to their sexual fantasies, the presence of women who talk about sex, and can openly desire and take pleasure, has meant that many men accept a sense of objectification in front of female lust. It's new and amusing to find a young girls' magazine like *Just Seventeen* running an article by a man in which he says: 'God only gave boys backsides for one reason – to give girls pleasure,' or to read in the *Sun* about a man who stripped on stage at a pub as a prelude to proposing to his girlfriend, as the audience yelled, 'Show us your tackle.'[29]

This may put men on the defensive: in recent American films such as *Disclosure* and *Basic Instinct*, we see men running scared of the female sexual energy that is being unleashed. But in British culture we often see men feeling easy about being taken as the objects of sexual desire. The British film *The Full Monty* dramatised this revolution. In this good-hearted comedy six unemployed men from Sheffield learn to benefit from the dramatic shift in sexual culture. They begin by commenting on women's breasts in the street, and end up stripping in front of a crowd of screaming women. Their action might be based on a desperate need for money in a society in which men's traditional work is disappearing, but it's also seen as an optimistic action that bodes well for their future relationships with their lovers, their friends and their families.

Just as men are feeling easier about being on the receiving end of sexual desire, so women are feeling easier about openly desiring them. Proactive female sexuality is in the mainstream now. It is part of the most popular, least rigorous swathe of our cultural lives. Women make the first moves in advertisements for coffee and cars, in articles in *Cosmopolitan* and the *Daily Mail*, in books by Sally Beauman and Jilly Cooper. 'I want you . . . now,' says the heroine of the Nescafé advertisements on the telephone to her lover, who is seen amid rumpled sheets. 'Give it to me raw' runs the slogan for a vodka advertisement, with the picture of a nubile young man, half naked. An advertisement for Ryvita shows a woman jumping on a young man in a bus: 'Who knows what you'll do when you're feeling good inside?' asks the arch caption. 'Girl power is . . . when you reply to wolf whistles by shouting "Get your arse out!"' the Spice Girls tell us.[30]

In this changed landscape, sex may sometimes be a battle, but it is not a battle in which women are always victims and men always oppressors. As the short story writer Helen Simpson writes of one bad relationship: 'They came together like this, almost in combat, gladiatorial. They turned cruel little blades on each other and wreaked havoc, and sulked; then made it up with a practised weariness.'[31] This sexual battle is an equal one. Giving and taking, her lovers turn their blades and then make it up.

These changes in what is seen as acceptable sexual behaviour make it easier than ever before for young women to define their own sexual ideals. They needn't feel bludgeoned by one particular aspect of sexuality. This means that the direction of feminism in this generation has changed. Women look back on the past with gratitude. The revolution in women's articulacy described at the beginning of the chapter was the foundation of our freedoms. But the idea that feminism now should be primarily involved in a movement to enable ordinary women to speak out about their sexuality is laughable. Women take for granted the articulacy and demystification that were once revolutionary. When a woman now writes a book called *Women's Pleasure or How to Have an Orgasm as Often as You Want*, she appears on the Jonathan Ross show and is interviewed in local papers, but is hardly seen as a standard bearer for the feminist revolution.[32]

Everywhere, women speak. There is no longer any revolutionary power in encouraging women to speak out about their sexuality. We can see the matter-of-fact loucheness of women's magazines that advocate speaking out, always speaking out: 'Tell your lover when you're enjoying sex', 'Trust has to be communicated and reinforced'; 'If you don't feel like having sex, tell your partner'; 'Tell him what you want'.[33] We can hear the uncoy speech of public health campaigns – 'When will you mention condoms?'; we can watch young women on television, on late-night chat shows like *The Girlie Show* or the *Pyjama Party*, as they romp around laughing about their sexual experiences. Young girls' magazines run advice on sexual positions and sexual pleasure. At schools, contraceptives are passed around and sexual pleasure for men and women is acknowledged. A Health Education Authority study reported that 94 per cent of parents are in favour of schools educating their children about human sexuality and most felt it should begin around the age of eight.[34]

When young women today read tales of women of earlier ages who went into marriage without understanding the mechanics of sexuality, they feel frankly amused. The stories Simone de Beauvoir tells of young women who believe they are dying when they have their first period look ridiculous to a generation raised on the aggressive advertising campaigns of brands of sanitary towels and tampons. By the time most young women lose their virginity today, they will probably have read hundreds of articles, dozens of novels, and watched scores of films that have filled them in on all shades of what that first experience might be like.

We all speak now. Speaking up is the *sine qua non* of contemporary society. When Catharine MacKinnon tells women that 'you learn that your reality subsists somewhere beneath the socially real – totally exposed but invisible, screaming yet inaudible, thought-about incessantly yet unthinkable, "expression" yet inexpressible, beyond words',[35] she is condemning women to a negative position which is at odds with reality. She seems blind to the cultural changes of the last ten or twenty years, which have been predicated on the understanding that women speak.

Given the cultural acceptance of women's speech and the diversity of these new sexual mores, even feminists may not reduce all the tangles that heterosexual women live through to the dead weight of patriarchy. Now that we have achieved such freedom, perhaps women can move on from the feminist insistence on the demystification of sexuality. After all, if the hostile strand of feminism is taken at face value, it costs us the acknowledgement that for many women heterosexual romance can be the site of the greatest beauty, the greatest mystery, the greatest delight of their lives. 'The dominant form of male sexuality *as we have all experienced it* takes the form of aggression, objectification, obsession with penetration, the ability to separate sex from emotion, affection or sensuality',[36] said one feminist in the eighties [my italics].

As we have all experienced it . . . such feminism required women to deny their own multifarious experiences of sexuality in favour of a monolithic sense of victimisation. Feminists now have begun to turn their backs on this hostile view of heterosexuality. Some of them do it by insisting that women can reassert their desire for romance since men can be as soft, as generous and affectionate as women can be. For instance, in *Straight Sex*,[37] the British feminist academic Lynne Segal suggests that heterosexual sex is predicated on male vulnerability and female power as much as vice versa. And in *Fire with Fire*, the American feminist Naomi Wolf makes her own experiences into a standard for gentle heterosexual romance. 'I've seen men delirious with affection,' she says, 'I have seen the word love trigger an erection.'[38] Others, like the American feminist Camille Paglia, argue that women should enjoy the occasional cruelties and dangers of heterosexual life rather than whinge about being victims: 'Surely we want to keep men virile and vigorous,' she insists. 'Deconstruction of the bourgeois code of "niceness" is a priority here.'[39]

Yet I'm not sure that on this subject, Naomi Wolf and Lynne Segal and Camille Paglia really have any more to say to young women than Andrea Dworkin or Catharine MacKinnon. Why do these feminists still believe that they must change women's own attitudes to sexuality? If feminism is to honour the revolution that it has created, it has to admit that it has no place in the bedroom any more. Feminism has to withdraw, has to acknowledge that it may not colonise women's private lives. Now, feminism has nothing to bring to women's sexual experiences; neither to warn them that heterosexual romance is dead, nor to reassure them that it exists. Women are grown up now. Feminists helped them to grow up and should stop treating them like children. Women no longer need to be told how to have orgasms, how to desire, what to desire.

This is not because sex is unimportant. But its language is so far from the language of a political movement that it is best for feminists to leave it alone. Individual women, individual artists, individual writers may explore sexuality, but no one can pretend to know what is good for other women. The language of sexuality is individual, where as a political movement speaks a mass language; it is extraordinary, where as a political movement must be commonplace; it is private rather than public; it is the language of poets and singers rather than teachers and lawyers.

Rather than attempting to codify women's behaviour, feminists should encourage them to free themselves from political interpretations of their personal lives, and move into the sexual realm without the baggage of political thought. This is the testimony of feminism's success, that personal freedom can be aligned with political equality.

Feminism will necessarily find a place in insisting that women's own experiences of sex must be respected, in lawcourts and public arenas, but feminists no longer need to try to define or mould those experiences. Individual women can do that for themselves.

what is to be done?

Feminists now may have little to say to young women about how they should live their sexual lives, as long as no one is getting hurt. But whenever violence or abuse is visible, that is where feminism has a role to play. Abused women still need support, raped women still need justice, men still need to be made to understand that violence is unacceptable. It is not women's private sexual behaviour that we want to change, but men's violent behaviour and the public response to it.

So feminism now has little to say to young women in trying to change their own attitudes to their sexuality, but it has a great deal of work to do in consolidating women's position in the public arena. This is the double-sided truth that we must confront: feminism has brought women great advances in enabling them to speak up about their sexual lives, but it has not yet achieved the concrete power for women that would give their speech real weight throughout society. That power is necessary if women are to protect themselves from abuse and from rape.

A recent survey by *Nineteen* magazine found that 22 per cent of young British girls said they had been forced into having sex against their will.[40] A larger survey published in 1994, *Sex in America*, echoed that figure: 22 per cent of women said that they had been forced to perform a sex act. When men were asked if they had ever forced a woman to do something she didn't want to do, only 3 per cent said that they had.[41] Other surveys raise that figure much further; a survey of 930 randomly selected American women in 1984 found that 41 per cent said they had been raped.[42] And yet fewer than one in ten of those rapes had been reported to the police.

Young women now have to turn their new confidence and articulacy about sex to greater advantage. They may feel confident and believe that now, at the end of the twentieth century, the distinction between a slut and an independent woman has broken down. They may feel able to chat men up, go out alone, wear glossy, gorgeous clothes, dance close to men, and choose whether to have sex or not and how to have it – romantically, languorously, or fast and loose. But they live in a world which has not yet caught up with them and in which, crucially, they do not yet have the power to protect themselves from men who have not moved towards the same ideals.

Women are learning to speak out about rape; the number of women reporting rape has more than doubled since 1983. But their new ease in speaking out isn't getting them where they want to go. Between 20 and 40 per cent of women say they have been raped; only 3 per cent of men say they have forced a woman to perform a sexual act: why does this gulf still yawn, and why is the masculine view still the norm in society? The conviction rate in rape cases is decreasing year by year, even though DNA testing now makes it much easier to prove that the accused has had sex with the complainant. The overall conviction rate stands now at fewer than ten per cent of reported rapes; compared to 24 per cent in 1985. Are nine out of ten women malicious liars? Or is it the case that although women's own attitudes to sexuality have changed, women do not yet have the concrete power in the criminal justice system to be able to bite where it hurts?

Even this figure of ten per cent does not reflect the depressing reality, since about a third of rapes and sexual assaults originally reported to the police are not recorded as crimes. This high no-criming rate in rape compares with an overall 'no-crime' rate of 3 per cent.[43] Taking this no-crime statistic into consideration, we can see that in fact 93 per cent of men reported for rape are not convicted, and remain free to rape again.

Furthermore, reported rapes are estimated by surveys of women to stand at only one in ten of the true total of rapes,[44] since the chilling effect of what women believe their experiences will be if they go to the police silences the great majority of them. One survey carried out in 1994 found that only 6 per cent of raped women had gone to the police. If we accept this statistic, the rapist who is convicted is a truly rare beast; 99.5 per cent of rapists walk around society, free to rape again and again; for every one man who is convicted, 199 are not.

The low number of rapists who are convicted leads to a strong belief among rapists that rape is not really a crime at all. Two researchers who interviewed 114 convicted rapists in the United States in 1980 found that this culture was depressingly evident.

The overwhelming majority of these rapists indicated they never thought they would go to prison for what they did. Some did not fear imprisonment because they did not define their behaviour as rape. Others knew that women frequently do not report rape and that in those cases that are reported conviction rates are low, and therefore they felt secure. These men perceived rape as a rewarding, low-risk act.[45]

We can assume that the same is true among rapists in Britain. Women who have serious injuries, who have pulse rates approaching a heart attack when they entered the police station to report the rape, who were raped in lonely cars in wastelands, who ran half-naked down streets to call for help after their attacks, who were given Aids and VD by their assailants, are accused of making false allegations and given no means of putting their case properly in court.

The thoroughgoing injustice in the legal system, that puts such a low value on women's experiences, is not questioned by the media. The press has used one or two grey-area date-rape cases, which were unaccountably allowed to progress to jury trial despite the fact that thousands of more violent, more distressing and more clear-cut cases that are far more likely to succeed are quietly dropped, to suggest that the pendulum has swung too far the other way, and that most rape cases are brought by malicious women. Although there may always be a handful of tragic women who do cry rape without foundation, the press has, oddly, ignored those cases that make up the majority of those at trial; in which women tell of brutal attacks and threats to their lives and bodies, and yet are denied justice because the structure of the trial is so weighted against them. Thus we have a backlash before we have achieved any concrete change in the legal system.

How is the criminal justice system weighted against women? In the discussion that follows, I am indebted to Professor Sue Lees, and her book *Carnal Knowledge: Rape on Trial*,[46] which probed the vital issues around rape and the British criminal justice system. In all the six ways that I have isolated to show how a woman finds the criminal justice system weighted against her, we see the same problem arising. The changes in attitudes and culture that second wave feminism brought us have not been matched by a corresponding increase in women's material power. Until women have concrete, thoroughgoing power they will always find their words and experiences devalued in the legal system.

First, the woman is allowed no influence on whether her case is allowed to progress to trial. Since the Crown Prosecution Service took over the decisions about whether or not a public prosecution should be brought on a case in 1986, fewer and fewer rape cases have gone to trial. In 1984 about a third of reported rapes went to trial, but in 1994 fewer than a fifth did. In evidence collected by Women Against Rape, we see that cases are dropped for flimsy reasons: because a woman waited two days before reporting the case; because she had drunk two vodkas; because there was no independent witness to the attack; because one witness, who was a friend of the assailant, had not supported the victim's story.[47]

In a striking indictment of the Crown Prosecution Service, the first private prosecution for rape in an English court was brought by two prostitutes in 1995. The CPS had declined to take their cases forward on grounds of insufficient evidence, despite the women's injuries. But after telling their tales of how they were tied up and threatened with knives, the two women won, and the case has become a *cause célèbre* in the campaign for justice that is more in tune with women's experiences.

Second, the woman is marginalised in the trial. Women who bring rape charges are not allowed any control or influence over the prosecution lawyers, and no direct representation in court. In the structure of the rape trial, the woman is simply the witness for the crown prosecution lawyer; she may not prepare the case with the lawyer or have any direct influence on what should be brought out in court. This means that women are often left as no more than spectators in cases that are played out without reference to their own experiences; evidence that they would like to have brought about the defendant's behaviour, their own actions and reactions, their own mental or physical injuries, is too often simply not aired. In one survey of women who were raped, 72 per cent of those whose cases were brought to court found their experiences there distressing, especially because they were not allowed to explain fully what had happened. Eighty-three per cent felt that they were on trial and not the defendant.[48]

The prosecution counsel is often bizarrely out of step with the victim, and fails to accord her words real significance. In one case in 1991, the prosecution – note, the barrister acting on the woman's side – asked the victim such irrelevant and intimate questions that even the defence barrister interrupted to say that such details were unnecessary. And he failed to ask her questions that would have allowed her to speak of crucial details – such as the fact that the assailant had been violent to her in the past and that he was carrying a weapon when he broke into her home. The victim asked Women Against Rape for their help and they advised her to give the prosecution barrister a letter listing the points she wanted to raise in court. But then Women Against Rape were accused of 'coaching' the victim, and she and they were taken to a police station for questioning. The man was acquitted.[49]

In one case where a 19-year-old man was accused of raping a 17-year-old woman, and was acquitted because she had been seen to kiss him before the alleged rape, the woman, Lianne Howard, commented afterwards: 'I didn't get the chance to say half the things I wanted to say. I thought I'd have the chance to explain how I felt the whole way through it, but any time I did try to explain, I was automatically fired back at or told just to answer the question.'[50] Why should rape victims be so silenced? Clearly, adversarial courtroom practice makes it impossible for jurors to hear the full truth of what has happened in rape cases.

In the famous Vicarage rape case, in 1986, the men got light sentences because, the judge commented, the victim had 'made a remarkable recovery'. The victim, Jill Saward, privately disagreed and later commented, 'What are we meant to do? Wear a sign? Nobody in the court ever asked how I felt, or asked anybody else how I was.'[51] Such mismatches between women's experiences and what is deemed important in the courtroom show us that the female experience still has too little weight in court. This mismatch between the victim's experience and what is seen as relevant in the courtroom is particularly obvious and leads to particularly grave effects in rape cases. These cases tend to rest on the question of consent to prove that a crime took place at all, and therefore they pit the woman's word against the man's. So the systematic downgrading of the woman's speech leads to constant miscarriages of justice.

Third, while female speech is marginalised in the courtroom, the defendant's speech is privileged. This privilege given to the man's words is part of the formal legal structure of a rape trial. If a man can show that he might well have believed the victim was consenting – reading screams as squeaks of pleasure, or resistance as play – he will be acquitted even if the jury believes that the woman did not actually consent. This is called a 'belief in consent' rather than 'actual consent' defence. No test of objectivity, of whether a 'reasonable' man would read the woman's signals that way, is legally required.

On the contrary, the judge often helps to privilege the individual man's point of view. In one case in 1993, a short dialogue between the judge and defendant went like this:

Judge: 'Did you find her attractive as a woman, a girl?'
Defendant: 'She was attractive enough.'
Judge: 'When you went into the bedroom you must have

thought it was Christmas and Easter put together when you found her naked in your bed.'[52]

Such reinforcement of the individual man's point of view, his libido and interpretations of a scene, means that the jury may feel pushed to put themselves into the position of the misogynist, and therefore acquit. This lack of objectivity is in striking contrast to other crimes, such as assault and homicide, where the jury must apply the test of whether force used in self-defence, for instance, is 'reasonable'.

Fourth, the woman's character and sexual history are still unfairly brought as evidence against her in court. The crime of rape seems to require a real rapee rather than a real rapist. And only a tiny minority of women can fulfil the conditions laid down for a rapee. If a woman goes out alone, or wears make-up, or wears cute underwear, or has had early or frequent sexual experiences, or has had an abortion, or is an unmarried parent, she must expect that this will be brought as evidence to question the possibility that she could be saying no. And this method, of using our new freedoms against us, almost invariably succeeds. Because more and more women now do go out alone, or go out late, or wear sexy clothes, or dance with men they do not know, or have had abortions or more than one sexual relationship, the misogyny that is still displayed in the legal system has led to a great spurt of acquittals. Women live in a different world from the archaic world they meet in the courtroom, and they are constantly reminded of this. Although the Sexual Offences (Amendment) Act (1976) required that leave should be sought from the judge to bring up a complainant's sexual history, in practice leave is given on flimsy excuses. A Channel 4 documentary in 1994 found that the previous sexual history of the complainant was brought up in 70 per cent of cases.

It is partly because the man's point of view is so privileged in the courtroom that leave to examine the victim's sexual history is so frequently granted. Since most trials hinge on the issue of consent, a woman's promiscuity or apparent availability becomes relevant, since, legal precedent states, that apparent availability may lead a man to believe in her consent. If, in such cases, the judge does not give leave to bring up the victim's sexual history, any conviction may be quashed in the Court of Appeal, which has stated that the law justifies 'such cross-examination under the [1976] section when the defence is that a defendant knew of the complainant's sexual history and in consequence had a genuine *or mistaken* belief that she was consenting [my italics]'.[53]

And even without bringing up her previous sexual history, the woman's reputation, and therefore ability to say no, can easily be questioned. Jill Evans, a barrister who frequently defends men on rape charges but who still sees the need for changes in the courtroom, told me: 'It's not the use of sexual history that's a problem so much as a general perception of the woman that is built up. If the woman initiated any contact, the jury finds it difficult to convict.'[54]

Fifth, although the woman's character is on trial, the defendant's is not. In other trials, a defendant's previous convictions must be revealed if any reference is made to the complainant's bad character, but in rape trials that is not mandatory. So the defendant's previous convictions are not brought as evidence; his previous attempted rapes and successful rapes and sexual harassment and domestic violence are deemed irrelevant, whereas her behaviour becomes central. Questions are rarely asked that aim to pin down his attitudes to sex, to consent, to the woman's personal signals. He is not expected to have sought consent in any way, however slight, yet she is always expected to have expressed in every fibre of her being evidence of total asexuality. Although previous sexual offences may be raised if there is a striking similarity between them, in practice even similar cases are almost never referred to, so that the jury has no idea that many other women have brought cases against the defendant. Sue Lees discovered one typical case of a man who is apparently a serial rapist, although he has never been convicted. He has been accused of rape by seven different women, and acquitted of the three cases that came to trial. At one of these trials, the police wanted to bring in evidence from two other cases, but leave was refused; he was acquitted.

Similarly, Orlando Baker, who has three convictions for attacking women while holding them prisoner, was acquitted of rape in 1994 after his victim, Ginny Rimmer, was subjected to relentless cross-examination. Jurors wept when his previous convictions were read to the court – he had been freed only eight weeks earlier from a seven-year sentence for rape. Ginny Rimmer said, 'I was outraged by what happened. The lawyers all knew his record and that I was telling the truth, yet they falsely called me a liar.'[55]

Although it is true that men must have the chance to make a credible defence even if they have been accused or even convicted before, there is surely a case for saying that if a woman's credibility is at any time put into question, so should the man's. In such cases, the jury should be trusted to use their discretion, under direction that previous offences or suspected offences cannot be held to prove guilt, to decide whether or not they feel that such offences illuminate the assailant's attitude to forced sex.

Sixth, myths about rape and violence are common in courts, and forensic doctors for the defence often imply that if raped, the woman should display injuries, and that if there are no injuries, there was no rape. It would be salutary for the jury to be given expert evidence on the other side, and told that in one survey, 81 per cent of women raped by strangers felt their lives were in danger, as did 42 per cent of those raped by acquaintances. Women do not easily forget news reports of women found sexually assaulted and killed. When a woman feels so threatened, she is right not to struggle and so she is less likely to be injured. In fact, the usual advice given to women who are assaulted is not to struggle, in case the man has a weapon. A significant proportion of the women who were surveyed and who did try to resist said the man became more violent in response to resistance that they offered – 47 per cent of strangers and 23 per cent of acquaintances.[56] Only two men in both groups (out of over 100) became less violent in response to the woman's resistance.[57] In many reported scenarios, the woman would have to have a strong deathwish to struggle: 'He got a kettle of boiling water and threatened to throw it over me if I didn't get undressed. He also picked up a knife and threatened to cut me. He . . . put the knife at the opening of my vagina and threatened to put it up if I resisted.'[58] But if these threats are not brought out in court, if the woman's fear is not given a hearing, if expert opinion is not called as to how a woman might be wise not to struggle, the jury is simply confronted with an uninjured woman whom they are pressed to believe is lying.

The difference between the relative weight given to the man's and the woman's experience make it now almost impossible to convict rapists in Britain. The sad truth is that any man with half an ounce of sense can get away with rape. And he can get away with it over and over again.

Yet previous attempts to change the way the criminal justice system deals with rape have had some effect, and women can learn from their previous successes in planning how the current situation might be changed. They have, for instance, changed the ways in which the police deal with rape. An episode of the BBC series *Police* in 1982 helped to change people's attitudes to the harsh interrogation techniques that police had used up to then with rape victims, and pressure from the Women's National Commission helped to produce new Home Office guidelines on handling rape cases. Female officers often stay with complainants throughout the investigation and better training has been introduced for police officers who deal with rape. These improvements may have contributed to the doubling of the number of reported rapes and sexual assaults over the last decade.

Courtroom practice has also changed enormously over the last decade. Anonymity for rape victims has been mandatory since 1976, and after pressure from lawyers and pressure groups, 1994 saw a change in legislation which meant that judges were no longer obliged to tell juries that independent corroboration was necessary to convict in rape cases. Previously, this warning not to convict on the uncorroborated word of the victim had been an irrational obstacle to conviction in rape cases where there were no witnesses. It was the reason for much justified fury from feminist groups and campaigns, since rape was the only crime in which the corroboration warning was given, which showed clearly that the woman's word was seen to be weightless and unimportant. Also, a long campaign by women's pressure groups and female lawyers made rape in marriage a crime in 1992, ending the bizarre injustice that made it impossible for women to protect themselves in their own homes.

Such changes remind us that the attitudes of the criminal justice system are not etched in stone and that those working for change need not become defeatist. In Australia, where a package of reforms has recently been implemented, perhaps most importantly that a woman's sexual history can never be examined in court, 75 per cent of men charged with rape are found guilty. It is vital that we reform the legal system in Britain even further. How will this be done?

Civil actions and private prosecutions can often point the way to justice for women who have been denied it. Still, the usefulness of such cases lies more in their strength as campaigns, when the injustices of the justice system can be highlighted, than as an answer to legal shortcomings. For instance, Linda Griffiths took her case to the civil courts in April 1995. She said she was raped by her former boss in 1991, and the Crown Prosecution Service decided not to prosecute on grounds of insufficient evidence. She won £50,000 damages in a civil action where, instead of needing proof 'beyond reasonable doubt', the court must decide 'on the balance of probabilities'. Her case was useful in highlighting women's dissatisfaction with the criminal justice system, but such actions only work if a man is solvent, since civil courts cannot give custodial sentences; and the regular denial of jury trials to rapists would be unjust.

The first English private prosecution for rape was brought in 1995, and as discussed above it served again to illuminate dissatisfaction with the present system. Particularly, because of concurrent campaigning by Women Against Rape and other pressure groups, it exposed some of the shortcomings of the Crown Prosecution Service, which fails to bring cases to trial even when the victim seemed to have a good case. Such publicity should encourage the Service to take forward more cases, and many journalists and politicians and campaigners are working to keep this need uppermost in the public mind.

Women have also begun to use European legislation to press for changes in the law in Britain. Julia Mason, a woman who was raped and then subjected to six days of terrifying cross-examination in court by the man who attacked her, waived her right to anonymity to draw attention to the injustice of her case. She is taking her case to the European Commission of Human Rights to argue that the 'degrading and inhuman' treatment she endured breached the European Convention on Human Rights. If she wins, the law in Britain will have to be changed to protect rape victims from extended cross-examination by their attackers. 'As a defendant, he had all the rights and I had none,' Julia Mason commented.[59]

Since women make up only 3,951 of the 27,205 officers in the Metropolitan police force,[60] and only 23 per cent of all practising barristers,[61] women don't feel like insiders in the courtroom, and the new values that arise from feminism cannot be easily understood there. This is a dangerous intersection: when old-fashioned cultural attitudes about female sexuality intersect with society's unequal power structures. The answer to this is, clearly, that women must come forward into the legal system, however alien to their values it may seem, and then gradually the system will change under the pressure of their attitudes in a way that it cannot do when only a tiny number of women are present.

Prosecution barristers need to be properly trained in dealing with sex offences, so that they can vigorously intervene to prevent the woman's experience being marginalised and the man's word being excessively privileged. Many barristers now support the idea that channels of communication must be opened between the Crown Prosecution Service and the victim. Currently, after a woman has reported a rape to the police, she has no contact with the prosecution service in preparing or discussing her case. As a mere witness for the prosecution, she is not involved with their deliberations and is given no chance to clarify her experience, hear their reactions, or emphasise aspects of the case that she finds important. Jill Evans, a barrister who often defends men on rape charges, is unhappy about the way the woman often feels sidelined by this courtroom practice, and would like to see meetings set up between the Crown's solicitor and the victim, and then the solicitor and the barrister, to discuss her case. Helena Kennedy QC also believes that it is important that there is 'closer liaison between the CPS and victims of crime, so that the victim is kept informed and involved throughout the process.'[62] If the defence is to use personal, malicious, vicious attacks, the prosecution must at least be in a position to refute them by reference to the victim's personal experiences and reactions to the attack. Empathy must be built up and the victim's own priorities recognised in the language of the court.

And we must see straightforward legislative changes. Clearly, current practice on bringing out the sexual history of the victim needs to be examined. Ideally, we would follow Australia and ensure that sexual history could never be brought as evidence in the trial. Then the jury would be able to keep their minds on the event in question rather than on an elegant web of innuendo. The system which allows any means to wreck the victim's story, and few means to question the defendant's, is too unjust to be viable.

If that change in legislation occurred, we would no longer find ourselves in the situation where 83 per cent of rape victims feel that they, not their attackers, are on trial. We might get to the situation where we began to close the gap between women's experiences and the law's response. We might get to the situation where all men realised that rape was a high-risk as well as immoral act.

Then we might also go further. Helena Kennedy QC has suggested that a warning on objectivity should be given by the judge to the jury, so that the jury is required to consider whether a reasonable man would have acted in the manner of the defendant, rather than being encouraged to acquit by the requirement to put themselves into the mind of the rapist. The Law Commission similarly has suggested that the law should be changed to allow a conviction of rape even if a man 'does not realise that the other person does not consent but that fact should be obvious to him'.[63] Such reforms would help to give equal weight to the word of the woman and of the man, rather than privileging the man's point of view. It would require the jury to consider whether an assault had in fact taken place, rather than whether the rapist believed it had taken place, which is a more reasonable and more just way to try to weigh two conflicting stories.

Such ideas prod us into imagining a world where women might find that the legal system does not automatically and systematically weigh against their words and their experiences. They would then find that the advances they had achieved in their private lives were also being lived out in public.

The injustice that raped women encounter extends to all sorts of other crimes against women. A recent report from Barnado's exposed the shocking reality of young girls' abuse on the streets of Bradford. While girls as young as 12 are working as prostitutes and being beaten and held prisoner by their pimps, and yet find no redress through the law, it is clear that the equality that women seek is still far away.[64] And women still find that although they have begun to speak out about the abuse they suffer in their own homes, they are very far from getting public support for women who experience domestic violence. They have not seen their own changed attitudes reflected in public debate and support. Domestic violence still tends to be seen as a trivial issue by men in Britain: when Paul Gascoigne was known to be beating up his wife, Sheryl, he went on playing soccer for England. Compare that to the fury that ensues when any sportsperson or even journalist is found to be taking drugs. In Britain today, abusing one's own body is still seen as a graver crime than abusing the body of one's wife.

Again, we are not looking to change individual women's attitudes to abuse. We are looking to get changes in the law and government services to make sure that women who are abused can find redress. As with rape, so with domestic violence: the criminal justice system has been found wanting. Recently, cases of abused women who killed their husbands – including Kiranjit Ahluwalia and Sara Thornton – that have been taken up by women's groups such as Southall Black Sisters and Justice for Women, have enforced a change in the attitudes of the courts, so that domestic violence is seen as the intolerable provocation that it clearly is.

But it is not only the criminal justice system that is problematic. Women are also looking for real support in society. Throughout

Britain, women suffer economic inequality, and this works against them when they try to leave abusive partners. In 1975, the Select Committee on violence in the home recommended there should be funding for one place in a refuge available for every 10,000 of the population. Currently there are only one-eighth of those spaces.[65] Organisations like Refuge and the Women's Aid Federation find that they have to turn away as many women as they can help. I remember visiting one refuge in Glasgow, and although it was run by optimistic, gentle women, I couldn't help thinking you'd have to be desperate to be there; it was small, smelly, tatty and miserable. Women who are being abused deserve better than this.

If women remember these undeniable horrors, the ways that women are ignored by the law, abandoned to their abusers and left to suffer attacks without justice, we will not want to spend our time interrogating our own attitudes to sexuality. Rather, we will find that we have concrete battles to fight on behalf of all women.

Campaigners, lawyers, police, politicians and journalists who are working towards changes that would protect women who suffer rape and domestic violence should not be deflected by the arguments of some feminists that any complaint about the abuse that women suffer simply positions women as victims. Katie Roiphe has criticised marches against rape because of this: 'The marchers seem to accept, even embrace, the mantle of victim status. As the speakers describe every fear, every possible horror suffered at the hands of men, the image they project is one of helplessness and passivity.'[66] And Betty Friedan has criticised the rape crisis movement: 'Obsession with rape, even offering Band-Aids to its victims, is a kind of wallowing in that victim state, that impotent rage, that sterile polarisation.'[67] But women and men who seek to change the laws about rape are not wallowing in the victim status of raped women. On the contrary, women are acting as victims if they do not turn their new ability to define their own sexuality into concrete equality. Women need to back up their new confidence with changes in the law and society at large, to send out the message that rape and abuse are not acceptable. The point of ensuring that more rapists are successfully prosecuted is not to make women feel vulnerable, but to make them feel safe.

This desire for justice in dealing with rape and abuse is more important than attacking the representation of sexuality. In the United States, pornography has become the central issue that feminists do battle on. But it is much more important to make sure that real abuse and violence and coercion do not go unpunished. Pornography hurts because we feel powerless to prevent real abuse; if we could consume it in an equal environment, would it frighten us in the same way? In many ways, women need pornography; they need a society that is frank and free in words and images and in which they can talk about their bodies and experiences without becoming social outcasts. It is telling that societies in which pornography is not at all acceptable also fail to accept free movement or rational dress for women. And although many state-by-state surveys in the United States have failed to find any correlation between the comsumption of pornography and the prevalence of sexual crime, one survey found a strong correlation between the consumption and availability of pornography, and women's equality, measured by 24 indicators of economic, political and legal equality.[68] So pornography and equality may go hand in hand in more tolerant, open societies.

Should we trust the monolithic demonisation of pornography? Or is it a travesty of the subtle ways that culture, even dirty culture, works through us and on us? Pornography can be good or bad, according to whether we are abused or free. Take two recent cultural moments in which women writers have examined the contemporary meaning of pornography for women.

In an April 1995 episode of the comedy series *Absolutely Fabulous*, the two kooky protagonists, Patsy Stone (Joanna Lumley) and Edina Monsoon (Jennifer Saunders), get so turned on by reading a copy of *Razzle* that they decide to set up an evening watching pornographic videos with two male prostitutes. When the two gentle guys are sitting in their room, Patsy makes the tacky come-ons we expect to hear said by a would-be James Bond to an innocent young girl: 'Has anyone told you you look like Robert Redford?' she says to the black guy; and 'That's a great shirt, I may have to rip it off you.' The video they finally watch features a friend of theirs.

Livi Michael, the Lancashire novelist who won the 1995 Geoffrey Faber prize for literature, gives us a very different scene. In one of her novels, a woman is locked in a relationship with a difficult man. She doesn't want to alienate him, because she will be lonely and miserable without him, but he has got into the habit of bringing pornographic magazines and videos to their house to look at before making love.

> The last time she'd seen Rob he'd brought a film as usual. Lizzie thought the girl on the screen looked about twelve, but Rob said she was older. She had little fatty breasts and almost no hair between her legs. She sat blindfolded between two men who were taking her school uniform off. Lizzie sat on the bed, trapped between sickness and desire. Turn it off, she told herself, turn it off, turn it off . . .[69]

When she decides she cannot bear to watch the girl being raped, she pulls out the video. Rob leaves her and she is plunged into loneliness.

Both of these scenes suggest that pornography alone is not the problem; the crux of the problem lies in the situations in which pornography is produced or consumed. In *Absolutely Fabulous* the situation is equal, without any suggestion of abuse, full of female friendship and power. But in Livi Michael's scene, the video is proof of a rape, and watched in an unequal relationship. Pornography here is used to support and produce abuse and violence; it is utterly unacceptable.

Pornography belongs in either context, and either context can be a reality in women's lives now. We live in a time in which our burgeoning humour and confidence about sexuality coincide with awareness about the reality of women's abuse. Pornography alone cannot prove either context is the whole truth.

Even when society is more equal, pornography will not just wither away. Many feminists have held to the ideal that when women are equal, sex will naturally be calm, affectionate and consensual, and pornography will be unknown. 'In a society in which equality is a fact, not merely a word . . . sex between people and things, human beings and pieces of paper, real men and unreal women, will be a turn-off. Artefacts of these abuses will reside under glass in museums next to dinosaur skeletons.'[70] But is this possible? Or is the idea of this marvellous golden age a distraction from the real business in hand? I think that it is not the business of feminism to clean up our mysterious desires. We can only work towards legal and social and economic and political structures that do not automatically weigh against women. The idea of changing our dreams and desires takes us frighteningly towards a brave new world in which we must involve the thought-police. But the new movement in feminism aims to separate the personal and the political, to reinforce women's personal freedom alongside our political equality.

There are, and still will be in an equal society, all sorts of dark corners of human desire, and women are not always innocent. Consensual, calm sex may have been the feminist ideal, but women often make their desires for domination or submission known. Nancy Friday has been collecting women's sexual fantasies since 1973, and in her latest book, published in 1991, she noticed that for the first time women were able to dream about domination, and that that could even veer into sadism. There is, she says, 'a whole new world of women's erotica that had opened up in answer to and because of the very real changes in women's lives.'[71] The two most notorious living figures of sexual sadism in Britain are women: Myra Hindley and Rosemary West. Even when women are in control, sex is not necessarily nice. Women must confront their own desires, and not shrug the blame for all sexual darkness on to men. Some of the best British writers who explore sexuality write towards this complicated truth. In the passage from Livi Michael that I quoted to underline the unacceptability of pornography to many women, we note the phrase 'torn between sickness and desire' as Lizzie watches the video she hates.

Similarly, we cannot assume a direct and easy link between sexual play and the real power structures of society. We are already easy with the idea that men can act out submissive fantasies in the bedroom, with Miss Whiplash or their bondage mistress, and the establishment does not come crashing down. Isn't it also possible to believe that a woman could be powerful and in control in her public life and enjoy submissiveness in bed, without undermining her commitment to real equalities? Feminists now realise that they can never clean up the hurly-burly of personal relationships, that sex will never be completely vanilla.

So feminists can concentrate on attacking concrete abuse, rather than trying to colonise all sex. Young women do now have a different attitude to sex from the one that Betty Friedan or Gloria Steinem fought to discredit. Young women feel far more confident, far more in control, than their mothers ever did. Any kind of puritanism resonates badly with them. So long as no one is getting

hurt, there should be private spaces, spaces that bear little explanation, in everyone's lives. Women need the legal back-up,
economic security and social support to gain redress for abuse, and
to ensure that their words are believed and acted upon. They do
not need feminism to prescribe certain attitudes and modes of
behaviour.

Feminism, like psychoanalysis, has weighed sex with so many
meanings that the idea of free, blank sex seems almost impossible
now. But is it? In *Mating*, a novel published in 1992, a male writer
speaks through a female character to describe this ascent into a
kind of blankness once trust has been achieved. In the most glori-
ously loving relationship, the woman thinks, 'There is another
kind of sex . . . My own name for it is blank sex. It's sex without an
order of battle. No program goes with blank sex.'[72] This bearable
lightness of being is a great ideal, and feminism can help to bring it
closer.

chapter 7

hello, boys!

'Try telling women's groups anything other than all men should be castrated at birth and you risk being labelled a sexist pig,'[1] warned one journalist recently. This image of feminism, as a movement of women who are personally hostile and vindictive towards men, is the most damaging part of the baggage that contemporary feminism has to carry. When I asked women around the country whether they were feminists, it was always that aspect of feminism that alienated them. 'I'm not a feminist,' insisted a woman who works as a cleaner in South London, after arguing strongly for the importance of women's equality and independence, 'I think men can be all right.' 'Oh no no,' laughed an unemployed woman in Glasgow, whose ex-husband had regularly beaten her up, when I asked her if she was a feminist. 'I haven't had much luck with men, but I wouldn't say they're all bad.'

This is the popular idea of feminism: that to be a feminist you must believe that all men are irredeemably bad. And this is not just a myth created by the media. Throughout the literature and history of the recent women's movement we do find, intermittently, a bitter, personal hostility voiced towards men. Men, collectively *and* individually, historically *and* here and now, are held to be simply the enemy, simply an obstruction to progress. 'All men are potential rapists',[2] some feminists insisted; not just in the biological sense, but because they believed all men individually enjoyed the fear that rape generated in women. 'They all benefit because they exploit our fear . . . These are all the same men – not a minority of sex-starved maniacs.'[3] 'Surely it is time for women to have their demands met,' wrote one woman in *Spare Rib* in 1987, 'Time for a national campaign for the use of castration!'[4]

Although men attended early meetings of the Women's Liberation Movement in Britain – and indeed ran the crèche in the very first national meeting of all, in 1970 – by 1973 a Women's Liberation centre in Covent Garden was completely closed to men, and that ethos prevailed in many other places: at Greenham Common, and in small women's groups up and down the country. The consciousness-raising movement was vital in giving a weight to women's experience that it had never before had and in allowing women to articulate the real prevalence and trauma of rape, child abuse and domestic violence. But as it took off, reproducing small, supportive, all-women's spaces throughout the country, the women's movement closed the doors to men. Women reviewed books about feminism, ran women's studies courses and set up women's groups.

I remember my father writing letters to *Spare Rib* and the *Guardian*'s women's page under an assumed name, because he wanted to enter a debate that would otherwise have been closed to him. Men were given the distinct sense that they were not welcome in feminist circles, and were often personally reviled if they did enter. Helena Kennedy's husband was once verbally abused at a Women in Publishing conference when he brought her newborn baby on to the stage for her to breastfeed.[5] A march against violence against women held in July 1986 fielded the chant 'Two, four, six, eight, who do we want to castrate . . . MEN', and when a lone man was seen in the crowd, he was hissed and booed until he left.[6]

In her autobiography Doris Lessing remembers a striking scene from her past:

> A building in London that houses a feminist publishing house
> has in it other offices, one of which is regularly visited by a
> friend of mine from the Middle East, as it happens an exem-
> plary husband and father. It took him a long time, he said, to
> understand why it was that every time he passed the door of
> the publishing house, one of the females came out and delib-
> erately stamped on his feet, as hard as she could . . . Not least
> depressing was that this kind of thing was thought of . . . as
> political action.[7]

Women who were attempting to put together ethical and political arguments that were completely new, understandably felt rather protective about them, and erected 'Keep Out' signs all over their new lawns. So, for instance, one group of feminists poured scorn on the idea that men should support the struggle against violence against women. They wanted to 'fight every step of the way against de-radicalisation of rape, against rape being amalgamated into the liberal consciousness' and against 'hoards [sic] of self-congratulatory men [saying] "of course I'm against rape"'.[8] That meant that although middle-class people have often been socialists, and white people were often active in the anti-apartheid movement, feminism, in many people's eyes, became a women-only arena.

Despite the massive success of feminism, this defensive attitude has not entirely disappeared. Mary Daly, a leading American feminist, refuses to take questions from men when she lectures.[9] Papers published after a conference on women's studies at Birkbeck College, London, in 1993 included an essay that referred viciously to men who wanted to join the feminist debate in academia.

> He 'espouses' anti-racism and anti-sexism, but skirts around serious work on masculinity which would necessitate his positioning himself within and as part of male culture. 'Posing' as a female/feminist (without having to claim victim status) along the way he manipulates women's realities, plunders their lived experience (of oppression) for course material, and may even do some serious 'fieldwork' (via sexual relations with one or more students).[10]

Such rhetoric provides a strong disincentive for men who might want to join in debates about equality; if he wants to talk about feminism sympathetically, he may be accused of 'posing as a feminist'; if he shows a commitment to anti-sexism he may be seen to be manipulating or plundering women's lives; his interest in the debates of his colleagues may be read only as sexual interest.

When feminists decide to hiss and boo individual men rather than attempting to persuade them, they may gain the strength of the moment – the wound-up crowd can shout together, differences can be forgotten, energy gained. But this gain comes with a longer-term expense. The wrongs that women are shouting about cannot be righted in this way; to find ways for all women to reach political and economic equality sudden anger must be tempered into pragmatic argument and persuasion.

The personal hostility to men that for a time became so visible within the women's movement was part and parcel of that over-identification of the personal and the political that I have attacked on other levels. If feminism was seen as a state of consciousness rather than a political movement, it made sense to insist that to be a feminist you had to have personal experience of oppression. There was no way that a man could understand inequality, given that he had not been oppressed, feminists argued, just as they also began to argue that no white woman could understand a black woman's weight of oppression, and that every white woman had to accept guilt for that oppression, and similarly for disabled women. This growth of 'identity politics' robbed feminism of much of its potential for concrete, collective change. If feminism is to succeed now, it must reconstitute itself as a straightforward argument for political, social and economic equality.

In such a straightforward equality movement, we will not have to ask individual men to bear the weight of their historical guilt. We can speak a language which remembers that individual lives exceed the social structures that surround them. Statements such as this, 'Men want women to be under their control and at their disposal. Men's sadistic fantasies teach them how to perpetrate unpleasant heterosexual practices and rape,'[11] crush all men into one demonic pattern. But in the new feminist movement, men are seen as individuals, some in favour of equality and some against. It is this division between the traditionalists and the progressives that is far more important now, than a simple division between men and women. Just as some women do not want to move towards greater equality, so some men are eager to throw off inequality. We do not need to make the weight of guilt a burden that every man is asked to carry, and the experience of being a victim an experience that every woman is required to share.

This idea that all men are feminism's enemies is partly just a result of sloppy argument. If women agreed that they were unequal in a society that gave men the advantage, some failed to tease out

the difference between a general condition and particular relationships and individuals. But it was also the result of extreme anger.
Can we say that the anger expressed towards men by some feminists
was a mistake? On one level, no; it was sincere, it drew women
together and in its heat new debates, especially on domestic violence and the sharing of domestic labour, were forged. But on
another level, absolutely: the vivid hostility towards men alienated countless women and men who would otherwise have been
sympathetic to the cause of equality. Women who found the idea of
unmitigated sisterhood boring and cloying were made to feel that
they were not feminists – although it was precisely from women
who naturally felt comfortable with men and insisted on their place
in masculine society, such as Mary Wollstonecraft and Simone de
Beauvoir, that feminism before the seventies had drawn its
strength. Above all, as I have been constantly reminded while
researching this book, this hostility just made many people forget
that feminism is simply an argument for sexual equality, and that
equality is now desired by most men as well as almost all women.

We also have to ask a difficult question. Has feminists' hostility
to men had the effect of driving them away from those very roles
that women would now like to see men embrace? The disgust that
feminists felt as they uncovered more and more evidence about
abuse in the family resulted in a kind of giving up on men. 'Women
are going to have to be the teachers and protectors for some time to
come,' Judith Herman, an influential writer on child abuse, wrote
in 1981.[12] Feminists in the second wave women's movement argued
strongly that men's contribution to family life and childcare was
always suspicious:

Nearly all of us could remember several incidents with relatives (male) which freaked us out in one way or another . . .
We see this as the subtle sexual abuse of girls . . . We do think

there is a connection between 'normal' and 'deviant' male behaviour to female children . . . We're saying that 'normal' behaviour isn't really so acceptable.[13]

Such vitriol directed at men's everyday behaviour in domestic and family life did not encourage men, who have never felt entirely at home in the domestic world, to insist on their place there.

So although women have moved into masculine roles with surprising ease, changing their clothes and their ambitions and their working lives without feeling that they have sacrificed their femininity, men are finding it more difficult to move the other way and take up an equal role in domestic and caring work. For instance, the number of male teachers in primary schools has dropped sharply, by 10 per cent in just 10 years. Within 15 years it is possible that there will be no men at all teaching in primary schools. 'Men are deterred from applying for jobs, particularly in infant schools, because of the concern created in society about the relations between men and young children,' one female primary school headteacher has said.[14]

This feminist suspicion of men's participation in family life has combined with the traditional masculine suspicion of effeminacy to create a culture that still militates against men who would like to shift into traditional feminine roles. One recent survey suggested that more than a half of all fathers said they spent five minutes or less one-to-one with their children on weekdays.[15] The absence of close fathering is exacerbated in families where the parents live apart: 750,000 British children do not see their fathers at all.[16] How much of that is caused by fathers' irresponsibility? And how much by a social work and legal system who do not see him as central to a child's welfare? As one woman in Glasgow told me, with resignation, her son had wanted to apply for custody of the child he had fathered with a teenage girlfriend. 'We did ring a lawyer but she told us that even if the girl was the worst drug-injecting junkie in the world, he wouldn't stand a chance.' That vignette, which surprised me at the time, was backed up by an experiment featured in a television programme in 1995. An actress and an actor visited solicitors separately, posing as spouses seeking a divorce and custody (now called a residence order) of their child. Although they both told the solicitors that the man had taken more responsibility for the child, while the woman had supposedly been more involved with her career and had also had an extra-marital affair, all the lawyers advised the woman to go for sole custody and told the man that he didn't have a chance of keeping his son. One commentator concluded that: 'These solicitors were not, themselves, anti-father, but were simply reflecting what they knew, or believed to be the reality.'[17]

Although legislation states unequivocally that the father and mother should be treated equally, in fact residence orders, as one barrister in family law assured me, 'would always go with the mother unless there was a compelling reason against her'. Many men are irresponsible about their children, but we should be alive to the idea that potentially responsible men may be pushed away from their families by a culture that sees family life as feminine terrain; a culture that both traditionalist and feminist have reinforced.

Yet in the long term, reducing abuse of children must rest, unequivocally, with building up men's care of and contact with their children. Then more and more men will see their children as subjects rather than objects, and will feel they have invested in an emotional bond that they do not want to break. In a carefully controlled study, two researchers have found that incestuous fathers were significantly less involved than non-abusing fathers in caring for their daughters in the early years.[18]

The challenge for this generation is to find ways of supporting

victims of abuse while still celebrating the beauty of close relationships between men and children, just as we can speak about
women's abuse of children without casting doubt on the whole
institution of motherhood. There is a way to heal this breach
between many men and their families without falling into the
rhetoric of the traditionalists about the need for the authority and
power of the father. Feminists have successfully asserted the ability
of women to fulfil masculine roles, but it is now time to move on.
We must now also admit and encourage men's ability to fulfil feminine roles. Then the circle of equality will be complete.

We can admit the vital need for fathers within families without
reinforcing the image of the father as a figure of patriarchal authority. On the contrary, the more fathers are involved with their
children the less likely the fathers are to be ashamed of feminine
behaviour, and the less likely their children are to be limited by sex-
specific behaviour.[19] Until recently, we tended to read that boys
brought up by their mothers became homosexual. But now the
opposite is suggested, that boys in single-parent families often react
by embracing traditional masculinity – or an ugly exaggeration of it.
A consensus is springing up among social policy professionals that
fatherless boys are likely to be involved in criminal behaviour, but
that boys with close relationships to their fathers – even if the
fathers themselves have been involved in criminal behaviour –
will be more law-abiding. Contrary to traditional expectations,
fathers have a vital role to play if children are to grow up at ease
with themselves and a changing world. Feminists should therefore
be unashamed in saying that men are central in family life, and
should be wary of speaking of the home as if it were a feminine
world.

It is time, then, to move on from the hostile years, when women's
anger erupted and men felt alienated from the equality movement.

Now, feminism belongs to men as well as to women. Indeed, if the impetus of feminism over the past century has been to give women the keys of the masculine kingdom, allowing them to work and play as men, to dress as men, to seek out sexual pleasure as only men once did, to vote, to drive lorries, to sit on the Speaker's chair in the House of Commons, so the impetus of feminism in the next century will be to give men the keys of the feminine kingdom. Here, they will discover the delights of caring for their children; of feeling secure and wanted at home; of being linked into strong social and family communities that do not just rely on their status; of being released from the unending burden of breadwinning. To make this happen women must be prepared to cede some emotional and ethical high ground at home, just as men have to cede financial and political high ground away from the home.

This turnaround in feminism is already beginning. Men are speaking about the changes they expect to see in themselves: 'The dilemma of the eighties woman was how to be a superwoman, how to have it all, and the dilemma for the nineties man is precisely that – how to have it all, a career, kids and a good relationship,' wrote one young journalist when he became a father.[20] And women are making moves towards them. Rosalind Coward, the feminist writer, has said, 'Men need to feel there is something in it [feminism] for them, while some women seem to need reminding it is a shared project, not a struggle to wrest power from people who already feel diminished.'[21] Sue Tibballs, a 29-year-old feminist who runs the Women's Communication Centre in London says, 'That confrontational feeling towards men has just gone completely. I don't know any women's groups that still have that attitude. I think feminism now has to be something that men share with women.'[22] The new feminist culture is something that is very bound up with women's relationships with men – at work, at home, in colleges, in politics – rather than a separatist ideal.

This isn't really new, of course. The hostility that I focused on above is only intermittently visible in the history of feminism. The women's movement does not, in general, rest on angry separatism. If we look back at our history, we can see that it affords us great examples of women and men reaching out to one another, attempting to find ways to right the wrongs of inequality together. From the Unitarian W. J. Fox, who argued for women's suffrage in 1832, to John Stuart Mill, who gave feminism vital political and intellectual support, to William Thompson, who wrote his *Appeal of One Half the Human Race, Women* with Anna Wheeler in 1825, to male politicians like Keir Hardie and Ramsay MacDonald who supported women's suffrage.

This is the history within which we can site ourselves, a history that takes into account both the public and the private support of men. Why should I deny my own experience, that my male partner has provided me with confidence in myself when I lacked it, that male editors have encouraged me to write at full throttle when I was holding back, that men have helped me achieve my potential just as much as women have? And I know this is nothing new. Always, everywhere, countless feminists have received support from countless individual men. I remember my father looking after me and my sister while my mother did her Open University degree. I know that Vera Brittain was given the feminist novel, Olive Schreiner's *The Story of an African Farm*, by her lover Roland Leighton, who 'had himself been a feminist ever since he discovered that his mother's work as well as his father's had paid for his education and their household expenses.'[23] Who can deny that Mary Wollstonecraft and Elizabeth Cady Stanton, Virginia Woolf and Rosa Luxemburg were supported by husbands and partners in their feminist journeys? Certainly, men are given the advantage by patriarchy; but everywhere individual men have chosen to question the justice of this advantage and to sympathise strongly with women's desire to throw off their shackles.

Perhaps this generation's impatience with the hostility voiced by earlier feminists partly stems from our luck. Young women now have the privilege of being able to form relationships with men who have grappled with the ideas of feminism as a natural part of their adolescent and adult development. Feminist women now expect that men will accompany us on our journeys through life, and not simply be obstructions, enemies, a dead weight. Women in the seventies did not have the luxury of frequently meeting men who took feminist ideas more or less for granted. Rather than blaming those women, we should thank them for creating the conditions for greater closeness between the sexes in their children's generation. But we can see how different our lives are from theirs, and how different our feminism must therefore be from theirs.

Rather than just berating men for not moving further into the feminist mould, we can also celebrate how far they have come. There is a long way to go in masculine culture, as there is in feminine culture. But when you think how far women have come in 100 years, from a time when education was held to be bad for their health, female suffrage bad for society and contraception a real immorality, we can be optimistic about where men might go in the next 100 years, from a time when close fathering is tolerated to a time when it is the norm, from a time when men's domination of politics is questioned to a time when it disappears, from a time when flexible working is discussed to a time when it is practised.

This hopefulness is particularly visible in Britain. American culture, with its exaggerated cult of masculinity, cannot provide us with many pointers towards new ways of thinking about masculinity. But in British culture we can look optimistically at the ways that men are moving on from traditional ideas of masculinity.

For instance, look at two recent books that show us how different British and American views on fatherhood can be. Compare *Patrimony* by the American writer Philip Roth, with *And When Did You Last See Your Father?* by the British writer Blake Morrison, published within two years of each other. Both are memoirs of the deaths of the writers' fathers. Both fathers die slowly, in the classic modern style, of terminal cancer; Roth's of brain cancer and Morrison's of bowel cancer. The titles are suggestive: Roth's rather grandiose and abstract word, with Morrison's uncertain, resonant question. Both writers find their fathers' descent into helplessness immensely traumatic, and attempt to deal with it in precise, physical detail. In particular, they look with anxiety at their fathers' ageing penises, their glances freighted with the great psychoanalytic mythology of patriarchy, that gives us the father's phallus as the site of authority. Here is Roth:

> I looked at his penis. I don't believe I'd seen it since I was a small boy, and back then I used to think it was quite big. It turned out that I had been right. It was thick and substantial and the one bodily part that didn't look at all old. It looked pretty serviceable. Stouter around, I noticed, than my own. 'Good for him,' I thought. 'If it gave some pleasure to him and my mother, all the better.' I looked at it intently, as though for the very first time, and waited on the thoughts . . . 'I must remember accurately,' I told myself, 'remember everything accurately so that when he is gone I can recreate the father who created me.' You must not forget anything.[24]

This is a reassuring passage. The father's penis is big and thick and substantial and young and serviceable and stout and pleasure-giving. By describing it Roth is making his relationship to his father seamless; by creating his father's penis in language Roth is participating in his father's role in creating him. They are locked into a seamless structure of authority, bigness, stoutness, manliness, which is not disturbed by illness or death. The book ends with a partial reprise of these words. 'He would remain alive there not only as my father but as the father, sitting in judgment on whatever I do. You must not forget anything.'[25] The father, even dead, is still the patriarch, still reassuringly judgmental.

Here, in contrast, is Morrison:

> Suddenly he tips his chair forward. The handkerchief scrunched between his thighs falls to the floor, and I see his penis scrolled up in its sac, a sad little rose, no engorgement. I remember how big it seemed when I saw it as a child at the swimming baths, and how I looked forward to being an adult so I could have one that big too. I think how as adult heterosexual males we rarely see each other's penises and never see each other's erections – least of all our fathers' erections – and I catch myself grieving that he may never have an erection again.[26]

'A sad little rose.' That is the father's penis, which as a child Morrison saw as so big and enviable. Morrison is honest that he is disappointed in his father; his father does not fulfil the promise of adult malehood. What's more, adult masculinity carries losses, being cut off from easy contact with other men. The passage is all about disappointment, estrangement and grief. But through this sense of honest disappointment, Morrison finds something else. He finds a new, fresh prose that is free from Roth's rhetoric and resonates wonderingly in our minds. His book is infinitely more moving than Roth's, because this father is a real man, not a symbolic father, a real man facing death without reassuring metaphors.

Morrison does not know, just as none of us know, what will happen after the patriarch dies, what kind of new relationships men and their sons will build. There is nothing programmatic, no definite symbols to hold on to in his work. He is honest that much of his relationship with his father was about missed connections, misunderstandings, disappointments on both sides. But he sketches a hopefulness into this uncertainty. At the end of his book, he remembers when his father was well enough to help Morrison out in his new house, by putting up a chandelier.

We turn the light on, and the six candle-bulbs shimmer through the cage of glass, the prison of prisms. 'Let there be light,' my father says, the only time I can ever remember him quoting anything . . . We stand there gawping upwards for a moment, as if we had witnessed a miracle, or as if this were a grand ballroom, not a suburban dining-room, and the next dance, if we had the courage to take part in it, might be the beginning of a new life. Then he turns the switch off and it's dark again and he says: 'Excellent. What's the next job, then?'[27]

Light shimmering through the cage, the prison. The next dance, that might be the beginning of a new life. We hear Morrison's yearning not just for his father's immortality, but for a new way of living with his father, a freedom, a closeness, a courage.

Another British book that focused this new ambivalence and optimism about masculinity was Nick Hornby's *Fever Pitch*, the bestselling book about the life of an Arsenal fan. This book has sometimes been seen as a regrettable work; a book that flashed up a new pride in laddishness. But *Fever Pitch* was so successful because although Hornby loves football, he did not, unlike other fashionable writers on the subject, fall for the grand, brutal, thuggish culture of the terraces. His football is a culture of little boys and ageing men, of losers and companionship, not over-endowed heroes. He injected a note of irony into football culture, and acknowledged that elements of masculinity, such as football fandom, must co-exist now with the loss of the traditional masculine world. 'It's easy to forget that we can pick and choose . . . it is possible to like football, soul music and beer, for example, but to abhor breast-grabbing and bottom-pinching (or, one has to concede, vice versa); one can admire Muriel Spark *and* Bryan Robson.'[28] Just like the young female rock stars who wear miniskirts but still talk about girlpower, Hornby clearly believes that men can like football without taking on the whole traditional freight of masculinity. Men can pick and choose, as he puts it, from the 'Masculinity Supermarket'. Hornby refuses to give up his love of football, just as new feminist women might refuse to give up their make-up, but he will acknowledge that masculinity isn't the thing it once was.

A fresh air of uncertainty breezes through Hornby's book. When he first takes a woman to see his beloved Arsenal, he asks the reader to step into her shoes, not his:

> I remember . . . how she responded each time Arsenal scored. Everyone in the row stood up apart from her (in the seats, standing up to acclaim a goal is an involuntary action, like sneezing); three times I looked down to see her shaking with laughter. 'It's so *funny*,' she said by way of explanation, and I could see her point. It had really never occurred to me before that football was, indeed, a funny game, and that like most things which only work if one *believes*, the back view (and because she remained seated she had a back view, right down a line of mostly misshapen male bottoms) is preposterous.[29]

Here we see, at last, a man becoming self-conscious and uncertain about his masculinity in front of a woman. It has often been said that women reflect men at twice their natural size; but young men of this generation are perhaps the first to find that they are not magnified in their girlfriends' eyes. And Nick Hornby is one of the first writers to express the tremors that creates in the masculine spirit.

In this new 'Masculinity Supermarket', irony is key. It is irony that allows men to giggle rather than glower over passages like the one above, where a girl shakes with laughter at the misshapen male bottoms that pay homage to the actions of shapely male legs; it is irony that allows men to take on various roles – 'caring and sharing', 'macho', 'laddish' – without feeling defined or compromised by any of them. Masculine literary culture in Britain is currently obsessed with treading this line of irony. Almost every young male writer and journalist writes in that self-mocking vein, examining elements of erstwhile masculinity with a bitter smile. Giles Smith mocked the figure of the pop star in his memoir, *Lost in Music*;[30] Mark Hudson took his family's mining tradition to pieces in his memoir, *Coming Back Brockens*.[31] Men also write obsessively about illness, as in Robert McCrum's memoir of his stroke, published in 1996 in the *New Yorker* and the *Guardian*, and rock musician Ben Watt's memoir of his intestinal disease, in *Patient*.[32] The enjoyment the men take in examining their frail bodies, and how they salvage an identity despite – or because of – their helplessness, their loss of potency, of power, is very telling.

The hugely successful television series, *Men Behaving Badly*, has again often been seen as a vaguely regrettable comedy that has resuscitated laddishness and sexism at a time when those qualities should be in retreat. Yet the satire it offers up is based on the absence of traditional masculinity. At every point the humour lies in the disjunction between the characters' vaunted laddishness and their real lack of sexual vigour, aggression or decisiveness. To prove his bravery, Gary (played by Martin Clunes) gets into a fight in the pub, but he feels he must hire his combatant. Similarly, he sleeps with another woman when his girlfriend is away, but in the encounter with the other woman, she is the one who instigates sex, she is confident and powerful in the bedroom, while it is quite clear that he is too gauche to follow through his desires. In this situation, his muttered chant the next morning, 'I did it, I did it,' is, as it is meant to be, only laughable. He does nothing. Only the women, in this world, can act. Similarly, his friend Tony (Neil Morrissey) may be obsessed with sleeping with Deborah (Leslie Ash), but he can never actually harass her or inflame her desire. He can only abase himself, he can only grovel and trip over his feet. The humour of the series always lies in the fact that the men's desires are betrayed by their actual effeminacy. *Men Behaving Badly* articulates the loss of masculinity, not its power, by giving us laddishness as a fragile pose.

The immense popularity of such books and television dramas shows us that British men are constructing a new culture around the loss of power. It is a good culture, a self-mocking, witty, resonant culture, that goes beyond any of the patterns of masculine culture that we have seen before.

The same optimistic note is struck when you look at the wash of social surveys and statistics which constantly suggest that feminine and masculine values in Britain are still moving closer and closer together. Men of this generation have taken on many of the precepts of feminism. When asked their response to the statement: 'Family life suffers if the mother works full-time', 80 per cent of men over 56 years old agreed. That clearly shows the weight of tradition women of that generation had to struggle against. But only 30 per cent of men under 25 agree with the statement. In one generation, 50 per cent of all men have changed their minds on this vital point. Among 25- to 35-year-olds, the correlation between men's and women's attitudes is almost complete. Thirty-six per cent of women agree with the statement, as do 37 per cent of men.[33]

Similarly, the pattern of domestic labour has also radically changed. We still have a long way to go, but the old cynicism that feminists felt about heterosexual relationships was encapsulated in the postcard slogan: 'It begins when you sink into his arms, and ends with your arms in his sink.' For a certain generation, that cynicism is still backed up by reality. Among working people over 35, women spend 18 hours a week on domestic work and men spend 6 hours; women do three times as much housework as their partners. But among working people under 25, women do 7 hours domestic work and men do 4 hours.[34] These women do less than twice as much as their partners. The gap is closing so fast that in a decade or so it may have equalised entirely. We should not underestimate the difference that this has wrought in men's lives. For instance, 82 per cent are now directly involved in everyday, practical caring for their children, more than twice as many as in the fifties.[35] The changes are still speeding on.

In this rapidly changing situation, many women don't want to harangue individual men, they don't feel that the individuals they know are perpetuating oppression. Rather, women and men can work together to create new structures of work and family life. Women need not always align themselves against men when defining what they want from social reforms. This is particularly true when it comes to one central potential reform: the move to flexible working. I will explore this issue in depth in Chapter 10, but it is worth noting here that the desire for flexible working is now being voiced by men as well as by women. Thirty-one per cent of working men under 35 say they would like to work partly at home, compared to 24 per cent of women.[36] We are recognising our common interest in such debates, and young men and women are coming together, working out ways of living together and working together that base themselves on equality. Feminists can celebrate this new equality between men and women, and not simply dismiss it as false consciousness.

It is often suggested that although women are entirely easy about entering masculine roles, men are entirely uneasy about going the other way. As I have discussed above, there is some justification for this judgement, as we see in the falling numbers of primary-school teachers. But is it really the case throughout society? One of the most striking results of the British genderquake is that as many men as women are now complaining to the Equal Opportunities Commission about sex discrimination in recruitment. I think it would be safe to hazard the conclusion that discrimination against men in recruitment for packing or secretarial or caring jobs is not in fact any greater than it has ever been before, but that men, like women, are no longer prepared to be constrained by traditional expectations of their sex. They therefore take it as a point of pride to take their cases to industrial tribunal, like the temporary secretary Jo Maugham, who was sent home from a law firm when the employer realised that the Jo was a Jolyon, not a Joanna;[37] or Alan Robinson, a secretary with 'outstanding qualifications' who took a secretarial agency to tribunal when he was refused a typing test. It looks as though things are on the move; one in five students attending Pitman secretarial courses today is a man, compared to one in 16 in 1991. Chris Marshall, the director of Pitman Training, has said: 'Ten years ago, it was almost unheard of for men to do a typing course. Now we are seeing a changing balance in the workplace, with more women filling managerial roles and men viewing secretarial work as fulfilling.'[38] Although a survey of personnel directors found that over half felt there was resistance to male secretaries, the culture is changing; and one regional director of Office Angels has said that senior female executives are particularly keen to employ male secretarial staff.[39]

Many commentators, feminists included, have chosen to see men's current journey as something that is only negative, only about ceding power. And therefore they naturally tend to talk as if men will only resist. Certainly, many men are resisting change. But many others are embracing it. In her book *Fatherhood Reclaimed*, Adrienne Burgess captures many of these delighted voices. Sebastian, a 39-year-old father, notes, 'It suits really well, working at home . . . The children love it. They love my presence in the home. I know so much more about their lives. More of it falls on me now.'[40] Jonathan Ross once said in the *News of the World*: 'It used to be a dilemma whether women went back to work after having children but these days it's a dilemma for men too if they should go back to work. Who wants to miss out on their kids growing up?' Hugo, a 59-year-old father, said:

> Sometimes I pinch myself and I say, how did I get such an extraordinary stroke of luck? Here I am, 59, with these two wonderful children. I get to see a lot of them . . . I think – this is incredible! Because the alternative was that I would have been working 9–6 . . . and missing it all. I couldn't bear the thought of doing that now. It's pathetic, why does anybody do it?[41]

A majority of men see their own fathers as 'negative role-models' and say they want to be very different kinds of fathers themselves; 'They will usually declare that they want to be closer to their children – both emotionally and physically.'[42] We can note the assertion made by the social researcher Helen Wilkinson on the attitudes that young men hold towards family life: 'The younger men interviewed . . . spoke warmly of the closer and more involved relationship that they have with their children.'[43] A European survey in 1995 revealed that 86.3 per cent of men and 87.4 per cent of women think fathers should be 'very involved in bringing the child up from an early age.'[44]

This gradual shift in desire means that images of fatherhood in our culture are changing. More and more, being a father is not just seen as a symbolic and distant role, but one that is complicated the way mothering is complicated, by day-to-day boredom and anger, and enriched the way mothering is enriched, by close and articulated love.

One of the most striking examples of this change is the way that Tony Blair talks about his life as a father. He does not just hold up his family life as a model of old-fashioned, decent values, he makes it very clear that he is as involved in caring for his children as his wife is. His ease with this role, like his wife's ease with her role as a working woman, is in tune with the values of so many of his supporters, and as he rightly says, not just middle-class supporters. 'Most people live their lives like that now,' Blair has said, 'I think a lot of rubbish is talked about it being just the trendy middle classes, but it's not. The working-class blokes in their twenties in my constituency, because their wives are working, are expected to and do help with the children.'[45] This caring role is a down-to-earth, realistic one, not a symbolic role. Once he was asked in an interview in *Marxism Today* what his first thought was in the morning, and he replied, 'Whether Kathryn's nappy needs changing.' One female interviewer said about him, 'Like many men of his generation, he seems a natural, physically affectionate father.'[46]

This understanding that men have and want much closer ties with their children is also seen in the way that the media treats working fathers, as men that might have a problem trying to juggle the two roles, rather than men that can simply rely on their families to bolster their power. A feature in *The Times* that focused on working fathers examined the lives of Howard Davies, 43-year-old director of the CBI, and Martin Taylor, 42-year-old chief executive of Barclays. The former said sadly, 'The children say they wish they could see more of me,' and the latter said, 'I feel I haven't seen as much of my friends as I would have liked over the past ten years, because I was determined not to miss my children growing up,' and explained that he goes away for at least five weeks a year with his family in an effort to keep close to his children.[47]

There is, similarly, more understanding that men might fail to be good fathers, as women might fail to be good mothers, if work makes them inaccessible to their children. Alex Carlile, a Liberal Democrat MP, recently decided to give up his political career in order to try to help his daughter, who suffered from depression. He said at a press conference, 'I am going home.' His other daughter has spoken about the difficulties she found in having a father who was so committed to his work, even though he was loving and kind. 'Behind the exciting holidays and interesting experiences was the shadow of my father's career . . . I grew up resenting my dad for his job as an MP and the fact that there was never enough time to tell him my problems or ask for advice.'[48]

This shift in the way men see their own lives suggests the beginning of a great revolution, just as the change in the way women saw themselves in the nineteenth century began a great revolution. This new revolution will be a revolution in everyday life – a revolution in the number of hours men spend with their children, in how flexible working will allow both men and women to give time to their families, in how they work with their female partners to negotiate power at home. It will take a long time, but the revolution in feminine attitudes has also taken a long time. At least this generation knows that they must now move forward together. There is a tentative, sometimes wary, sometimes uncertain but sometimes overjoyed partnership between men and women to be found in feminist debates today.

chapter 8

the new feminism embraces power

Have we ever seen women in quite these ways before?

'I want you to consider me for the promotion,' says a quiet, determined Helen Mirren as Jane Tennison in *Prime Suspect*. The most striking image of the 1997 election was a photograph of more than 100 Labour women MPs, standing together and waving after the first meeting of the Parliamentary Labour Party. 'She excelled at everything she did,' another tabloid says about the first female firefighter to die on duty.[1] The news journalist Kate Adie's 'authority and compassion' make her women's most popular heroine in a national survey.[2] For the first time, in 1995, the government appoints two women to its team of economic advisers previously known as 'Wise Men'. The London *Evening Standard* runs a picture of the first female ambassador to Ireland, Veronica Sutherland, meeting the first female President of Ireland, Mary Robinson.[3] In 1996 we hear that businesses headed by women are twice as profitable, and grow twice as fast, as companies headed by men.[4] Northern Irish women launch a Women's Coalition Party to send delegates to the 1996 Peace Process talks, and contrary to expectations, they win two seats. The first women's forum based on female heads of state is held in Stockholm in 1996; seven present or former female heads of state attend, including the President of Ireland and the President of Iceland.

Despite the inequality that affects the life of every woman in Britain, such evidence of women's growing power is a real change. It cannot be denied. It means that feminism can no longer only be associated with the voice of the outsider and the downtrodden. The new feminism is also the movement that celebrates women's growing success. As women break into every corridor of power in Britain, we can see that we are in the final stretch of a long feminist revolution, that is taking women from the outside of society to the inside, from silence to speech, from impotence to strength. Despite the fact that we haven't yet reached the finishing tape, let's remember, sometimes, to be glad about how far we've come and to recognise that this growing power is changing our view of ourselves and our goals.

Compared to every other age, women now have more power measured by any gauge – by money, by influence, by representation in culture, the media and politics – than ever before. The greatest achievement of the nineteenth-century women's movement was to get women out of their stifling homes and into the larger spaces of work and public debate, where their voices could be heard. Women have always worked, but until the feminist movement took off in the mid-nineteenth century, their work was almost never a route out of dependence and poverty. The World Anti-Slavery Convention held in London in 1840 refused to let the female delegates speak. In 1869, the first public meeting on women's suffrage fielded just two female speakers, and their daring was so extraordinary that they were criticised for their unwomanly behaviour in the House of Commons.[5] Nineteenth- and early twentieth-century literature is riddled with the cries of stultified, desperate women: Caroline Helstone in Charlotte Brontë's *Shirley*, Dorothea Brooke in George Eliot's *Middlemarch*, Lily Bart in Edith Wharton's *The House of Mirth*. Although women still delight in nineteenth-century novels, there is always a shudder mixed with their delight, a fear of the narrow social mores that could lead even women like Anne Elliot in Jane Austen's *Persuasion* or Isabel Archer in Henry James's *The Portrait of a Lady* into a frozen, claustrophobic existence. Florence Nightingale memorably described the useless life of a woman in 1852:

> Women are never supposed to have any occupation of sufficient importance not to be interrupted . . . and women themselves have accepted this, have written books to support it, and have trained themselves so as to consider whatever they do as not of such value to the world or to others, but that they can throw it up at the first claim of social life.[6]

But women have now broken through the walls that closed them off from public life, activity and ambition. There are now no legal barriers to prevent women taking their places in the corridors of power. The journey to this point has been a long one. Women first attended the Trades Union Congress in 1875, were first accepted for a medical degree in 1877, were first allowed to own property on the same terms as men in 1882, first entered the House of Commons in 1919, were first admitted to the Bar in 1921. At all these turning points, women were changing society culturally as well as legally. They were revolting against the iron grip of femininity that had silenced even feminists.

In the seventies the last legal barrier to power fell with the Sex

Discrimination Act in 1975. Although women are far from equal, that doesn't stop individual women from cracking the glass ceiling in many different places. Even in the past few years, we have seen the first woman Prime Minister in 1979, the first woman head of MI5 in 1992, the first woman chief police constable in 1995, the first female chief executive of a FTSE-100 company in 1997. Such women create ripples that go far beyond their own success; they provide inspirations and dreams for countless other women who are now in school or taking their first jobs. Although feminism still has a long way to go and many battles to fight, a whole generation of women has grown up who have expectations of their lives that even their mothers can hardly understand.

This change in young women's expectations means that the new feminism looks and sounds very different from feminism at any other time in history.[7] However revolutionary previous feminists may have been, they were still bogged down in a culture that denied power to women as a matter of course. Because of this, many early feminists emphasised that they would not encourage women to seek publicity or throw off traditional femininity. Josephine Butler, the great nineteenth-century feminist who led the campaign against the degrading Contagious Diseases Act, once said of the women with whom she worked: 'The utter absence in them of any desire for recognition, of any vestige of egotism in any form, is worthy of remark. In the purity of their motives they shine out "clear as crystal".'[8] Even feminists, clearly, were not to seek recognition or betray egotism, their hands would be clean of such dirty power-seeking.

And there were certainly feminists in the seventies who turned their backs on the growth of women's worldly power. They moved away from feminism's earlier emphasis on equality towards an emphasis on difference, and women's difference from men was shown, just as Josephine Butler had said, in their lack of egotism.

As Polly Toynbee once wrote: 'If any sister appeared in the press she was accused of ego-tripping, so statements were issued anonymously.'[9] Or as Beatrix Campbell and Anna Coote said about the seventies women's movement: 'Those who put themselves forward were commonly dismissed as opportunists.'[10]

This kind of feminism relied only on the romantic and utopian power that resides with the outsider. It insisted that women should always be defined through their difference from men – more virtuous, less sexual, more peaceful, less eager for worldly power, able to exert their influence indirectly through moral or spiritual means rather than directly by taking an equal stake in lawcourts, media or politics. Fundamentally, both the radical feminist and the reactionary concur: women are not satisfied, and should not be satisfied, by playing to their own egos or their own success. And radical feminists could be vicious about the woman who stepped into roles that seemed masculine. Mary Daly, for instance, argued that women 'are allowed into pieces of patriarchal territory as a show of female presence'. Daly called such a woman the 'painted bird' who masked male power. 'She is herself . . . an intensifier of the common condition of women under patriarchy.'[11]

This idealistic feminist rhetoric encouraged women to turn their backs on hierarchies; patriarchal power was perceived as a ladder, feminist power as a web. Men worked in death, destruction and money; women in creation, healing and emotion. Sylvie Pierce, who is now the chief executive of the London Borough of Tower Hamlets and was involved in the women's movement in the seventies, spoke to me about 'the tyranny of structurelessness, in which you couldn't have a chair of a meeting', which infected the movement. In Britain, this sort of feminism found a visible outpouring in the peace movement, especially at the Greenham Common peace camps that were set up in the eighties. Here, the shift that feminism had undergone, from striking out for equal opportunities to a female-centred culture, was made concrete. 'As feminists we believe there are no good hierarchies,' one feminist peace group wrote in 1978,[12] and in the eighties the first protests at Greenham began to enact 'the anti-patriarchal maternalist separation.'[13]

Important as Greenham was in terms of the peace movement, for feminism it created a double-edged sword; beautiful, utopian, and dangerously prescriptive, as pragmatism was 'overtaken by talk of witches and goddesses and being nice to trees'.[14] This thorough-going criticism of traditional society can certainly be attractive to many women, and few women could swear that they are entirely without irony and a sense of distance when they go to work in places such as Parliament, national newspapers, the Bar, or big businesses. To say that women are distanced from the culture that exists in such places is a simple description of their experience. But it is unnecessary to make distance from power into a prescriptive theory. Women can be insiders who change things, rather than eternal outsiders. But the theory of women's absolute difference from men and male power-seeking bolstered women's diffidence about breaking into power structures. This diffidence is still seen in feminism today, although it is being gradually washed away by a less wary generation.

For instance, I was told at a seminar about young women's involvement in women's organisations in July 1995 that 'should' is an unfeminist word, when I expressed the view that feminist organisations 'should' communicate better. Various women at the seminar argued that women's organisations could not become too highly professional or campaigning, since then they would not be seen as 'safe places' where women could feel secure.

This inability to accept worldly female power is most clearly shown in the way that the women's movement disowned Margaret Thatcher. Margaret Thatcher displayed no problems about dealing with hierarchies and structures, displaying ego and opportunism.

She showed her pleasure in power and her misery when she was ousted from it. These were qualities that put her beyond the pale of mainstream feminist opinion.

But now things are beginning to change. The power-seeker is beginning to look like a positive figure for women, rather than a source of shame. So let's start with Margaret Thatcher. No British woman this century can come close to her achievements in grasping power. Someone of the wrong sex and the wrong class broke through what looked like invincible barriers to reach into the heart of the establishment. Her transformation from an uncertain minister to *Private Eye*'s 'Thatch, supreme ruler of the universe', was a grand, bewitching metamorphosis. And yet it did not involve denying her femininity. 'Just think,' she once said, 'the women of this country have never had a Prime Minister who knew the things that they knew, never, never. And the things that we know are very different from what men know.'[15] She did not believe that women had to become masculine to wield power. She once said, 'The best compliment they [men] can give a woman is that she thinks like a man. I say she does not; she thinks like a woman.'[16] She tapped traditional, mythical images of female power and made them flesh: in 1983 she was depicted on the front of the *Sun* as Britannia,[17] next to the lines: 'There is just one compelling reason why the Tories are heading for an emphatic victory in today's election . . . The reason is a lady . . . It's Margaret Thatcher all the way.'

She made constant references to 'Victorian values' and in one rally before the 1983 election spoke about the new renaissance that was about to envelop Britain, which she made analogous to the Elizabethan era.[18] She clearly liked to be able to use these examples of other ages when Britain was ruled by women; she was well known and well mocked for referring to herself as 'we' as if she too were Queen. Her colleagues were rather mesmerised; in the diaries of Alan Clark, one of her ministers, we are constantly aware of the slight bedazzlement he felt at the very presence of 'the Lady' – far in excess of any admiration he had for his male superiors. And by feeding the language of power with feminine tropes – the household economy, learning to 'carve a joint',[19] the shopping basket – Margaret Thatcher began to map out a language women might feel comfortable about using even when they were running the country's economy or sending troops to war. Again, in her dress, which was an interesting mixture of hardness – helmet-like hair, sharp suits – and softness – the lowered voice, the lipstick – she made female power look positively decorous and acceptable.

Yet she never held back because of her sex and she broke the most apparently resistant bastion of male power in the Western world. In photographs and television clips today we see an image that already seems almost mythical, almost impossible: the woman in colour among the men in grey. She was physically brave; when the IRA bomb went off in the hotel she was staying in during the party conference in Brighton in 1984, 'There was discussion about whether I should return to No 10, but I said, "No, I'm staying."'[20] She was indifferent to criticism. She was proud of her escape from the traditional feminine role, commenting that she only cooked eggs and cheese, microwaved ready-cooked meals or hacked at things in the fridge. She relished combative situations; in her very first meeting of heads of state in the European Union she noted with pleasure that she was able to swing the agenda off course: 'Most of the other heads of government were furious,'[21] she said delightedly. She allowed British women to celebrate their ability not just to be nurturing or caring or life-affirming, but also to be deeply unpleasant, to be cruel, to be death-dealing, to be egotistic. It was cathartic for us to acknowledge those possibilities in the female character, writ so large.

Women who complain that Margaret Thatcher was not a feminist because she didn't help other women or openly acknowledge her debt to feminism have a point, but they are also missing something vital. She normalised female success. She showed that although feminine power and masculine power may have different languages, different metaphors, different appearances, different gestures, different traditions, different ways of being glamorous or nasty, they are equally strong, equally valid. That ability to show, in practice, the different-but-equal nature of a powerful woman is far more impressive than, for instance, the fake power-feminism of Hillary Clinton, who rode to power on her husband's back and then made a song and dance about her independence and feminism.

Margaret Thatcher's legacy is everywhere. Every time a journalist or a historian tries to deal with, say, why Britain is in the state it is, or what the true qualities of a leader should be, we suddenly see the unquestioning masculinity of their references snapping. No reflection on Britain in the eighties, no reflection on the free market, no reflection on power, is complete without the necessary obeisance to Margaret Thatcher. No one can ever question whether women are capable of single-minded vigour, of efficient leadership, after Margaret Thatcher. She is the great unsung heroine of British feminism.

But even now, many, many years after she took power, feminists are unable to celebrate her achievements, not just because of their political colour, but because she has been demonised as a freak. Bernadette Vallely, the founder of the Women's Environmental Network, said solemnly to me, 'Margaret Thatcher was a man, after all.' She was not, she was a woman. Because of this insistence that Margaret Thatcher had 'become a man', many women denied their daughters a point of identification into the corridors of power. They made her seem deviant.

But young women who grew up in the eighties have been positively affected by her status. As Oona King, the second black woman to become an MP, said to me: 'I don't care if Margaret Thatcher was the devil, it meant so much to me that I was growing up when two women – she and the Queen – were running the country.'

This generation of women is much less likely to experience feminists' erstwhile ambivalence about taking on power. Now that women are streaming in – or trickling in – to all areas from the law and politics, to publishing and television, to medicine and business, they are more confident that they can shape those areas in their way. They no longer feel so worried about getting their hands dirty, now it is clear how many good things can be built with dirty hands, covered with the grit of determination and the oil of money.

The women's movement was weakened by its excessive attachment to a politically correct idealism. The idea that women should naturally tend to non-hierarchical and consensual and utopian methods of organisation meant that truly independent women were often forced away from the women's movement, to the movement's loss. Many women who could have drawn strength from groups of inspiring, like-minded thinkers became isolated and weakened, while the lack of tangible figureheads, money and points of influence in turn weakened the movement itself. Paradoxically, just as a generation of women were growing up who were easy with power and independence, the feminist movement could only speak the language of the group and the victim. Many of the women whom I interviewed who recognised the need to attack discrimination and who believed in equality on all levels, still absolutely refused to call themselves feminists because of the image it brought to their minds of a sorry victim, rather than a laughing, independent, ambitious optimist.

One of the most striking aspects of the new feminism is the belief that worldly power is important and valuable, and that we should build on the power that we have rather than seeking to disown it. If feminism in the nineteenth century was defined by its outsider status, in that feminists then were forced to speak from the edges of society; and feminism in the seventies and eighties was defined by its sense of difference, in that feminists then wanted to mark out a separate space for themselves; so feminism at the beginning of the twenty-first century is defined by its insider status. It is enunciated by women who may be Members of Parliament or cleaners or novelists or environmental activists, but they will be damned if they will be forced to go into a separate space to talk and take action.

As part of this insider movement, the pursuit of equality in the corridors of power is vital. Women will only be equal when every woman working on a shopfloor feels that she has the same access to training and promotion as every man; when every woman who joins a union feels that she can become a national officer if she wants; when every woman who trains as a barrister feels that she can say, like Cherie Booth, 'I want to be a judge' without being mocked; when every woman who goes into journalism feels she need not work on the fashion page, and can become a news editor if she prefers.

For too long, feminist writers have kicked around the problematic football of power, wondering whether women really want power, what kind of power women want, and whether women in power would really change society. To such questions, I would put the most basic answers.

Yes, women do want power. They are tired of having less than men everywhere, less money, less influence on decision-making at work and home, in shops and offices, in Parliament and lawcourts, in issues from road-building to health care. They want to be present everywhere, in every office and every boardroom where decisions are taken that affect their lives.

And they want all kinds of power. Perhaps power can be thought of in three ways. First, there is an almost negative power, the power over our bodies and little else, that just asks that women should not be threatened and harassed and can live their lives undisturbed. Then there is the power to work and vote and speak, buy and sell as we want, freely in society. And lastly, there is the power to influence others and take decisions that affect others' lives, even in the most exclusive and difficult places in the land. This last form of power might look like the icing on the cake, but it is important to understand that all three aspects of power are interlinked, and the first two depend on the third. Women do not feel free from violence and harassment unless they have some economic security and secure rights to work, own property and gain legal redress. And they will never have such economic and social and legal rights on a level with men until they are fully represented in decision-making everywhere.

The question remains: will women in power really change society? Do they use power differently and to different ends from men?

Many women want to believe that this is the case. Clare Short MP believes that the level of debate in the House of Commons will become more forthright and straightforward when more women are able to join in. 'Women in Parliament are much more honest and direct,' she told me. 'They are completely uninterested in all that public-school braying.' Barbara Follett MP also told me that she believes 'men tend to talk in abstracts, whereas women want to ground the theory in how it will affect people's everyday lives'. And Alison Parkinson, who is active in the Association of Women Solicitors, told me that women's style of discussing issues in meetings was much 'more conversational; the men declaim, and then the women come in, saying what about such and such, and steering them back to brass tacks'.

But I think we should be extremely wary of making such claims for women. It is precisely such ideas about the way women naturally behave that has kept them out of power for so long. And once they get power, men often see women as women have traditionally seen men. One male midwife, Nicholas Royle, says: 'I've found women colleagues are more domineering, aggressive and uncommunicative.'[22] When Sue Douglas took over the editorship at the *Sunday Express* in 1996, she was quickly taken to an industrial tribunal (although the case for sex discrimination failed) for sacking older men rather than younger women. Graham Jones, the former assistant editor, said he was 'discarded like a used toffee wrapper', that it was 'like King Herod in reverse – not the babies being killed, but all the men over 35'.[23] One male doctor who was victimised by female consultants won more than £3,000 in compensation for sex discrimination from a Yorkshire hospital in 1996. The doctor, Michael Fish, commented on the stress he had experienced after being victimised by two senior women, and saw the problem as one of simple abuse of power. 'Hopefully,' he said, 'no more junior male doctors will be subjected to discrimination by senior members of staff.'[24] And when an all-female bench of magistrates jailed a father who fell behind with maintenance payments, his barrister said that there should have been at least one man on the bench, suggesting that women, like men, could not be trusted to listen sympathetically to testimony that lay beyond their own experience.[25] Such cases show that women in power might behave to men exactly as men have often behaved to women: unfairly and aggressively.

Powerful women can also undermine other women. In one striking case, a young telesales operator took her female boss to an industrial tribunal for woman-to-woman sex discrimination. She said that her boss had made comments about her big breasts and made her discuss her sexual experiences with her.[26] Such an experience is far from the web-like network of caring women that has been idealised by feminists, but these experiences are becoming more visible as more women become powerful.

Women now have to confront their own ability to dominate and exclude. It is impossible for us to know whether, when women are equal in power, they will be any nicer or gentler or more reasonable than men. The face of female power is the face of Catherine the Great as well as the noble, gentle face of Aung San Suu Kyi; just as the face of male power is that of Josef Stalin as well as the noble, gentle face of Nelson Mandela. Everything that women do may be coloured by their femininity, but they still have the ability to be good or bad, generous or cruel. Women are no more a monolith than men are.

Yet although I wouldn't like to make any claims for women's ability, individually, to be more caring and sharing than men are, I think it is true that when women come into any area of work or any profession, the culture in that profession becomes more humanised. Not feminised, but humanised. It becomes less and less possible for the culture to remain split between masculine professionalism and feminine caring, masculine authority and feminine compassion. This is not because women are nicer than men, but because their sphere of traditional expertise and knowledge tends to lie with the patient rather than the doctor, the victim rather than the soldier, the outsider rather than the insider. They share their knowledge with the men around them, just as men share their understanding of power and professionalism.

So we have seen issues like childcare, education and health pressing forwards in political debate as women move into more powerful roles in politics. All opinion surveys of women confirm that these are the issues that matter most to them; while men put taxation and the economy ahead. The construction of the welfare state would not have taken the form it did, with its emphasis on health care and family support, without the influence of women in local and central government, in pressure groups and unions.

We have also seen great shifts in the culture of reportage as more women have entered journalism. As the journalist and MP, Martin Bell, said on *Newsnight*,[27] foreign news reporting has changed enormously over the past decade. 'We used to focus on the generals and the armies, now we focus more on the people . . . It's a more humanised and compassionate agenda.' It is unlikely to be coincidental that this different agenda has arisen as more and more women press into news reporting. During the war in the former Yugoslavia, male reporters even began to feel that they were on the sidelines. It was a female reporter, Maggie O'Kane, who broke the story of organised rape in Bosnia, and one male reporter, when asked by his newspaper why he wasn't sending them similar stories, replied, 'You have to be a woman to get those stories out of people.'[28]

We have also seen a much greater emphasis on the experience of the patient as more women have moved into health care, and the unquestioned authority of the doctor has correspondingly declined. An intriguing example of how the movement of women into power may have changed the culture of the health system was once given by Edwina Currie. When she herself was in labour, she had asked for an epidural to relieve the pain, but her doctor ignored her request and gave her pethidine instead, which, in her words, 'made me as high as a kite but did nothing for the pain. I was furious.' She remembered that experience many years later: 'Long afterwards, when I was health minister and involved in developing the consent form for patients, I insisted they should have the right to decide and that doctors should not be able to overrule them.'[29]

Women's power can, therefore, change society. As powerful women enter various spheres of activity that were once dominated by men – from government, to journalism, to health care, and beyond – they make them more human, they open them up to the full range of human experience. Certainly, women want power for the sake of this greater good. But they also want power for the sake of ordinary, concrete justice.

Women want power for their own security and freedom, because unless women are more accepted and less exceptional in powerful positions, every individual career will always be more vulnerable, every individual woman's presence always an anomaly that might be smoothed out. They will always be unsure about whether they are there as tokens or on their own merit; or about what part their looks play in their success. They will always be slightly ill-at-ease in an alien culture. They want women both above and below them so that they don't find their presence questioned. Indeed, contrary to popular myth, women now prefer to work for women.[30]

Justice will not come for women without power. In an unequal society, all inequalities bolster and mirror one another. The discrimination that a female doctor encounters personally (there are twice as many suspensions of women doctors as men, but only half as many are finally upheld)[31] mirrors the discrimination that a female patient suffers personally (women must be much iller than men to get hospital treatment for heart disease), because they are part and parcel of the long undermining of feminine behaviour.

Similarly, fewer women in lawcourts and police stations mean that women find themselves disadvantaged when they come into contact with the criminal justice system because their voice and their experiences are those of an outsider; fewer women in the media mean that priorities associated with women are still made peripheral and that women are the object rather than the subject of debate; few women in business and the City mean that power and money are always seen as masculine attributes, and that a woman who demands them is always seen to be rocking the boat. More women in power will mean a better deal for women throughout society.

So the battle for greater equality in the corridors of power is a battle worth fighting, partly for the individual woman facing up to her future, partly for the interests of women more generally, and partly for society at large. It is a battle that this new generation of young women is ready to fight.

If feminism now is becoming franker and more upfront about women's straightforward desire for straightforward power, that is down to a great cultural shift that has occurred among young women. Women still live and work in unequal conditions, but their lives are unequivocally better than women's lives have ever been before. Particularly if we compare the situation of women in Britain today with that of any other age, we can see that feminism has been an especially great success for young, middle-class women. The young, educated woman at the end of the twentieth century is a new kind of woman, with quite different experiences and ambitions from her mother's generation.

For instance, there are now more female professionals under 35 than over 35. And although the ratio of female to male wages among full-time workers in Britain is around 75 per cent, that's very different for women under 24 years old who have a degree or higher education; they earn 92 per cent of their male counterparts' wages.[32] Among certain professionals – such as solicitors – newly qualified women now outnumber men. Unsurprisingly, these successful young women feel far more positively about feminism than older women do.[33]

Gillian Shephard has said, 'Young women are marvellous – a different species. They have no gender problems, and huge confidence. I think we have done this. The climate we have created has made them into the people they are.'[34] Women may differ from one another as much as they ever did, and much of our psychology is naturally not available to policy-makers and survey-takers, but there is a new archetype growing up, quite different from the minx-like, flapper-style 'New Woman' of the twenties, or the embattled feminist of the sixties. The new feminist is a confident creature, who both embraces and exceeds old notions of femininity. She may be feminine in her dress, or feminine in her desire for marriage and children, but she is feminist in her commitment to equality.

In a way, this new feminist is a fantasy, a creation of advertisements and sitcoms, novels and women's magazines. But she is also real, a real distillation of women's new desires and experiences. She appears in surveys and statistics, in the news, and in the voices and experiences of ordinary working women.

What do the surveys tell us? A wide-ranging mixture of research undertaken by the think-tank Demos has suggested that while the gap between men's and women's values is clear among people over 40, 'it virtually disappears among the youngest age groups'.[35] They have noted that young women report almost as much attachment even to masculine traits like violence, hedonism and detachment as young men do. Similarly, 'psychological testing' of 1,000 people showed that personality traits once considered exclusively male are becoming increasingly prominent in young women under 30'. The emergent generation of females has, according to Dr Robert McHenry, chairman of the Oxford Psychologists' Press, 'started to acquire male arrogance, leadership qualities and a tendency towards dishonesty'.[36]

Harder statistics underline these ideas. The new feminist no longer suffers from the old handicap girls seemed to find at school and university. Against all expectations, she has begun to surpass her male peers at school. Until very recently, it was taken for granted that girls began to fall behind boys at puberty. Now, at GCSE level 37 per cent of boys are achieving five or more A to C grades compared to 46.4 per cent of girls. This success is not confined to traditional feminine subjects: in physics, 73.7 per cent of girls get A to C grades, and only 69.2 per cent of boys.[37] These figures have often been treated with alarm rather than excitement: Peter Osborne, headteacher at Shenfield School in Essex, a comprehensive with nearly a thousand pupils, says, 'The boys are worried because the girls are so assertive.'[38] Women under 35 are three times more likely than women over 55 to have degrees.[39] This higher level of education translates into higher expectations and ease with independence. If a young woman today rejects conventional professional and employment structures, it is likely to be a choice that arises from autonomy rather than domesticity. Young women are now more likely than men to want to 'travel and see the world' before launching their careers.[40]

Going out into the working world, such a woman is determined to be treated the same as her male colleagues. In surveys on the incidence of sexual discrimination, it is very notable that younger women report more experience of sexual discrimination than older women despite their shorter working lives;[41] this must be partly due to their greater impatience with any kind of inequality. Rachael Davies, a 23-year-old employee development consultant at Lucas Industries, says she is not a feminist, but insists, 'The one thing I do fight for is that I refuse to fill any stereotypical feminine role at work. I won't do much clerical work. I have to prove that I don't have to do it. I hope that I am considered equal to the men.'[42]

This kind of feminism relies on the desire to be seen as an insider rather than an outsider. A group of young women architects that I spoke to were very keen to point out: 'If we talk about women's architecture, that doesn't mean that we just want to do domestic buildings. There was an old feminist approach that seemed to push women into small-scale, community building. But women want to design banks and galleries too.' The more powerful the new feminist becomes, the easier she feels about smaller instances of sexism that may still surround her. One young barrister told me: 'When I was a pupil at my chambers, and saw the *Sun* lying around in the tea room, I hated it. I felt so powerless and that seemed to underline it. But now, I couldn't give a damn.'

The new feminist will probably still have her eyes on marriage, although she takes for granted that it will be a partnership of equals rather than a relationship with a dominant and subordinate partner. Ninety-two per cent of young women disagree with the statement, 'A husband should earn and a wife should stay at home.'[43] Such a young woman also takes contraceptive and abortion rights absolutely for granted, in order to control her fertility as far as possible. The average age for having a first child is now 28 in Britain, the highest it has ever been. And the number of women in the UK having babies after the age of 40 has increased by more than 50 per cent in the past 10 years.

This means that women can look to a lifetime of increasing power. They can see their careers as a progression rather than a cycle that stops and starts around their family. Now that there is a generation above them who first broke the glass ceiling, they can, if they want, look to senior women in the cultural world, in hospitals, companies and politics for images of future success. Colette Dowling wrote in *The Cinderella Complex* that a woman 'without an adequate role model is in a deep psychological quandary'.[44] But many women now would be puzzled by such a notion: they do have vivid role models.

Many young women identify that figure early on in their working lives – a junior doctor I talked to always called her senior registrar on her first job 'my role-model', with only a trace of irony; some younger journalists at newspapers said they semi-consciously imitated female senior editors in working practices; young women in architecture talked to me about the female partners in their firms as rather romantic figures; young women MPs have told me that they see female ministers as signals of their potential success.

If they aren't in fields with such definite ladders of success, they look elsewhere for such images. Emma Must, a leading environmental campaigner, spoke about Germaine Greer and the visible ex-director of the charity Shelter, Sheila McKechnie, as older women who command her respect. This intent identification of themselves with senior women increases such young women's sense of self-worth. They now know they needn't disappear as they get older.

Given that 38 per cent of all professional jobs are now taken by women, young professional women are now rarely alone at work in the way that their mothers' and grandmothers' generation of high-achieving women were. Not only can they identify with the women above them, they also have a peer group around them in which large numbers of their closest friends are other ambitious working women, egging them on and laughing with them. In 1971 Germaine Greer could write, 'Of the love of fellows women know nothing.'[45] But all the young women I spoke to knew very well the love of their fellows, and relied heavily on a close-knit peer group, with its own strong jokes and judgements and gossip. Indeed, one survey found that young men are now more alarmed than women by the idea of life without a steady romantic relationship, while women were more concerned with developing platonic relationships.[46]

In journalism, the profession I know best, there is certainly a 'girls' club' that runs alongside and inside the traditional boys' club. The suggestion that women don't know how to network, which is still constantly put about, is nonsense. Working both as a commissioning editor and as a freelance journalist, I have found that most women journalists, like most men, are locked into a dense network that brings them lunches, commissions, jobs, and – when they're really lucky – friendship. Like all such networks, women's networks tread a constant line between friendliness and out-and-out venality, and women seem just as happy as men in treading that line. Most of

these women don't seem to need any help in learning how to network; they'll go to it with a ferocious will in the office canteen, on
the telephone, in a Soho restaurant, at a party, or caught on the hop
while shopping in Marks & Spencer or waiting for a bus.

In more embattled arenas, those networks of women are even
more obvious. Clare Short MP has spoken vividly of the support
that women MPs give one another, in the face of the sometimes
aggressive behaviour of the men in the Commons. 'You can get in
behind her, pay her a compliment. We all know how we protect
each other,' she says.[47] Teresa Gorman, the Conservative MP, has
paid tribute to the way this support can operate across party lines.
'As a newcomer,' she once wrote, 'Labour's rottweilers, Skinner
and Sedgemore, were giving me a bad time. Clare soon shut them
up. And on occasion I've done the same for her.'[48]

As young women move up in their work they are now often
keen to bring younger women on. This is another sign of women's
growing success, that they can feel bolstered rather than threatened
by their younger counterparts. Annie Hockaday, a 30-year-old barrister, told me, 'I went on to the pupillage committee in my
chambers because I wanted to provide a point of contact for young
female pupils – the kind of contact with a senior woman I didn't
have when I was in their position.' Nina Gordon, the vocalist, gui-
tarist and songwriter with the band Veruca Salt, says: 'I love it
when young women come up to me after shows; in a way it means
more to me [than the men]. We've played some all-ages shows,
which are the best because when a 16-year-old woman – girl? –
female person? – comes up and says, "Ooh, that was so great, I play
guitar and I want to do this too", it's a really cool feeling. It's inspiring to feel like you may be inspiring somebody else.'[49] This kind of
relationship provides women with a funny buzz of pleasure; they
take positive delight in steering new recruits into their groups, in
giving them points of contact and access to their knowledge. It's

like the buzz that you get in a new town when someone asks you the way; you have become the pathfinder.

Clearly, the fact that women increasingly identify themselves with work rather than home is one catalyst for the rising rates of divorce. The rays of self-enlarging relationships expand at work. We can never box women up again into believing their worth hangs on their husbands. And we must be glad of this when we remember what the marriage relation for bourgeois women used to entail. Think of poor Rosamond Vincy in *Middlemarch*, a clever, worldly woman who would have done very well in PR or advertising, with nothing to do but whine at her husband for not bringing in enough money. Think of Charlotte Brontë, who married after writing three of the greatest novels of the nineteenth century, and was reduced to seeking her husband's approval for writing letters to her best friend.

More recently, compare the wives of the Labour leaders in the last generation, and you can see a shift that highlights the quiet revolution in the attitudes of women to the getting and keeping of power. Glenys Kinnock was the first leader's wife to have a career and a political persona, but she was unable to keep the career going. She trained as a teacher but gave up full-time work when she had children, in order to concentrate on her family and support her husband. Her teaching career stalled, and despite her charity work she became totally identified with her husband and family. 'I felt the pressures were so enormous on all of us that something had to give.'[50] It wasn't until after her children grew up and her husband resigned his leadership that she was free again to pursue her career, and stood for election as a member of the European Parliament. Apart from the wonderful finish, her story echoes that of myriad women in their fifties who took maybe 20 years out of a possible career in order to concentrate on their family; and then, if they could, tried to re-enter working life.

In comparison, Cherie Booth, Tony Blair's wife, who was born in 1954, earns more than he does and works long hours as a Queen's Counsel. Rather than identifying herself with her husband's struggle, she is a separate person with her own career. She is an outstanding lawyer in her own right; she keeps her own surname. When I once interviewed Glenys Kinnock, she saw Cherie's different life as an almost inevitable outcome of belonging to the younger generation. 'Maybe if I was your generation,' she said to me, 'or like some of my friends, like Tony and Cherie, it would have been different. That's a different generation and they have different options.' Cherie Booth sees her career as solidly linear, a straightforward path to individual power, rather than the cyclical pattern that Glenys Kinnock fell into. 'I want to be a judge,' Cherie said when she became a QC in 1995.[51]

Many younger women have taken cues from both these positions. They do want it all, even if some of them may also have decided that they can't have it all at the same time. Geraldine Caulfield, a 27-year-old production manager at Northern Foods, says that although she would like to take time out of work when she has children, 'I don't want to compromise. I want to come back in a senior position.'[52] Debbie Hinks, a marketing executive who has given up her job until her children are at school, said, 'I am a career woman, it's just that I'm going to have two careers.'[53]

In other words, the twenty- and thirty-somethings coming up in the professions, business and politics are dismissive of those who question their right to be there. They don't feel like rebels. They feel that they are taking on their birthright. Every woman in such spheres that I spoke to told me they had always assumed they would have a career. Perhaps, like Deborah Saunt, a 29-year-old architect, their mother worked and they used her as a role-model: 'I always assumed I'd do the same as my mum did – I saw that she didn't stop when she had children.' Or, like Philippa Smith,[54] a 29-year-old barrister, their mother did not work and they had learnt from that: 'I saw what it did to her sense of self and autonomy. The effects of economic dependency are devastating.' This shows how young women are able to build on both the failures and the successes of their mothers. They are finding a new orientation for their femininity, one that older women can only regard with admiration and some jealousy. As Edwina Currie said of these 'young revolutionaries': this is a solid, unimpeachable bourgeois revolution that has utterly transformed the lives of young women, who see 'nothing odd in having a bank account, a driving licence and a credit card or two, in going halves on a meal out, in planning a home and a family and a job and helping to pay the mortgage, for that is how all their friends are doing it.'[55]

All these statistics and evidence of women's professional success can feel rather dry; as though women could be defined just by their briefcases and their job titles. Yet we see a kind of romance with power beginning, as women imaginatively flesh out the changes in their lives. For the first time in British culture, having power has begun to be part of women's dreams and desires.

On television as a whole, women have only a third of the speaking roles, but this varies widely from the news, in which women take one fifth of the speaking roles, to drama, in which they are much more evenly represented. They even outnumber men in serial dramas, and tend to take dominant roles: 22 per cent of women take major roles compared to 18 per cent of men.[56]

In television drama we now see women's new dreams taking flight. From the charismatic Helen Mirren as the police chief in *Prime Suspect*; to the prison governor in *The Governor*, we watch women exploring the hunger and pleasures of power. The toughest doctor on screen in the nineties was a woman, Helen Baxendale as Dr Claire Maitland in *Cardiac Arrest*. Her story showed a crisp, hardheaded doctor finding that she could not compromise her standards to the level of the current health system. The story of the conflict between an orthodox health-care system and the individual doctor who has a more human vision has been told often enough for a male doctor – as in George Eliot's *Middlemarch* – and was here recast with a proud, clever woman at its heart.

Life and art have begun to entwine and feed off one another. When Pauline Clare was appointed Britain's first chief police constable, her physical similarity to Helen Mirren was noted. When Liz Cross was appointed as an Anglican vicar in Wedmore, Somerset, in the teeth of fierce opposition, reporters commented on her resemblance to Dawn French in the television series *The Vicar of Dibley*.[57] The first real female manager of a football club, Karren Brady, wrote a glitzy blockbuster in which the feisty heroine ends up running a football club.[58] Edwina Currie fleshes out her own hunger for power and that of the women around her in Parliament in frothy novels, in which she attempts to entwine power and sexuality.

In the advertisements that break up the drama we are confronted by more women playing up their authority, women whose charisma is seen to rest firmly on their worldly power. Cherie Lunghi in advertisements for Kenco coffee runs rings round her male colleagues; harassed executives for Gold Blend insist on working late; female bosses give pep-talks to their team for British Telecom. An advertisement for mobile telephones figures a peripatetic business-woman telephoning her stay-at-home husband, who is, naturally, thrilled to see her when she eventually returns. The mums and babes may still dominate the images of women in advertising, but beside them this new and striking female figure has moved in even on the lowest rung of our imaginative lives, a powerful woman who is also a point of identification and desire. Next to her, men in power are often presented with bitter irony, as people who have sacrificed too much or who are behind the times. The 'chief executive's wife' on AT & T advertisements queries her husband's excessive dedication to work; on British Telecom advertisements the male middle-manager will never catch up with new developments.

Clearly, television scriptwriters and advertising executives have realised that women do fantasise about worldly power. Perhaps that idea entered popular culture in the thirties, when popular fiction written by and for women began to play with the theme of getting and using power. Scarlett O'Hara was the great figurehead of that change in the dream-life of young women; she may have been punished, but she was a heroine whose sexuality was inextricably entwined with her desire for money and land and business. Other popular writers, from Jackie Collins to Barbara Taylor Bradford, continued those fantasies, and now popular writers assume that one female fantasy they must gratify is that of power, how power will make the heroine beautiful, rich, and beloved.

In *Career Girls*, an unapologetically brash, breezy and trashy bestseller about two women clawing their way to the top in journalism and the music business, the 23-year-old British writer Louise Bagshawe makes it clear that when men lust after her heroines, they are partly lusting after their power and success. These girls are feminists, but they are feminists with money and greed and lovingly described designer suits. Here is her future husband falling in love with one of the heroines, Topaz Rossi:

> Topaz Rossi was under Joe Goldstein's skin, and he didn't like it. She annoyed him and she bothered him and she made him mad . . . Rossi refused to get out of his mind. Maybe it was the harsh feminism, but he met a lot of feminists. Maybe it was her personality. That brash, bold, in-your-face way Topaz had about her. She seemed to be everywhere he went, shouting

encouragement to the *Girlfriend* staffers, carrying great stacks
of layouts past his office or her own, greeting everybody in the
goddamn building like they were her bosom buddies . . .
'Compromise' was not in her dictionary. That girl would argue
for two hours rather than concede anything. She was fucking
relentless. Maybe it was her dress sense . . . Totally inappropriate for the working environment, he thought severely.
Always showing off her figure. Bright colours. Designer names.
Rich fabrics. He'd never met another redhead who could wear
a shocking-pink suit by Vivienne Westwood and get away
with it. It was just so – so – off-putting, this bold, brassy, ballsy
Italian girl storming around the place like an ongoing nuclear
explosion.[59]

Clearly, this is Scarlett O'Hara's daughter. The bright colours, the
inappropriate clothes, the relentless desire to control everyone
echo Scarlett's driven nature. But Topaz Rossi has certain advantages over the earlier heroine. She doesn't have to work through
men to get power, and so her love of display becomes a badge of
independence as well as a lure for men's desire. When marriage
comes, it is an unlooked-for luxury, an addition to rather than the
centre of her life. And she can have friends. Unlike Scarlett, who
ends up alone and unloved, Topaz Rossi ends up naming her daughter after her best girlfriend. This is all good wish-fulfilment stuff,
and such heroines tell us something about women's dreams now;
they want to be desirable, but also powerful, independent and in
control.

Women's magazines also celebrate and extend this cultural shift.
As Germaine Greer wrote in her new introduction to *The Female
Eunuch*: 'Women's magazines are now written for grown-ups, and
discuss not only pre-marital sex, contraception and abortion,
but venereal disease, incest, sexual perversion, and, even more

surprising, finance high and low, politics, conservation.'[60] Away from the narrow agenda of overtly feminist magazines, they have been able to break the feminist taboo on power. The biggest selling women's magazines, *Cosmopolitan* and *Marie Claire*, contain careers advice and parade role-models. *Vogue* will run features on the new Labour women, on new political pundits (including Suzanne Moore, Helen Wilkinson and Anne Applebaum), or on powerful literary agents (including Felicity Rubinstein, Georgina Capel and Alexandra Pringle), or women in business, or influential women in newspapers. They provide images of power that women can buy into easily, since those images, swathed in Calvin Klein and Armani, look so calmly glamorous. At the same time these magazines acknowledge and reinforce women's longings to be sexually active and desirable. Thus women acting, and acting powerfully and well, take the stage alongside women who simply look. Such magazines prove that women can be both object of lust and subject of power, and this double fantasy is clearly immensely attractive to the young women who buy the magazines.

Similarly, newspapers are becoming much more tolerant and even celebratory of powerful women. Their femininity, or lack of it, is not always to the fore. In one consideration in the *Daily Mail* of politicians jockeying for the Tory leadership in 1995, while Michael Heseltine was described as 'blond' and Kenneth Clarke as 'portly', Gillian Shephard's physical characteristics were not even mentioned. New female Labour ministers find that their new power was taken for granted: Harriet Harman has 'the self-confidence of someone born to rule',[61] and Tessa Jowell is on 'route to the top of Mr Blair's government'.[62]

The media also dots in this new culture of power with tiny stories, providing a colourful patchwork of upbeat moments and continually reminding young women that success is natural and desirable. One day, you will read about the number of women who now drive cars; 40 per cent of all new cars are now bought by women, so that Honda, for example, is developing a training programme to improve their sales staff's approach to female clients.[63] Another, about the second wealthiest woman in Britain, who started life as a bus-driver's daughter.[64] Another, about the first woman ever to be granted a licence to be a boxing trainer.[65] Another, about five female chess grandmasters, including 18-year-old Judit Polgar.[66] Another, about women winning the right to go into combat in the army.[67] Another, that women are now pulling ahead in endurance sports, and may soon be beating men into second place in marathon running.[68] Another, about the woman who climbed Everest without oxygen.[69] Another, about the women in the SAS who participate in undercover intelligence work.[70] And so on. All these stories provide new images of women; women who fight, who run, who drive cars, who make businesses grow, who beat men at chess. And so young women see all kinds of possible reflections of themselves; a range of glittering mirrors that would have been unthinkable even one generation ago.

We can take heart from these images in popular literature, the press and television, but we need not insist that all our culture should be transformed to fit it into such a cheerleading frame. We should be aware that cultures with a plethora of strong female images do not always take those images to heart in everyday life: fifth century Athens gave us Medea and Antigone, the cool Athene of the Oresteia and outstanding feminine artistic and moral forces like the Muses and the Furies, but women of the time were not generally literate or allowed to participate in public life.

The clearest examples of women's attractions to power today are not to be found within art, but within everyday life – in the behaviour of young women and their changing expectations of their lives. In the meantime, art often questions this attraction to power, and shows that culture and everyday life, the personal and the political, are not always identical.

Without doubt, when we look at the changing lives of young women today, we can see a spring of optimism bubbling up. Young women need not apologise for wanting power and equality, and can confidently believe that their desires are going to be fulfilled. We can acknowledge that inequality exists, and still celebrate how far women have come. We can see that changes sometimes create stress and uncertainty, and yet hold on to the underlying truth: we've never had it so good.

chapter 9

not just for the few

The popular understanding of feminism, both of contemporary feminism and of the historical women's movement, is that it appeals only to middle-class women. From the *Daily Mail* journalist Richard Littlejohn telling us that feminism now consists only of 'middle-class professional women talking to each other',[1] to the respected American social scientist Christopher Lasch claiming that the movement for women's suffrage was 'a middle-class movement addressed to the middle-class woman's need for self-expression',[2] the narrow social horizons of feminism have often been taken for granted.

If true, this would be a damning critique of feminism. Even today, how could one put one's faith in a new feminism that failed to speak beyond the middle class, that had no goals that other women could sympathise with, whose ideas of power and equality appealed only to a small fraction of society? But this image of feminism should not be taken as a given. It is true that feminism now tends to be associated with MPs and lawyers, journalists and television actresses, rather than with women who are living on benefits or working as secretaries or cleaners. But that is not necessarily a problem about feminism so much as a problem about the media. Perhaps we have to go beyond the most obvious vignettes, the faces of Cherie Booth or Anna Ford or Harriet Harman, to try to see what impact feminism has had on other women and whether it is true that feminism, today and in the past, has had little effect on most women's lives.

The evidence that exists suggests that it is, in fact, completely wrong to suggest that feminism today appeals only to middle-class women. In 1995 the *Mail on Sunday* commissioned a MORI poll on aspects of feminism and sexual politics. Unsurprisingly, given the results it obtained, the newspaper published few of its findings. One of the discoveries that has languished unpublished in the MORI offices for the last three years is that there was no difference across the social groups in the responses to the question: 'Has feminism been good for women?' and 'Has feminism been good for men?' and 'Has feminism been bad for men and women?' All classes recorded staggeringly high positive responses to such questions, and the negative responses were lower among working-class than middle-class women. So although 16 per cent of AB women feel that feminism has been bad for both men and women, only 13 per cent of women in social groups D and E feel that way.

Similarly, there is a popular misconception that only middle-class women have chosen to renegotiate household roles in line with their feminist beliefs. Most people believe that although you may find a few middle-class men in Hampstead or Islington loading the car with expensive groceries and packing smart toddlers' clothes into a shiny washing machine, in the homes of less advantaged families you will find the housework done much as ever, by a harassed working-class woman as her husband snoozes in front of the television.

Again, that myth should be laid to rest. The same survey by MORI found that there was no class difference at all in the sharing of household tasks. Twenty-four per cent of AB women say that cleaning and housework is equally shared between themselves and a partner, whereas 38 per cent of women in DE social groups say so. This telling statistic has also not been published until now, but it throws an interesting light on the penetration of feminist beliefs throughout the classes. Again, 28 per cent of AB couples say that they share childcare equally, and 30 per cent of women in DE social groups.[3] Such statistics suggest that it would be entirely inaccurate to argue that feminism is a narrowly middle-class movement that has had no impact on the attitudes and behaviour of other women.

Not only is contemporary feminism visible throughout all levels of society, the history of British feminism is not just the history of middle-class women. In Britain many of the most important struggles of feminism have been fought outside drawing-rooms or boardrooms. Throughout the nineteenth century, working women struggled to be taken seriously by their male colleagues and to be paid decently by their employers. Their strikes and protests, their organisations and their mutual support form an often forgotten narrative of female power, always bubbling under traditional social structures and threatening to overturn them. The progress that working women made throughout the nineteenth and twentieth centuries makes up a vivid story of women's ability to change their lives.

The greatest women's movement of all, the movement for women's suffrage, was always a movement that sprang from working-class as well as middle-class women, and that put the interests of working women to the fore. The manifesto of the Suffragette organisation, the Women's Social and Political Union, circulated in 1905, cited one reason alone for giving women the vote: 'The working women of the country who are earning starvation wages stand in urgent need of the vote . . . The vote is the worker's best friend.'[4] Indeed, Christabel Pankhurst at one point felt that the campaign for women's suffrage, 'was too exclusively dependent for its demonstration upon the women of the East End', and argued for the necessity of bringing in more middle-class women. 'It was the right and duty of women more fortunately placed to do their share . . . My democratic principles and instincts made me want a movement based on no class distinctions, and including not mainly the working class but women of all classes.'[5]

Working women have a long tradition of campaigning for dignity and equality in their working life. They began with sporadic instances of independence. In 1780, for instance, the Sisterhood of Leicester Women Wool-spinners protested against child labour being used to undercut women's wages. One woman, 'having more spirit than discretion, stirred up the sisterhood, and they stirred up all the men they could influence (not a few) to go and destroy the mills erected in and near Leicester.'[6] Women workers set up all-women friendly and benefit societies throughout the eighteenth century, and throughout the nineteenth struggled to organise unions. Journalists reacted in horror; one wrote in 1833, 'Alarmists may view these indications of feminine independence as more menacing to established institutions than the education of the lower orders.'[7] During the first half of the nineteenth century there were unions of female shoe-binders and straw-bonnet makers, weavers and lace-runners, tailors and upholsterers and even of domestic workers. In 1825, for instance, Edinburgh maids organised the Maidservants' Union Society and threatened to strike if they did not get their Sundays off and their mistresses' old clothes.[8]

The confidence of the woman wage-earner makes a striking

contrast to the usual picture we have of the frail and passive Victorian woman, as in this telling anecdote from 1844, of a woman worker drinking in her club:

> A man came into one of these club-rooms, with a child in his arms. 'Come, lass', said he, addressing one of the women, 'come home, for I cannot keep this bairn quiet, and the other I have left crying at home.' 'I won't go home, idle devil,' she replied. 'I have thee to keep, and the bairns too, and if I can't have a pint of ale quietly it's too tiresome. This is only the second pint Bess and me have had between us; thou may sup if thou likes, and sit thee down, but I won't go home yet.[9]

Working women's organisations were helped along by the creation of the Women's Protective and Provident League in 1874, later the Women's Trade Union League, which quickly became a national federation of unions of women workers. Gradually women succeeded in putting the case for the dignity of their work to hostile male trade unionists, and constantly showed their strength to surprised employers. In 1911, for instance, 14,000 women confectionery workers marched into new power when they struck for better wages – and won.

> One morning . . . the women in a big confectionery factory suddenly left work, came out in a body and marched down the street. From factory and workshop as they passed, the workers came out and joined them as though the Pied Piper were calling. The doors of great jam, biscuit and food preparation factories, of workshops where girls were making sweetstuff, glue or tin boxes, of tea-packing houses and perambulator works, opened and gave forth their contingents, to swell the singing, laughing procession.[10]

And through the Women's Co-operative Guild, which was founded in 1884, working women voiced their desires and were able to take part in campaigns that influenced government policy, particularly in areas such as maternity benefit and improved healthcare for mothers and children. The Guild's network of local groups linked to a national framework empowered ordinary women. One such woman, a millhand who later became a Poor Law Guardian, wrote movingly of going to Guild meetings and feeling her own potential beginning to stir: 'I had longings and aspirations and a vague idea of power within myself which had never had an opportunity of realisation. At the close of the meetings I felt as I imagine a War Horse must feel when he hears the beat of the drums.'[11]

After the wars, as one historian of working women put it, 'the new women's emancipation movement rolled on, regardless of what the mass media considered newsworthy.'[12] Although to some it looked as if the second wave women's movement came out of nowhere, the story of working women shows a seamlessness and a progression that did not need any sudden jolt into consciousness. Their long struggles for equal pay matured, and in 1968 a lead was given by a strike of women at Ford's Dagenham car factory that garnered massive publicity and sympathy. One hundred and eighty-seven women machinists demanded upgrading of their work to take account of the skill involved; the first industrial action ever undertaken on the principle that women should be given equal pay for work of equal value.[13] At around the same time, there was also a small but militant revolt of bus conductresses against the trade union policy of not allowing them to be bus drivers.[14] Out of such grass-roots beginnings grew the Equal Pay Act of 1970 and the Sex Discrimination Act of 1975, with their far-reaching effects on the culture of work.[15] This legislation was not achieved just by the pressures of middle-class women, but also by the force that working-class women brought to bear on a Labour government through strikes and union action.

Similar struggles go on in women's lives today. Women continue to exercise power in their working lives to try to put an end to discrimination. For instance, in 1995, three school dinner ladies whose pay was cut to less than that of men doing work of equal value won a victory in the House of Lords. They had been supported by Unison, the public service union, in their effort to get back pay of about £1,500 each for 1,300 dinner ladies working for North Yorkshire County Council. The Council had cut their pay, their holiday and sick pay entitlements after putting the service out to tender against private competition. The men with whose work they had previously been compared had continued to enjoy the same terms and conditions.[16]

In 1997 four female nursery nurses, earning around £11,000 per annum, took Gloucestershire County Council to industrial tribunal to argue that their work should be seen as equal to the council's waste technician or architectural technician, in other words, that they should be paid up to £7,000 more. And they won. One of them, Clare Whelan, said: 'I think in the past women have just accepted that their chosen professions aren't well paid and that's starting to change.'[17]

Now, working women no longer have to struggle to be recognised by trade unions. Indeed, now that the power of trades unions is declining, unions are courting women rather than vice versa. They are constantly seeking to reassure women that the union has their interests at heart and will try to attain equal pay, or flexible working conditions, or maternity leave schemes for them. The Transport and General Workers' Union, for instance, has run women-only recruitment campaigns; Unison has worked successfully to remove sex discrimination in the electricity supply industry and has helped many women to secure childcare facilities by putting pressure on employers to supply vouchers, workplace nurseries or out-of-school care; the GMB has reserved ten seats on its

executive council for women since 1987.[18] If women's member-
ship of unions is declining it is not because women are not
investing as much energy and spirit as ever into working life, but
because they can see that the unions are now often bogged down in
the past while women are moving forward into an ever more hope-
ful future.

Employers are also responding to women's increasing fire and
verve in the workforce. Many employers are creating equal opportunities policies which are not aimed just at graduates in managerial
training schemes. For instance, Elkes of Northern Foods has
encouraged women machine-operators to train as 'setters', that is,
to carry out machine-adjusting tasks. In order to encourage women
to move into process jobs like mixing and operating ovens, they
have made the jobs more accessible for women by converting them
to a fixed-shift regime, working from 8 a.m. to 5 p.m. or 5 p.m. to
10 p.m., rather than the previous 6 a.m. to 2 p.m. and 2 p.m. to 10
p.m., worked on alternate days.[19] And the bank First Direct
designed its offices in Leeds with a crèche for 150 children and
improved security for women working at night.[20]

Given this narrative of the power of working women to change
the culture of work, employment law, the attitudes of unions and
employers large and small, we should not be dazzled by the more
often told stories of middle-class women's successes in getting access
to higher education and the professions. The tradition of female
power is not confined to boardrooms and universities, it runs
throughout society.

So when we hear that women are feeling more powerful, do we
tend to imagine only neat ranks of middle-class women in chic
suits? We could imagine other women. A young woman unloading
boxes of wholefoods from a heavy lorry, for instance, and an elderly
woman pausing to admire her work: 'Do you drive that thing?' says
the elderly woman to the young one in boots. 'I wish I could have

done that.'[21] Or a 16-year-old girl on a grim estate in Glasgow, working for £50 a week because she'll do anything to escape from the life of claustrophobic dependence that her mother fell into.[22] Or a 16-year-old single parent, who is still intending to do her A levels and go to university: 'I know my baby isn't going to prevent me achieving my goals. In fact, he's made me even more determined . . . It annoys me that the press are so down on teenage mums . . . Having a baby has made me take responsibility for things in my life.'[23]

The newly powerful women that are becoming visible in television, cinema and literature often look very like ordinary women. British television serials, unlike their glossy American counterparts, are especially vivid in that regard. Mandy Jordache in the soap opera Brookside, played by Sandra Maitland, was best known for her horrible velour tracksuits until she displayed an unexpected ability to cope with domestic violence and her own trial for murder. In the wake of her trial, record numbers of women called Women's Aid helplines; clearly women all over Britain could identify with her desire for freedom from violence. The prostitutes in the gritty television drama *Band of Gold* get out of prostitution by setting up a cleaning business; it's not exactly the fairy-tale ending given to the prostitute in the Hollywood film *Pretty Woman*, but it may be more appealing to down-to-earth British girls.

Some British films field heroines along the same lines. Take the women in Mike Leigh's award-winning and irreducibly British film *Secrets and Lies*. These women hardly float through life; they are committed to hard graft. We see each of them not just at home, or in bed, but at work. One is found in an optician's, where she is a skilled optometrist, one on the streets, where she is a road-sweeper, and one in a cardboard-box factory: 'I'm the only one on slits,' she says proudly. Their struggles to forge authentic emotional lives are founded on their ability to realise their own independence through work.

British literature also explores the changing lives of women beyond the middle class. Take the women in Kate Atkinson's novel *Behind the Scenes at the Museum*, which won the Whitbread Prize in 1995.[24] The heroine, Ruby Lennox, comes from a line of shop-keepers, servants, milliners and factory workers, but ends up as a poet, aiming to write the tales of the women in her family. Is that, to some extent, Kate Atkinson's own story, a woman who has worked in many fields, from being a home help to being a teacher, before becoming a prizewinning writer? Or take the women in novels by Catherine Cookson, one of the most popular and un-mistakably British writers around. Certainly, Catherine Cookson's novels are more or less fairy-tales, in which wish-fulfilment follows hard on the heels of unimaginable disasters, but the heroines often come from a kind of earthy, fleshy reality. In *The Golden Straw*, the heroine is a plain working girl, a milliner with an illegitimate baby, who builds up her own business and takes pleasure in bringing on the girls who work with her.[25]

Or take more frankly realist novels like Pat Barker's *Blow Your House Down*, in which the lives of prostitutes are invested with power and sympathy. The presence of a Ripper-style murderer in the town does not create glamorous landscapes of death and desire, but rather a kickback of common sense. The prostitutes talk directly to the reader about the problems of their work, in a matter-of-fact style: 'We took car numbers. Right? I think the majority of women do take car numbers now . . . There's two reasons. One, you scare the bloke, because he knows your mate's got his number so he's less likely to try his little tricks. Two, if he does, the number means you can trace the car.'[26] Despite its harsh subject matter, this novel is not about despair, but survival.

This kind of gritty female power reminds us that the

genderquake in Britain goes far beyond banks and boardrooms. One development that binds women of all classes and backgrounds together is the new sense of the importance of paid work in their lives: this is the least expected and most far-reaching social change of the last 20 years. In 1971, 37 per cent of the labour force were women, in 1994, 44 per cent were. In 1961, just under half of all women of working age worked. In 2001 three-quarters of them will probably be at work.[27] For women like me, born in the late sixties, the difference between our mothers' generation and our daughters' generation is nowhere more marked than in this fact. If our mother worked she was unusual, if our daughter does not, she will be extraordinary. This quiet social revolution has shaken the relations between the sexes in Britain to the core throughout all levels of society.

Although working-class women have always worked, paid work has now taken on a new importance in their lives. Work is no longer just a stopgap. When asked if they would like to have a paid job even if they already had a reasonable living income without working, 76 per cent of all working women in 1989 replied that they would, and only 72 per cent of working men said they would. This positive figure for women has jumped by a remarkable 10 per cent in just 5 years; clearly women are finding more fulfilment at work than ever before.[28] Another survey among men and women in accountancy, law, banking, construction and information technology found that just 37 per cent of women say they are only working because they have to, compared with 54 per cent of men.[29] Recent research undertaken in Scotland found that women with children who work are much happier than those who don't, and that the more hours women worked the happier they are. 'In statistical terms the contrast is quite marked,' said Howard Kahn of Edinburgh University, who conducted the research.[30] Those women who did not work were found to be vulnerable to anxiety, panic attacks and constant but unexplained fear, depression, and debilitating ailments.

We cannot begin to quantify what it is that women like about work: one may like the contact with people, another, conversely, may like to escape from her family and spend the time with computers or machines; one may like exercising power and controlling other workers, another may like being released from responsibility and following others' decisions; one may like the frisson of personal creation, another may like to let her mind drift as she copytypes other people's letters; one may feel she is contributing to the wider social good, another may feel her work is all about enhancing her own status and glamour. Who knows? And yet the extraordinary thing is that so many women like working so much that three-quarters of them would do it even if there was no financial need.

This is changing the traditional relationships between men and women. More than half of all couples are made up of a man and a woman who are both earning, and the number of women earning more than their partner has trebled from one in fifteen in the early 1980s to one in five in 1995.[31] In 30 per cent of households, the woman is the main or the only breadwinner. Women are much more likely than ever before to continue working even if they have children. Nearly half of married and cohabiting women with children under five are working today compared with just a quarter 15 years ago.[32] This trend is growing: employment rates among women with children grew faster during the eighties than among women without children. Two-thirds of working women returned to work within nine months of giving birth in 1989, compared to only a quarter of women in 1979,[33] while in the early fifties, it took five years for a quarter of women to return to work after giving birth.[34] Women with young children tend to work part-time, but they are still working women as well as mothers, and still see their participation in paid work as central to their financial and emotional independence.

Given that most women will have two children or fewer, it is impossible for young women to see mothering and home-making as their only role. Given that one in three marriages may end in divorce, it is impossible for women to think they will not have to earn their own living. The decision to work is no longer a choice, it is a path that is already mapped out for women as it is for men.

This generation of working women has redrawn the map of femininity. The distinction between women who work outside the home for money, or inside the home for nothing, has collapsed; the vast majority of women work both inside and outside the home. They might see their abilities as including, say, repainting their kitchen or teaching their children to read or cooking apple pie, as well as arguing over their hours of work or applying for training. Although the media like to mock this crossover as 'superwoman', the 'having it all' chimera, what woman doesn't put energy into both worlds? A woman doesn't have to be a middle-class, educated high-flier to find that she is constantly crossing from home to work. This generation of women is the first that does not have to confine itself to either realm, home or work, that can stretch boundaries without fear of social ostracism. Although women would like to find ways to sort out the inequality they still face, they would not like to expunge this revolution at the core of femininity. No, more than 90 per cent of young women believe that married women should do paid work; and 85 per cent of women say that economic independence is very important to them.[35]

The new significance that all women, not just middle-class women, attach to their work is reflected in their growing intolerance of discrimination. They are feeling powerful at work, and will try to gain redress if anyone challenges that power. So the numbers of women lodging cases against their employers for alleged sex discrimination rises all the time; in 1995 there were 5,506 cases, a near 10 per cent rise over 1994.[36] We tend to associate such cases with high-flying women, and that's often correct. One of the most striking recent cases was brought by Christine Esplin, a personnel manager who sought compensation for equal pay, unfair dismissal and sexual discrimination when she discovered that she was being paid substantially less than a man working in a similar job in the same company. Her employer settled out of court for £120,000.[37] Helen Bamber, a 32-year-old city bond dealer, was awarded £81,000 by an industrial tribunal after she brought a successful sex discrimination case against her employer, Fuji.[38]

But we shouldn't forget that less glamorous and powerful women also look to the law to get justice in their working lives. A 13-year-old schoolgirl took a newsagent to an industrial tribunal in 1996 for refusing to contemplate employing girls to do his paper round. Natasha Ford said that Mr Parvaz had been 'old-fashioned' and 'sexist' in not allowing her to earn £7.50 a week on the paper round.[39] Or consider Kathless Porter, who serviced lavatories for a hygiene company in northern Ireland. She received £34,000 in an out-of-court settlement after being pushed into compulsory retirement at the age of 60.[40]

These stories are not just isolated spots; they show us a new world of work, in which women can invest their own struggles for equality with cultural and moral weight. They are feeling their strength and their capacity to make others do their will. Now that women tend to see their work as a vital part of their lives, their commitment to work and the pressure they put on unions and employers is far greater than ever before. More than any other change in women's lives, this shift in the numbers and influence of working women alerts us to the fact that it may, now, be possible to reach forward to real equality.

*

Whatever kind of work women are doing, they have started to talk a language of self-respect and ambition. The desire for more power and equality is not just heard from middle-class women. A group of female shopfloor workers gave these responses about why work matters to them: 'For me work gets me out, it gives me independence, the chance to meet other people,' said one; 'I'm married but you still want your independence. I want to do my own thing, you know. I don't like asking him for money,' said another. 'I really like saying I'm off to work. I live on a rough council estate and my job gives me confidence, it makes me feel like I'm somebody,' says another.[41]

Women in all kinds of work echo one another. Among the women I interviewed, I heard almost uncanny repetitions of the same experiences and desires. Rachel Finnah, a home carer in south London, says that although she has children, 'I couldn't sit at home all day, I'd go mad, all my friends feel the same way.' This investment in work has transformed the attitudes of women like her, they see their paths going onwards and upwards. Rachel is studying health management part-time as well as working, and intends to become a social worker. She believes work is as important for women as it is for men, and that women's commitment is only enhanced if they have children. 'Work is definitely as important for women as it is for men, especially for women with children. If you've got children, they're looking at you to move ahead, to give them an idea of what they can achieve.' Susan Fuller started work as a cleaner and is now a street-cleaning supervisor for her local council, managing a team of 20 workers, all men. They resent her, off and on, but she doesn't care. 'I give as good as I get. If they tell me a woman's place is in the home, I make a joke of it.'

At Suma, a workers' co-operative in Halifax, I sit in the sun outside the warehouse, talking to the women who pack goods and drive trucks alongside the men. 'I'm glad I've done this, I've proved something to myself and to the men I meet,' says Deb Matin, a

34-year-old who drives heavy goods vehicles. 'Everywhere else I've worked I've had to fight and fight to be treated equally.' Suma is a special place, where all the jobs are shared equally among men and women. It makes for an atmosphere where women are stretching themselves without the fear of any backlash. Leonie Hilliard, who has been with the company for ten years, says, 'Gender really does cease to matter here at all. You see women changing – they become a lot more aggressive when they're driving trucks – and you see men changing, they lose some of their arrogance.' Jenny Stein, a 31-year-old who has only been with the company for two months, says, 'I've always believed there's nothing really that women can't do, and here everyone accepts that. There are no doubts.'

So to track the genderquake, you can't just go to the beige, air-conditioned offices of city solicitors or hear from the smart, articulate women who work in the media. Elsewhere in Britain, the change is often even more profound, more in-your-face, more extra-ordinary. In Stoke-on-Trent, a city built on the mining industry, the pits were systematically closed down throughout the eighties and the nineties. Everyone in Britain remembers the men on the picket lines, and the battles between the miners on the ground and the police on their horses with their batons. It looked like a boys' own struggle, in which one side, the miners' side, lost unequivocally, losing their jobs, their culture, their communities in the process. But that isn't the whole story.

Brenda Procter was on the picket lines too, with her teenage daughter Melanie. She's 46 now, her daughter is 21, and we sit in her neat, colour-coordinated terrace house where a budgerigar squawks when we talk too loudly. Brenda shows me videos of the news reports of women occupying Trentham pit when it was threatened with closure in 1992; Brenda is in the occupation, emerging bleary-eyed after three days; Melanie is among the group of women outside, trying to bring food to the occupiers.

Nothing in Brenda's previous life had prepared her for that kind of confrontation. She was born and bred in Stoke. 'My dad and my granddad and my uncles were all miners. My life was built around my dad in the pits.' She got married to a miner herself at the age of 19, and when she had her two children she left her job in the potteries and stayed at home. 'I missed working. I missed the company. You get into a rut when you stay at home.' She did some homeworking, some lithographing. 'It was hard, looking after children all day and then working at night under a false light. But I wanted to do something. It was a trade, you see. A lot of women were doing homeworking, just earning a few pence an hour, rather than doing nothing at all.' But it looked as though nothing would change, nothing would make her life very different from her mother's and her grandmothers', until the strike.

'When they came out in 1984, I thought the women should be doing something, so I sent out a letter, to try and get a support group together. We ran the food centres, we made up parcels of food to keep the men going. The food centres became community centres. They were hives of activity. It changed my whole life. From being at home bringing up the children, I became politically active. I started going on marches, going to rallies, speaking in public. I realised I could do more than I ever thought possible. I dealt with the media, I got up and spoke to 500 people.'

So the strike wasn't just a miserable time, I ask, it wasn't just a defeat? 'No,' says Brenda, smiling nostalgically, 'the strike was a positive thing for me. It opened new doors. It brought me alive.' Now, Brenda is doing a master's degree at Keele University, and wants to become a lecturer. Her husband, on the other hand, whom she divorced seven years ago, seems to have taken more of a knocking. He's still in work, as a mechanic, but, 'He misses the mines.'

Brenda's daughter Melanie hasn't taken on her mother's political feistiness, but she is independent in a way her mother could never have dreamt of being at her age, even though she already has an 8-month-old baby. 'I trained as a machinist. I don't want to get married, to be tied down. I've got a choice now.' Does her boyfriend mind that they aren't married, does he wish for a more traditional set-up? I ask. 'He's happy with it. He doesn't know no different.'

From Brenda's house, I drive through endless quiet streets, lined with old but well-kempt terraced houses, to the edge of Stoke. Rose Hunter is sitting in her sunny front garden in Biddulph, a old mining village, with her best friend, Carol. Rose is 36. Again, her father and her husband were miners. Again, she got married at 19 and stayed home to look after her children. During the strike in 1984–5 she took a while to get involved. 'They said, come to this meeting on Sunday, and I thought, what the hell is Dave going to say if I say I want to go out on a Sunday?' She too is nostalgic about the days of struggle, about the way it catapulted her into life outside her home. 'The strike was the starting point for everything.' In the strike she learnt to go out on her own, to speak in public, to sing in public, to organise protests. If she thinks back to the woman she was 15 years ago, how have things changed? 'I'm more independent now, I'm more powerful. Before that I was afraid to speak up.' Her best friend Carol, who is round for the afternoon, wasn't active in the support groups herself, but, she says, 'I feel the same. You feel the difference in the community.'

'It changed everyone's lives,' Rose says definitely. 'Even those women who weren't politically active, it made them feel stronger. When you go down to the pub now, there are more women out with their friends. Relationships have changed. The men have had their cake and ate it for too long. Now they're getting a taste of their own medicine. They feel threatened, but that's their problem. Women who have got financial independence will act independent.' Her husband is dead now. 'There was some violence.' But she's come through. She knows her life is completely different from her mother's: 'There was a lot of things holding her back. I can't believe it when I talk to older women and they keep saying, "I couldn't have done that," and I think – why not? They should have just gone and done it.' And, she believes, her children's lives will be different again. They will build on the opportunities that she has grasped. 'I want them to be dead independent,' she says, looking dreamily into their futures.

It is impossible to escape from the spirit of this female power. You can go anywhere you want in Britain, right to the places where optimism should, rationally, peter out, where you might feel justified in saying, here feminism has not reached, and find it beating. Greater Easterhouse is one of the most deprived areas of Britain, a sprawling area on the outskirts of Glasgow, where ranks of concrete flats, paint peeling on the iron balconies, give way to boarded-up shopping areas, every door barred except the new sign of the unemployed resource centre. An unlikely place to go looking for the new spirit among women. You should really come here to write harsh, elegiac pieces about the loss of working-class community, about joyriders and crack, about street corners and redundancies, about lost boys and disgruntled men.

And yet it comes at you from all sides; another spirit, another kind of community that seems to be taking the place of whatever it was that got lost. Gaille McCann, who lives in Easterhouse, says, 'You won't find a greater fighting spirit anywhere.' She got married and started having children at 16. She was working as a cleaner, from six to nine in the morning and then after half past three in the afternoon, in the local school where two of her children were pupils. She got drawn into community action when the school was threatened with closure, and went on with it. 'I used to have no confidence, but then you just think, I'm going to deal with this. Now, I've seen the things that you can change.'

Gaille now runs a community health project. I meet her in its office – a small flat in one of those faceless, run-down blocks that make up Easterhouse, turned into an office with the help of a couple of pinboards and a fax machine. She is a woman who exudes confidence. Her project fosters all those ideals of self-reliance that the media would like to believe have died out in such communities. It has helped local women to set up co-operatives in nurseries that supply milk in return for the milk tokens given to families on income support; the profits are then ploughed back into providing fresh fruit for the children. It has brought local people together to supply evidence to the health authorities about what they think would improve their health; among other things, that has brought the area a GP referral system that gets people on income support, who otherwise couldn't afford it, into the local sports centre.

While I am talking to Gaille, another woman pushes open the door. Carol Giblin is also one of Easterhouse's new women. She has three children and a fourth on the way, and lives on benefit with her similarly unemployed husband. Feckless dependents waiting for a handout? Hardly. She points out the logo on her powder-blue sweatshirt: 'The Greater Easterhouse Breastfeeding Promotion Project'. Along with six other women, Carol works between five and seven days a week, for no money apart from transport expenses 'and a little bit of help towards childcare', to support women in Easterhouse who are breastfeeding. Currently, just seven per cent of women in Easterhouse breastfeed their babies, but the number is rising, as Carol and her team trundle around Easterhouse, day in, day out, making door-to-door calls followed by workshops, hospital visits, and just being there, for other women, at the other end of the telephone. 'They're amazing,' Gaille says frankly, looking at Carol. Carol laughs back, 'Well, I don't think many other people could do this.'

Even feminists often find it hard to stick up for women who are single parents in areas like Easterhouse. There are at least 2,543 single parent families in this area of 15,480 households.[42] Parts of the media have been so clever in drawing up and colouring in their idea of the quintessential single mother: young, amoral, without a thought for the future, living on benefits, feeding her children on nothing but biscuits, spending her benefit on cigarettes and videos, that it is hard to remember that single mothers are as various as other women – except that single mothers are more likely to be poor, more likely to be unemployed, more likely to be in council housing than other women.

But single mothers also bear witness to the new kind of female power. Laura McCreadie helps to run the Greater Easterhouse Lone Parent Forum. She, like the women in the five groups that the forum supports, is kicking against the myth of that quintessential single parent. We meet in the Forum's current office, a cramped room with a view on to a bleak square, but the plans for a new centre are laid out on her desk. With a grant from the National Lottery Charities Board, the Forum is moving into a building where it can offer more training – from personal presentation to computing; more childcare, and more support for single mothers who want to change their lives. Laura, a single parent herself, tells me why she thinks it works.

'This organisation is run by local women. If you have a stake in this place and a say in how it is run, it gives you a feeling of having power, of being in power somewhere – it might be the first time in your life you've felt that. Most people are fed up with officials; professional people just fob them off. They want the real thing. They want to make the best out of their lives. I have seen women change so much here; they start training, they get proper qualifications, they start talking about the future instead of living one day at a time.'

*

These little organisations run by women like Gaille McCann and Carol Giblin and Laura McCreadie make up a large network in Easterhouse, a network that sometimes seems to be the only thing that stands between people living on the edge, and people falling off the edge. In a women's centre, I meet Joyce Dobbie, a local woman, smart and sharp in her heels and lipstick, who has recovered from alcohol problems. 'If you'd seen me when I first came here you wouldn't recognise me now. I was at death's door. These women saved me.'

Women tend to be more active than men in community organisations, even if they aren't specifically women's groups. Gaille McCann has also organised a tenants' association that aims to form a housing association to take over run-down properties. 'Women are more active,' she says. 'I think women take the community's problems to heart more and they feel they have to do something about it.' Mhairi Stewart, who works for the local Women's Aid Centre, agrees that women make community action peculiarly their own. 'Political parties really aren't so important for them. They don't see the political road as very effective. But they are taking their own kind of political action through community groups. They can make a real difference on a local level.' Mhairi is sceptical about the idea that old working class communities ever had more to offer women than they do now. Her father-in-law, who is now in his sixties, used to live nearby: 'He lived in the old Glasgow tenements with a courtyard in the middle. He said as a child you could hear them, night after night, men beating the women up. It was completely accepted. It was like a joke, you'd just say, oh, there's so and so at it again.'

The new kind of communities that these women are trying to build rest on a new ideal of equality. They look towards a feminist future just as much as middle-class women or other working women do. If more successful feminists ignore their struggles, they do women everywhere a disservice. These women remind us that disadvantaged women want power and equality just as much as more advantaged women. And as this new female power goes from strength to strength, we can see a different Britain being brought into being, one in which equality and respect can thrive throughout society.

chapter 10

where do we go from here?

This is the double-sided reality of women's lives. Women are unequal: their voices are drowned out in the corridors of power; they earn on average half as much as men; they are more likely to live in poverty than men do. But individual women are also feeling powerful. They are freer than ever before, and they are using that freedom to gain a hold in the workplace, to live their lives as they want and to look with optimism into the future.

How can these two truths be reconciled? It is time for feminism to look outward again, and to forge this sporadic sense of power into a movement that will bring equality for all women. We have begun to see a new feminism arise that is free from the political correctness that once dogged the women's movement. Let's make this new feminism work. We can join hands with one another, and with men, in order to create a more equal society in Britain.

Clearly, some of the obstacles that women face can be overcome by individual effort. It is wonderful to see individual women choosing to live their lives their way, fulfilling their ambitions at work or at home without feeling stifled by a weight of traditional expectation. It is great to see individual couples creating their own environments; new kinds of partnership, new homes where men are as involved with their children as women are. But many obstacles require a push greater than the efforts of a single individual or a single family. There are some real goals ahead for the new feminism, which will only be achieved if individuals work together, not alone. The masses of young women who are now taking their places at work and dreaming of their bright futures are impatient of discrimination and eager to challenge anyone who stands in their way. They are keen to see a more equal society; but if they are to create it, they need help from government, from men, from older women, from the media, from the law, from all of us.

What are these goals? For a start, if we are to see real equality we will have to revolutionise the organisation of work. This is by far the most ambitious transformation that the new feminism has in its sights, the creation of a new balance between work and home.

Second, women need a new national network of childcare. Even if we create a better balance between work and home, parents still need better, safer and less expensive provision of daycare. Although some women manage within the current services, new patterns of work require different systems of care and education. New after-school clubs and comprehensive provision of childcare for all children under five whose parents want it would allow women to make real choices about whether to work or whether to stay at home.

Third, we need to see men taking on the same responsibilities as women at home. Their efforts in that direction must be helped by flexible working practices and the encouragement of young men to go into traditional feminine working environments.

Fourth, women must be supported in their own and their

families' journeys away from poverty. Individual women are currently dragged down and pushed into disadvantage by an outdated working culture, an unresponsive benefits system, the absence of childcare and the lack of support given to their own efforts to improve their neighbourhoods and their own lives.

Fifth, we need legislative and welfare support for women facing sexual and domestic violence. Every woman who experiences violence must feel that she has access to justice, and every woman should be able to move into a safe environment if she is facing abuse at home.

All these changes are achievable if women and men work together. If you look back at the past 100 years of feminist achievement, and the changes that have been seen in women's status and education and work, as well as the revolution in cultural and social behaviour, this new feminist agenda does not look utopian, it looks natural and achievable.

one: the new feminism gets to work

First, let's concentrate on the organisation of work, the most far-reaching revolution that the new feminism is aiming for. Work, it is true, is a dull and unromantic sphere, more usually the subject of government statistics and Equal Opportunities Commission reports than the site of urgent idealism. And yet we cannot go on averting our eyes from work, since this is where the ground of women's inequality is laid, and where it is played out. All our great ideals stumble over the barrier of women's inequality at work.

If you doubt this assertion, pause for a minute. You may say, for instance, with Catharine MacKinnon and Andrea Dworkin, that what keeps women down is their fear of men's violence. Yet women have moved mountains in raising people's awareness of sexual and domestic violence. If they are still at a disadvantage in getting justice for women who are raped or finding protection for women at risk in their homes that is not because their arguments are not stirring and compelling. Rather, it is because there are not enough women in the police forces and in lawcourts to give full weight to the woman's word; not enough women in Parliament and the civil service to draft legislation that makes sense for women. Only when women are as well represented as men in the police force and lawcourts will women who are raped find justice. Only when women are equal players in Parliament and Whitehall will legislation treat women and men equally. Only when women and men have equal financial independence will women be able to escape from abusive relationships when they want to; and if they decide to stay we will know that it is their own choice. Until that bedrock of material inequality is swept away, women will not be free.

The inequality inherent in working life proceeds from the fact that work is still structured on the premise that a worker's domestic life will be taken care of by somebody else. The gap between home and working life opened up hundreds of years ago, and has yawned ever wider. From the start of the industrial revolution, when factories and businesses were set up that demanded all of a worker's time and attention, men and women have been forced into an unequal double-act. In order to keep a family going in such a working environment, the man would work long hours away from the home for a decent wage and the woman would work long hours in the home for nothing. In this traditional separation of the masculine and feminine sphere, the division between two working styles was defined by many characteristics. But above all the split between masculine and feminine work was seen in one characteristic: men's work was linear and women's work was cyclical.

The traditional image of masculine work was that it lay either in manufacturing or managerial occupations. It was full-time, leaving few hours for the man to take on a role as a parent or anything else – a gardener, a reader, a cook or a socialite. He had a strong community at work to which he would give allegiance: the company itself; or the community of workers, the union. The work took place in a clear workplace: a factory or an office, and home was left behind during working hours. But most importantly of all, a masculine job was a job for life, in which a man trained in a firm to which he would then give life-long loyalty. So he had a linear working pattern, with incremental promotions leading to seniority in old age. He would be expected to move up a clearly defined hierarchy: to begin in a junior, badly paid role designed for a young man and to finish up in a senior, well-paid job where he would be surrounded by other elderly men.

This kind of work could be well rewarded, but it was inflexible. Because of a woman's traditional commitment to domestic life, she could rarely work to this pattern. And so her work was rather different. Typically, the woman would move into and out of work, with intervening time to devote to the domestic sphere. So she had a cyclical working pattern, and would constantly return to the same level, or even lower, when she re-entered working life. Hierarchies therefore put her at a disadvantage. Because of her broken working pattern, she had much less allegiance to the company or the union. Her work was generally seen as an extension of her natural, domestic role, rather than an autonomous role in itself. So she often worked in service areas – nannying, waitressing, serving in shops, and so on. She often worked at home – either in other people's homes, or in her own home, taking in washing, doing piecework, minding children – or she might work short hours or odd hours. All these characteristics made her work more flexible, but also less well rewarded and less powerful. The cyclical nature of her working life particularly put her at a disadvantage. She would gain skills, loyalty and experience, but then take a break and be thrown back on her original, low-status work.

This distinction between the linear and cyclical career still persists. Men are still encouraged to pursue full-time work, in which they become alienated from home life and give their allegiance to another organisation or ideal. Women are still encouraged to envisage their work as a broken pattern that shatters around their domestic life, especially if they have children.

As I mentioned in chapters 1 and 2, Mrs Typical loses over a half of the income that she would have earned throughout her life if she has children, while having children typically makes no difference to the lifetime income that a man will earn.[1] This imbalance shows how far men's and women's lives are still moulded by the conventional split between the linear and the cyclical career. All kinds of women are affected, in all kinds of work, by the sudden and often unforeseen clash that occurs when their domestic life fights for space with their working life. Single parents suffer most obviously from the split between work and home. Because the mechanisms – the childcare, the benefits system, the working practices – that might help women to combine working life and family life still hardly exist, Britain has fallen into a situation where 600,000 lone parents stay at home, dependent on state benefits,[2] even though most of them say they would like to work if childcare were available. This is an extraordinary situation, that condemns millions of children to grinding poverty, and that forces adult women into dependence. Because they often lose their connection with the training and working world entirely, this dependence can continue long after their children grow up.

But the split between home and work affects all women, not just mothers. A woman does not have to have children herself to find difficulties arise from this traditional split. Even a childless woman will find her male colleagues may make assumptions about her commitment to work based on the belief that she *will* have children. Even a childless woman may find that she dislikes the growing isolation she faces at work as more and more women drop out to have children and then return in junior, part-time roles. Even a childless woman will find that the lack of women in public life militates against her values being taken seriously by legislators and executives. Even a childless woman may find that she comes up against men's hostility at work, a hostility based on the fact that they are still used to seeing women in unpaid and servicing roles rather than powerful positions.

If we do not revolutionise the organisation of work women will never be able to challenge men's ability to pull away from them as they get older, and as they take on the rewards and success that are still associated with masculinity rather than femininity. This systematic inequality is embedded in the very structure of working life, and attacking its root cause, rather than the symptoms, must be the priority for feminism today.

In the past, feminists have usually taken one of two attitudes toward attacking the inequality embedded in the organisation of work. Sometimes they argued that women should be left to pursue their powerless, cyclical careers, but should be given special treatment from employers and the state to compensate them for the worst effects of inequality. At other times they argued that women should be encouraged to remake themselves in line with the traditional masculine working pattern, and learn to fit in with the full-time, whole-life route to power. Both attitudes have a long lineage, but neither is sufficient any more. Women don't want to beg special treatment or to have to fit into the old straitjackets of working life. They want to forge a new way of working that will be more in tune with their priorities and their desires.

If you look more closely at those two earlier positions: that women should beg special treatment from employers or that they should remake themselves in the masculine pattern, you quickly see the disadvantages of either stance. Among those feminists who have embraced the first position, that women should be left to the domestic sphere, was the campaigner and politician Eleanor Rathbone, who enunciated a feminism that was based less on equal rights than special needs. She argued at the beginning of this century that 'feminists should work for reforms which reflected the reality of women's interests, rather than those which aimed to make them equal to men on men's terms.'[3] Particularly, she wanted to see women being paid for their domestic labour, so that she saw women remaining in the cyclical career, but wanted special efforts to be made by the state to redress their financial disadvantages. Similarly, feminists in the seventies agitated for women to be compensated by the state for their contributions to domestic labour and childcare. Women in the Wages for Housework campaign argued that this would put an end to women's dependence: 'We demand that employers and their governments pay us for the work we do free. We want money of our own.'[4]

Women have undeniably benefited from the ways that employers and social services have responded to their special needs. They have benefited from child benefit, maternity leave, from schemes for flexible working, from state support for women with children. We should never underestimate how these changes have revolutionised women's lives. But this kind of special treatment can only go so far in making women equal players at work. Some women in Britain have expressed fear about the other effects it may have on women's employment. Two-thirds of the 200 female members of the Institute of Directors said that they thought that job prospects for women were being damaged by extended rights of maternity leave and high compensation awards for those sacked for being pregnant. Dr Ann Robinson, head of the Institute's policy unit, said that the findings showed how female directors were worried about women becoming 'different and more expensive' to employ. Similarly, one in three heads of small businesses has said that they would avoid hiring, promoting or training a woman of childbearing age in case she left to have a baby. They preferred older women who had had their families, since they resented footing the bill for maternity pay and found it difficult to adjust to the demands of working mothers.[5]

In Nordic countries, where far more has been done to try to help women into equality at work, it has been seen that concentrating flexible work policies on women has led to an entrenchment of different behaviour by men and women. The split between the linear and the cyclical career has not disappeared. Men and women still work in very different ways, with women slipping out of employment for long periods when they have children, with consequent ill effects on their subsequent employment, and men staying solidly in the workplace, consolidating their power. Clearly, if all help for domestic labour is targeted on women, the split between the linear and the cyclical career remains in place, and women still find that they are expected to cede power in the wider world to men. We have to ask whether targeting more and more special help on women may not have the effect of exaggerating traditional roles for men and women, and preventing a real revolution taking place in working patterns.

Other feminists have argued that women must remake themselves in line with the masculine tradition, and take on the linear career, working full-time and for their whole lives, maybe in traditional masculine occupations. So when Eleanor Rathbone put forward the arguments for family allowances before the First World War, she found ranged against her many feminists who wanted women to commit themselves to work, not to the home.

Ada Nield Chew was one of those who strongly disapproved . . . If 'babies were cared for during the hours the mothers were at work by trained mothers in special baby homes . . . the Lancashire married women would lead the van in the intelligent progress of their sex and class.' Child allowances should be combated by all enlightened women . . . The children must be cared for . . . But not by paying poor women to be mothers. Women must be financially independent of men. But not by paying poor women to be wives.[6]

The opinion of Ada Nield Chew, this early twentieth-century feminist, was clearly that equality could only come through women's devotion to work. Unless they were the 'trained mothers' working in 'special baby homes', women should deny their maternal instincts.

The demand of the Women's Liberation Movement in the seventies for '24-hour nurseries' showed the desire for something similar. Indeed, throughout the literature of the second wave women's movement the alternative to sexual inequality is often seen to be rigid communal organisation of domestic tasks. Shulamith Firestone, the radical feminist, argued that women should give up bearing children altogether. She agitated for 'the more distant solutions based on the potentials of modern embryology, that is, artificial reproduction',[7] and idealised a society where the family would disappear and childrearing be carried out collectively. Contemporary feminists may not go so far, but they still often assume that the career woman is the only real feminist. For many women, especially ambitious and qualified women, the move into a linear, full-time, whole-life career spells freedom. But this ideal does not strike a chord with all women.

Indeed, neither of these two positions: that women should beg special treatment from employers to compensate them for their weaker positions; or that women should simply mould themselves into the traditional pattern of the linear career, can provide us with the answer we are seeking today. We have to go beyond them, and try to mark out a third way, that would build on recent social changes to create a revolution in the organisation of work.

This new way of working would release men and women from the impossible choice between well-rewarded and dehumanising linear work and insecure, flexible cyclical work. Currently, for too many people, work resembles a badly designed building, whose entrances and exits are difficult to find, with an artificial climate and a clamour of white noise. The ideal is to build a more beautiful, vernacular building, to open the windows, to catch the light from outside and the sound of children playing, to let people come and go more freely.

This is the generation that has learnt that you can have it all, but you can't have it all at the same time. Few people can simultaneously answer the demands of their ambitions and of their families or their private lives. But everyone can, if they want, answer them at different times. If we break down the idea that there are only two working patterns – the linear, secure, inflexible, grey, exhausting, 45-year career, and the cyclical, colourful, insecure working life – and believe that there is another possibility, the patchwork career, we are halfway there. The patchwork career has certain periods of hard graft and dedication, but it also contains time out, time when there are hours to watch a child play or watch the light through the trees. It allows a woman to reach for power, but it also allows a man time to become a beloved person within his family, and to help to create a fine living environment for those he loves.

That means that the balance between forward movement and stillness, between achievement and consolidation, that most people feel is essential for a full life, would not be achieved by the simultaneous contrast between women in the home and men at work, but by each individual balancing work and home over the years, falling for their ambition or their family in turn. So a new balance between work and home, and a new balance between masculine and feminine would be created.

After all, women's distance from masculine working culture has not only put them at a disadvantage. It has also given them a great advantage. Because women's lives were not swallowed up by the tick of the working day and the inexorable, linear movement of the working career, they have traditionally had a different relationship to time. They have been able to exploit their cyclical working patterns to become more aware of the cyclical wheel of birth and death, and the seasons and the stillness of domestic life.

The difference between the linear and the cyclical way of living has often given women a rich and buoyant way of life that has provided a vital contrast with the arid march of men's traditional culture. Men – and some women – have often celebrated the charm of the angel in the house in ways that women understandably find restrictive and undermining. But we should be wary of turning our backs on the domestic sphere entirely. If we revalue the domestic sphere, alongside working life, we can transform the organisation of work.

In Virginia Woolf's novel *To the Lighthouse*, this difference between linear and cyclical life is the difference between Mr Ramsay and Mrs Ramsay. Mr Ramsay, a philosopher, is obsessed by how far along the ladder of success and knowledge he has gone. Mrs Ramsay, on the other hand, displays a constant ability to create anew. 'The whole effort of merging and flowing and creating rested with her,' the narrator muses during a family meal. She creates a balance between knowledge and love, theory and sensuality, work and home. Mr Ramsay goes to her 'to be taken within the circle of life, warmed and soothed, to have his senses restored to him, his barrenness made fertile, and all the rooms of the house made full of life.'[8] Mrs Ramsay's life, although bounded by the domestic sphere, is still, with its emotional depth and her closeness to her children, infinitely richer than Mr Ramsay's.

Or take the experience of Anna Wulf in Doris Lessing's *The Golden Notebook*. In one day, described in precise, minute detail, Anna's lover Michael begins by rushing off to the hospital where he works. She, however, has time to watch her child, who 'has the lazy bumbling movements of a bee in the sun', and to buy food for the evening – 'It is a great pleasure, buying food I will cook for Michael, a sensuous pleasure'[9] – in a quieter, more ruminative frame of mind, before going to her work. The slow stacking up of detail which Lessing uses to describe Anna's mind seems to make time stand still. As her lover and other men whirl by her, she is deeply involved with every sensual impression of her day.

In these examples, we see how women's writing often connects us to the unique poignancy of domestic life. That poignancy is often rather inarticulate, made up of sensations and images rather than words, and women artists remind us of those inarticulate strengths. The works of the impressionist painter, Berthe Morisot, differ from the work of her male contemporaries in their concentration on domestic life, on women hanging out the washing, women sewing or minding children in gardens and rooms, women laying the table for lunch. She doesn't just look in at this world, she and her own family appear in it; Berthe Morisot dressing with her daughter and Eugène Manet with his daughter are scenes from her own domestic life that she reframes in her art. But she turns her enclosed and well-known world into a source of artistic experiment.

Similarly, Judy Chicago's famous artwork, *The Dinner Party*, is an experimental work that reaches deep into the traditions of women's domestic life. First shown in 1979, it consists of a vast triangular table with 39 place settings, each with a carefully worked plate, chalice and embroidered runner, each commemorating a woman from history or myth. The choice of the dinner party for this meeting of powerful women is resonant; it shows that Chicago saw the domestic sphere as the right place for celebrating women's power.

Women have often celebrated their closeness to the family, to the home, to food and to small sensual pleasures in these ways. They have even infused their link to the domestic world with moral importance, and seen the home as a place where selfless, sharing, gentle values can be practised and enunciated. As well as the strong attachment to domestic life voiced by artists and ordinary women, female writers and analysts from Penelope Leach to Alice Miller have encouraged us to believe that love and joy in a child's early years are the most precious gifts any human being can give another.

Feminists now should not think they have to jettison all the artistic, sensual, emotional and ethical richness that women themselves have long associated with the domestic sphere. Much feminist writing has been devoted to breaking the hold that the domestic realm has exercised on women, and that was the right channel for feminism in previous years, when women were still reluctant to break out of the home for fear of poverty and ridicule.

But in this generation, feminism can afford a rather different emphasis. The problem of this generation is not so much that women must be encouraged to break free of domestic life, but that men must be encouraged to come towards it, and unless we can remember and celebrate what is poignant and exciting about domestic life, we will lose some of our most precious culture without having anything to put in its place. And then who will care for our sick and elderly people, who will take care to give children a sense of security and belonging, and who will prepare the meals where families can make a space of their own after battling with their work?

After all, if two people try to make a home together while they are both pursuing a full-time, whole-life, linear career, they will often begin to feel that something is missing. This is true for men as much as for women. In New York City, the proportion of men reporting significant conflict between work and family increased from 12 per cent to 71 per cent between 1977 and 1989; that is, from a small minority to a large majority.[10] Rather than requiring men and women to turn their backs on the home in order to reshape themselves as the perfect worker, feminists should remind us of the joy that domestic life can bring to men as well as women.

This is certainly the time to prepare for a better balance between work and home. Partly, this is the right time because women are becoming more powerful, have more allegiance to work, and are more impatient of anyone who stands in their way. But this is also a unique time because of the way that men's and women's values are moving so much closer together. As I explored in chapter seven, the earlier hostility towards men evinced by feminists, and vice versa, is breaking down. Men are beginning to realise that they, too, can gain from the equality movement. Men too want to change the balance between work and home; they too want to construct a new pattern of work. Thirty-six per cent of working men under 35, compared to 33 per cent of women, would like to take a year's leave from their work. And 18 per cent of men compared to 21 per cent of women would like to work at home.[11] These men are eager for change, eager to find a new balance in their lives.

Interestingly, it is therefore from men that we find some of the most impassioned arguments for finding a new way of working. Men have always had their own tradition of dissent from the model of the perfect worker. Throughout nineteenth- and twentieth-century literature and philosophy we read the words of men railing desperately against the model of the perfect worker. From Charles Dickens to H. G. Wells, from George Orwell to John Grisham, men have written out their loathing of the organisations that forced them to be workers rather than people. Amitai Etzioni, the American writer who has influenced both American and British politicans with his vision of 'communitarianism', exemplifies this trend. He is keen to see society embrace a way of life in which the community and the family are given as high a priority as the career and self-advancement. In his vision of that, he does not see women being driven back into the home and a return to traditional family life. He looks for ways forward in the possibility of reorganising the structure of work and the greater involvement of men in their families. These are, as far as I'm concerned, feminist goals. He likes the idea of more flexitime, more job shares, more shiftwork, all to 'increase the all-important parental presence' at home.[12]

Similarly, the management guru Charles Handy, who has influenced the way that many British and American organisations are structured, looks to a future in which men as well as women will lead a more flexible working life, with a better balance between work and home. 'No longer will the office or the plant be the home from home of most men . . . No longer will a career mean climbing the ladder of jobs in an organisation . . . No longer can one expect to sell 100,000 hours of one's life to an organisation,' he insists.[13] Instead of the linear career of the past, he imagines a life in which we strike a balance between paid work; gift work – or voluntary work; home work – parenting or caring for older relations; and study work – or further education.[14] This is an attractive vision for men who are recognising that they cannot work all hours and still be a complete person, and for women who would now like to extend their power without giving up the advantages of a cyclical working life.

So this new feminist programme can count on the support of men as well as women. And it can also count on the support of more impersonal economic forces. Economic changes are already pushing forward new ways of working, and beginning to heal the old split between feminine and masculine, cyclical and linear work. Feminists can take heart from these widescale economic changes and force them to bring forward a new equality.

What do these economic changes entail? Above all, the

emphasis in working life has shifted away from the full-time career in manufacturing or management. Workers in Britain are now much less likely than before to be engaged in managing other people or manufacturing goods. Instead, they provide services to other people – in shops, employment agencies, hospitals, public relations, hairdressing, counselling, restaurants – or they are what Robert Reich calls 'symbolic analysts' – they are lawyers, financial analysts, academics, journalists, information technologists, management consultants.[15] Since 1950, 5 million jobs in manufacturing have disappeared in Britain and 8 million have been created in services.[16] In these new worlds of work, the old distinctions between male and female work slip away. Work now requires skills that women are easily acquiring, or have always had.

This breakdown of those old distinctions between manufacturing and service work means that it is more and more common for men and women to work side by side, not in separate environments. Although segregation is still very prevalent, it is decreasing. The younger a woman is, the less likely she is to work in an exclusively female environment; the proportion of women in occupations where there are roughly equal numbers of men and women is only 21.5 per cent among women over 55, but 34.7 per cent among women under 25.[17]

The distinction between male and female patterns of work is breaking down in other ways too. There has been a vast surge in part-time work. In 1951, 831,000 people, or 3.75 per cent of all working people, worked part-time. Now more than 6 million people, or 22 per cent of all workers do. Most of these part-time workers are women, but one in five are men, and they can be involved in any kind of work. Seven out of ten major companies employ part-time managers, and 80 per cent of employers believe that part-time working for managers will become increasingly popular.[18] Many people would like to work part-time for at least some of their lives, perhaps when they have young children or an elderly relation to care for, or after retirement, or when they are pursuing other projects or voluntary work – or simply because they want a break.

Men and women are taking more conscious control over the way they will work and what they will do. More people than ever before work for themselves rather than for an employer; self-employment has more than doubled in the last 15 years. Many people are recognising that they cannot rely on their bosses to look after them, to control their places and patterns of work, their education and movements. Instead, such people believe that it is vital to drive one's own ambitions. Perhaps women take easily to this self-reliant ideal because they have never been able to build up the same loyalty to organisations that men have; they are more accustomed to moving in and out of organisations, building up their own networks, and making a career out of a disconnected working life.

Indeed, the job for life, with a slow, reliable pattern of promotion has become a thing of the past. Job tenure is becoming shorter; even among men, only 54 per cent have held the same job for five years or more, down from 62 per cent in 1984.[19] In every area of work, it is becoming more and more acceptable for people to change occupations and employers many times during their working lives. And this new way of working is having the effect of making men's and women's working patterns draw closer and closer together.

The end to the old dichotomy between the linear career and the cyclical one is also being signalled by a change in the culture of the organisation, where relatively unhierarchical forms of organisation are now ubiquitous. The old organisations, with their huge, centrally directed workforces, are obsolete. This breakdown of hierarchy is seen in the informal office culture. Managers are called by their first names and secretaries retitled administrators; office buildings are designed, as in the new headquarters of First Direct in Leeds, without executive suites or boardrooms. It is also seen in the formal management structure. As Charles Handy has said, 'Work, itself, is no longer organised as it used to be. Organisations are not now drawn as pyramids of boxes. British Steel is said once to have an organisation chart which, when unfolded, stretched across a room. Those charts now have circles and amoeba-like blobs where the boxes used to be.'[20] In such organisations, the centre may set standards and provide goals but it cannot direct workers or control their working environments.

This breakdown of hierarchy leads to a different way of imagining the relationship between the employer and employee. What was once seen as a monolithic stand-off now relies on a more consultative, consensual approach, and women, because they have invested less in the old forms of hierarchy, are assumed to be better at responding to these patterns of communication. Sylvie Pierce, chief executive of the London Borough of Tower Hamlets, told me, 'This is a style of management that is available to men and women. It's not just about being an autocratic boss, but about being someone who leads and engages with the people that work with one.' Rebecca Thomas, a director at Framlington Investment Management, said that when she joined the company ten years ago there were no female directors, and now five out of 12 directors are women: 'The culture of the place has changed totally in that time. Once, the nitty-gritty was discussed in the men's loos, now everything is open, everyone is involved. We all go out together socially, from secretaries to directors, and everyone is on a level.'

Now that hierarchies are breaking down, it is impossible to fit workers into a ladder of promotion that will only be finished when they are reaching retirement. The idea of career progression has become very blurred. James Reed, a director of Reed Employment, has written that 'many companies are trying to remove the emphasis on promotion as the only way forward. Instead, they encourage people to move horizontally within the company so that they gain a broader base of experience.'[21] Given that the rigid hierarchies of old, which took a lifetime to climb, no longer exist, the imperative for a powerful, successful worker to keep a cumulative working pattern no longer exists.

These developments can now be moved on and strengthened by new employment practices. Currently, many of these economic changes are causing misery and disruption; flexibility is often seen to work in the interests of the employer rather than the worker. But if we are honest, we know there will be no return to the jobs for life, the hierarchies and the predictability of the past. These developments must be harnessed in the cause of equality. There is now almost no job that cannot be done on a job-share or part-time basis. The organisation of the work may differ; for some jobs, say in daily newspapers, part-timers might need to work three long days rather than five or six half-days; in others, particularly repetitive jobs, half-days might be far more productive. It takes bravery on the part of people in work to learn that they can job share or work part-time without losing control or status. It takes imagination on the part of their employers, to understand that people who are not in their offices or shops or factories all day, every day, are still committed and energetic workers. It takes effort from all of us, to support people working in new ways.

The acceptance of career breaks might be the most important single change that could release men and women into a more equal working world. In Sweden, this has already happened, and a comparison with 'Mrs Typical' there and here is telling. When the Swedish Mrs Typical has children, she loses just one-sixth of her lifetime earnings. This is partly because of the subsidised childcare provision that exists in Sweden. But it is also because of the existence of paid parental leave both for the time of birth, and also for taking care of sick children. Fathers can take advantage of these as well as mothers. And parents have a right to cut their hours of work to 80 per cent in the original job while their children are under eight.[22] If these factors were also true of Britain, we would not see the same disenfranchisement of women from equal status at work and an independent income.

These breaks might be seen as primarily parental leave, but they may just as well be imagined as breaks for learning and living. Many countries have already moved to make career breaks a natural part of the rhythms of working life; in France and Belgium, workers have a legal right to 6 to 12 months off. These career breaks might naturally be for education as much as parenting; in Singapore, a Central Provident Fund requires compulsory contributions from employers and employees into a personal fund that can be drawn down for education as well as retirement.[23]

Such a cyclical, broken work pattern would respect people's desire to balance work and home across each individual life. Our new ideal of employed work might be, then, that when parents have children, generally in their twenties and thirties, they would take long breaks into part-time work, or out of paid work altogether. For up to five years after the birth of each child, employees would be legally entitled to expect employers to do their utmost to accommodate such breaks and flexible working packages. If the parents on leave were paid a statutory allowance by the state rather than the employer, that would keep the costs to the employer down, and the consequent churning of jobs would not result in more people in total drawing down benefits than at present.

After these few years of home-centred life parents would build up their working hours again, and they would work altogether a longer working life than is now the case, not retiring fully until they are 70, to make up for earlier lost earnings. Such a system might require a different kind of social insurance, in which people borrow earlier and make up their debts later, rather than storing everything up for old age. This pattern would make for a cultural shift that assumed a career path would level out for a few years in the earlier half of the working life; and such a cultural shift would also allow childless people to take breaks, for learning or living, if they wanted. More importantly, this pattern would allow parents to care for their children if they wished to do so. This would be a departure from a working pattern that requires parents either to leave their children in daycare or with nannies even if they would prefer to spend time with them themselves, or to fall into poverty and marginalisation if they break their working lives. The testimony of men and women who look to their parenting future in fear, or who speak of being torn and drained, relationships being harmed and emotions stunted, when their working and domestic lives clash, demands such a change.

Now, it would be old-fashioned for women to tailor themselves to a rigid ideal of a worker that is falling out of date – and that was never much loved, even by men. Rather than confronting the inhumanity that lies at the core of the workerist ideal, feminists have often closed their eyes to it as they argue for an equal place in those strange organisations. That attitude is understandable, but outdated. Women now can try to consolidate their growing power without falling flat on their faces in an effort to run ever faster up the escalator of work. This is the most pressing feminist realisation of our times. We want equality, but not equality on the understanding that we must jettison everything, always, from the old feminine way of life. As I argued earlier, in many areas of work – health care, news reporting, teaching – we can see that even a minority of women can have an immense difference on the culture around them. They do not just disappear into existing traditions. And that shows us that women now have the potential not to assume that they must fall into step with old masculine models of behaviour. Instead, we can forge a new ideal of work, a fresh and more human ideal. It will combine the advantages of both male and female work; women know that flexible working and a closeness to domestic and civic life has brought them advantages; men know that linear work and the power and influence it brings gives them advantages.

There is a crying need to make working more flexible. If the wall that has been set up between work and the home could be knocked down, we could move into a more equal society. And we would all have a better time. One social researcher described the first generation of factory workers in this way: 'Unlike today's workers, men were not task-oriented. To their employers' annoyance, they wandered about, chatted to workmates, stretched out their midday breaks to two hours, took Mondays off when the spirit moved them, and saw it as their right to attend a wide array of holiday festivals.'[24] Workers now need to be able to reclaim some of that human spirit.

Many people, who are locked out of work altogether, or who are locked into work that demands excessive hours and energy, feel that we have never been further from achieving a real balance between work and home. But a revolution at work is already beginning, and it could soon move much closer, much more quickly. Partly, it can be and is being brought closer simply by individual decisions, by individuals making their needs known to employers and one another. We need to see a more concerted effort for change. We need legislation to give workers the right to periods of parental leave and flexible working packages. We need to see a cultural shift on the part of employers and workers so that they accept that part-time and job-share workers can be as committed to the organisation as full-time workers. And we need to see ordinary women and men raising their voices and demanding the revolution in working life that they desire.

two: a new strategy for childcare

A real balance between work and home is the single most important change that the new feminism wants to see. But there are
other changes on the horizon. Next up comes a new strategy of
childcare. Again, this is not something that individuals can achieve
by themselves. Currently, the high price that having children
exacts from British women is hugely exacerbated by the absence of
a good network of childcare in this country. In France, where pre-
school and after-school daycare is subsidised and public support is
given to childminders, when Mrs Typical has children she loses
only 8 per cent of her lifetime's income.[25]

No woman should feel that she has to leave her children in daycare if she doesn't want to, and that is why we want a better balance
between work and home; but every woman with children should
feel that she can choose to do paid work if she wants to. The realisation of the need for a better childcare strategy – both for parents,
and for children – is gradually seeping into the rhetoric of central
government. In 1995 Tony Blair promised parents 'quality childcare
and universal nursery provision', and in 1997 he emphasised that
single mothers should be entitled to good quality, low-cost childcare. Women MPs with children, especially Labour MPs such as
Tessa Jowell, Harriet Harman and Margaret Howell, have been
active in popularising and extending such debates, and the entry of
more women into Parliament has pushed it on even further. When
I spoke to the new women MPs who entered Parliament in 1997,
the one issue that they returned to over and over again when they
were discussing how they could help women to achieve equality
was the need to put in place a national childcare strategy. Ruth
Kelly, an economist who was 28 years old and eight months pregnant when she entered Parliament, said, 'Childcare is part of the
political agenda now. It's important for all women, including single

parents and poor parents. It's not exclusively a women's issue, but it's very dear to my heart.'

But these ideals are not, currently, being matched by results; women in Britain still have to struggle with a ridiculously low and patchy level of childcare provision. Everywhere I went in my research for this book, from lunch with the editors of a glossy magazine to tea with community activists in Scotland, I kept hearing the same refrain: 'We need childcare.' Recently, a regional policy commissioner from the European Community said that when she toured the UK she had found herself in the 'surprising situation' of being presented with bids for European finance for basic childcare to enable mothers either to take a job or enter training schemes. She said, 'Facilities are desperately needed. Is the organisation of childcare services a European or a national task in a rich country like the UK?'[26] A surprising number of grants from the National Lottery Charities Board are made to childcare organisations – after-school clubs and playgroups. But women in Britain must force the government to recognise that desperate need for better childcare is not something it can just shuffle off to European grants, individual charities and lottery funds.

We need a national strategy that will make pre-school, after-school and holiday childcare free at the point of use. Politicans must support parents' needs, since the development of a good system of childcare is not something that can be achieved by individual women and men. There has been a gradual movement away from public provision of any kind of welfare services; but this rigid ideological position is putting equality out of the reach of too many women. Individual women cannot be expected to bear the costs of childcare all by themselves; it is this expectation that drives so many women into poverty and dependence and forces women out of work for many years or for their whole lives. All of society should share the costs, through the state-funded provision of a full system of childcare for all children whose parents want it.

Together with the new organisation of work, this would mean that women and men could make real choices about whether they wanted to work or to look after their children themselves. This is a choice that we would all like to be able to make, and it would make the most far-reaching change in the lives of single mothers. They need support with the costs of childcare if they are to enter training and paid work, a movement that would raise their living standards and those of their children. The current British situation, in which one in three children is born into poverty, must be remedied as quickly as possible. Solving this problem would help women primarily, but through women it would help a whole generation of disadvantaged children to step out of poverty and expand their narrow horizons. The pressing need for a new childcare strategy must not be underestimated.

three: men in the home

The new feminism wants men to have unequivocal faith in their central role at home and in bringing up children. This is partly down to individuals, down to men themselves having the courage to take a full part in domestic life, and many individual men are now eager to make that journey. But wider organisational change is essential even here.

Flexible working and parental leave must be available for men as well as women. The current system, which confines them almost wholly to women, cuts women off from equality at work just as it cuts men off from equality at home. Take a case like that of Susan Edwards and the London Underground. She sued the Underground on the basis of sex discrimination for not arranging flexible working times for her.[27] Such an argument – that flexible working is due to women because they are women – effectively cuts men out of possible legal redress if they find themselves in the same position. Instead, such flexibility should be available for both parents of children under school age. Paternity leave should be a universal, non-transferable right for all men who become parents. We need to see a revolution in expectations, where employers will assume that men as well as women will have to make arrangements to fit work around childcare and vice versa, and where men will assume that having children will impinge heavily on their lives.

We also want to see a change in the culture of the caring and education professions. The movement of men into domestic life deserves the kind of public recognition that the movement of women into work has achieved. For instance, while initiatives have existed for decades to encourage women to think of moving into science and engineering, or information technology, or public life, why are there no initiatives to encourage young men, whose traditional employment opportunities are shrinking, to think of moving into, say, primary school education, childcare, cleaning and nursing? After all, even if children are growing up in families where their parents have successfully renegotiated their roles to share out caring and paid work more equally, they will still go to schools and hospitals and nurseries where the face of caring will almost always be female. And this will constantly discourage young boys from feeling that masculinity and caring are complementary.

We also need to see a conscious shift in the attitudes of the legal and social work profession to encourage men to become and stay more involved with their children. This is especially the case for men who are separated from their partners. Currently, too many men are not encouraged not to become active fathers, and the ongoing breakdown of traditional family life is harming women's growing power. One and a half million women bring up their children effectively alone, and nearly half of them find themselves cut off from the responsibilities and rewards of paid work because of that. To re-create a more equitable balance between work and home, strenuous efforts must be made to bring separated men, where appropriate, to care for their children. This does not, by any means, stop at financial care. The Child Support Agency, by focusing attention on the financial relationship between a father and his children, may even have made the problem worse. It is only the day-to-day involvement of fathers with their children that will allow women back into work and create greater equality between men and women.

Conservative forces have recently taken over the debate about the importance of family life. But this is a ridiculous scenario; feminists have traditionally been, and should always be, in the vanguard of asserting the importance of family life, the rights of children and women to live happy lives at home. To this end men should be welcomed into the home, to share fully in the responsibilities and delights of home life.

four: opening the poverty trap

The new feminism is an inclusive, not an exclusive movement. Women in disadvantaged areas, women living on benefits or low wages and women bringing up their children in poverty know how heavily inequality presses upon them and how desperate their need is for a fairer society.

The new organisation of work, that will bring us a new balance between work and home, will attack inequality not just among highly qualified and educated women and men, but throughout society. Currently, there is a great divide between work-rich and work-poor households. In work-rich households, both partners work, and often overwork, and can afford all the trappings of a middle-class lifestyle that still may not feel like luxuries to their time-pressed beneficiaries. But in work-poor households no adult works, and the family slips further and further away from the financial and personal rewards of working. These inequalities weigh hardest on women, since in each type of household they will have less time and smaller incomes. It is almost always the women who will find that they have no time at all for themselves in between cooking meals, emptying the washing machine and taking the children to school around their long working hours; or the women who go without food so that their children will not be hungry or who wear the same worn-out clothes for years so that their children can have decent shoes for school. But if the entrenched demarcation of working and domestic life broke down, we could imagine work being shared out rather differently among British households. We would see a greater equity between the work-rich and the work-poor.

If people did not give up their entire lives to a linear career, they would find more time to devote to other kinds of work: to unpaid work at home; to voluntary work; to work in the neighbourhood – in a playgroup or a school or a tenants' association or a refuge or a local exchange-trading scheme. Such work is currently dominated by women and seen as unimportant. The experience that people gain from such jobs is not given full respect by employers, and voluntary and community workers are given little support by local or central government. But if men and women were able to participate in such work as a natural part of their patchwork working life, we would see it moving into a more central place in our culture, and given far more respect and importance.

This change would make a difference both in advantaged and disadvantaged areas. People who had achieved success at work would still welcome the chance to spend more time with their families or in their neighbourhoods, enlarging and reassessing their sense of themselves and their place at home and in society. They would be able to explore their hinterlands and be less likely to feel that they had spent their lives dancing to other people's tunes. But such a change would also make a great difference in disadvantaged areas. In poorer areas it is always obvious that there is a great deal of work to be done, even if there are no jobs. But if people were supported in trying to find ways to work without a clearly defined job and a clearly defined employer, they would be able to tackle many of the problems of such areas. When I visited some of the many community groups in Greater Easterhouse, in Glasgow, I met women who were managing to break through the stagnation of unemployment and poverty by creating their own kinds of workplaces – community health groups, women's groups, refuges, tenants' associations – where they could get to grips with the needs of their neighbourhood even without the traditional structures of a job or an employer. Tragically, all their organisations were chronically underfunded and fragile because of it, and their energies were often wasted on endless fund-raising and self-promotion. But the ideas and potential that they were exploring were wholly inspiring and extraordinary. That is the energy that needs to be tapped, not just the energy of women in traditional, linear careers.

As well as the revolution in the organisation of work, women in poverty need specific help now. They need a minimum wage set at a realistic level for survival, so that they need not see all their working efforts swallowed up in derisory pay. As well as the minimum wage, women and men should work side by side, not in separate environments. It is only when men work beside women that women find their work becomes better paid and more valued; it is only when women work beside men that men find their work can be made flexible and tailored around family needs. Again, these reforms cannot be achieved solely by individuals; campaigns such as Opportunity 2000 and Take Your Daughters to Work Day encourage women into men's work and could be used to work the other way too; while unions and industrial tribunals give those women who want to make a stand on equal pay the ability to bite where it hurts.

More women than men live on benefits, and we should listen to what they say. Most of them state that they would like to work, but that they cannot take up the work that is available because the wages wouldn't cover their rent after they lost their housing benefit, or because they wouldn't be able to pay someone to look after their children, or because they are terrified of the delay in starting up a new claim if the job didn't last. This poverty trap must be sprung open. We need to see reform of the welfare state that will allow women to work part-time, or participate in voluntary work, or take up temporary employment, without immediately losing all the benefits that keep themselves and their families above water.

The new strategy of childcare would also help women in poverty. Pre-school and after-school and holiday care must now be free at the point of use so that women on low incomes can be enabled to build up a better future for themselves and their families by participating in training or paid or voluntary work. These concrete changes in everyday life would mean that we could no longer define millions of women just by their poverty; they would be free to live out their individual ambitions and desires.

five: support for women experiencing violence

The new feminism does not want to follow women into the bedroom or examine their private sexual lives. But it does want to ensure that women who experience sexual or domestic violence find redress and support. First, we need legislative changes to ensure that justice is done on behalf of raped women. We have to send out the message that rape is not acceptable by ensuring that more than one out of ten rapes is reported and more than one out of ten reported rapists is convicted. As I discussed in Chapter 6, this can be done by straightforward legislative changes such as ensuring that a victim's sexual history is never brought as evidence in court, as well as wider reforms such as opening up channels of communication between victims of sexual violence and the prosecution service.

We also want to see support for women who experience other kinds of abuse and violence. As women benefit from other changes in society, they will find economic equality and will find that they will be less in thrall to abusive partners. But until that equality has arrived, we want to see much more support and many more refuge places available for women in need. Currently, only a fifth of the necessary places are available, and funding must be put in place to ensure that all women who want to can escape easily from violent men. Such a change would allow women to live free from fear, to know that if they are abused they can look for justice just as a man would.

These five goals are not impossible ones. They are already being brought closer every day by the extraordinary efforts of individuals, and if we work together then we can bring these dreams into reality. Then we will see women living free from the worst effects of abuse and poverty. We will see women and men sharing power and bringing up their children with dignity. We owe it to ourselves, to the dreams that we have of lives that are not moulded by fusty and outdated social structures, not to give up. We owe it to the women before us, who fought much bigger battles in the face of much greater odds, and won. And we owe it to women younger than ourselves, who are still to put their dreams into practice, to ensure that they do not find themselves thwarted by inequalitites they never built and to which they have never felt any allegiance.

These ideals are the right channels for the new feminism. Too many women with all kinds of dreams – dreams of being a great artist, a charismatic leader or simply a respected mother who can give her children good food and good care – are still being thwarted by material inequality. Let feminism now only turn its attention to those material inequalities, and we can move into a new and brighter future.

epilogue

the future is feminist

I am writing these words in a bar in London in the spring of 1997. I'm drinking a glass of beer and watching people go by outside the window. This is a simple, easy pleasure; resting and watching other people come and go; savouring the cold drink after a long day's work; thinking of what the evening holds. One winter evening in 1930, two women tried to have a cup of tea before catching a train. The two of them went bravely into a hotel, but the manager rushed up to them. "'I'm afaid you can't stop here. We can't serve you. You must go . . ." He was regretful, but rules were rules. We were females entering the hotel without a man. Out we must go. And out we went. We walked up and down the bleak, chill, damp, draughty platform', wrote Winifred Holtby, who was one of those women.[1] There was a day, not so long ago, when women couldn't even drink tea unaccompanied by a man; now we can sit alone in bars without a second thought.

I am wearing a trouser-suit, and my hair is loose. I look like all the other women on the street outside the café, my clothes are quite simple and minimal, like theirs. They move around gracefully and easily. Many of them look hardly different from the men around them, while others have laid claim to a more decorative way of dressing. So a woman in jeans and sloppy sweater will walk by, followed by a woman in a sharp skirt and heels, followed by another woman in jeans. Rebecca West once wrote about the unavoidable uniform imposed by the fashions she and her contemporaries had to wear at the beginning of the century: 'The adult costume of our sex waited for us round the next bend in the path, as a handicap and a humiliation, heavy, crippling, loaded with rows of buttons and hooks and eyes that were always coming off and had to be sewn on again, and boned in all sorts of places.'[2] Without that handicap and humiliation, I can take real pleasure in the clothes I buy; my wardrobe contains pretty silk dresses and spindly sandals as well as stout clothes in dull colours to wear for gardening or walking or working.

I will pay for my drink with my own money, that I earn from my own work. Ann Veronica, H. G. Wells' nice middle-class heroine, ran away from home to the horror of her father, and tried to get a job at the beginning of this century. What did she find?

No work that offered was at all of the quality she had vaguely postulated for herself. With such qualifications as she possessed, two chief channels of employment lay open, and neither attracted her, neither seemed really to offer a conclusive escape from that subjection to mankind against which she was rebelling. One main avenue was for her to become a sort of salaried accessory wife or mother, to be a governess or an assistant school-mistress, or a very high type of governess-nurse. The other was to go into . . . a photographer's reception room, for example, or a costumier's or a hat shop . . . all these things were fearfully ill-paid. They carried no more than bare subsistence wages, and they demanded all her time and energy.[3]

Ann Veronica's inability to find work threw her under the protection of a man she disliked and then forced her into early marriage. My ability to find work allows me to pay for this drink, a small freedom, but it also gives me all the other freedoms and dignities that women before the middle of century rarely knew: to choose whom I should live with and where I can go in the evenings and how I can spend my time. Now, not all women have access to fulfilling work, but many do. The world of rewarding, respectable work is no longer an alien mystery, as it was to women at the beginning of the century.

When I have finished my drink, I will go and meet my partner. We aren't married, though we share a house. Remember the reaction to poor Lydia Bennet, who tried to live with her lover before marriage in *Pride and Prejudice*. 'She is lost for ever,' observed Elizabeth Bennet; 'Loss of virtue in a female is irretrievable . . . one false step involves her in endless ruin . . . her reputation is no less brittle than it is beautiful,' agreed Mary Bennet; 'The death of your daughter would have been a blessing in comparison of this,' added Mr Collins.[4] Think of the unimaginable transformation that has occurred now, so that free love is no longer an eccentric and shocking dream, but an everyday reality.

Tomorrow I will get up and my easy life, full of the ordinary freedoms that make women's lives so much happier than they used to be, will carry on. I don't think about those freedoms. I don't think about the fact that I wear comfortable clothes, that I drink in bars, that I work, that I can love a man outside marriage. Yet all these everyday transformations, as well as others – that I use contraceptives, that I work at a newspaper, that I got a degree from a university, that I am paid much the same as my male colleagues, that I can vote, that I own a flat – were only brought to me after the struggle and argument of previous feminists.

Feminism in the twentieth century has already achieved half a revolution. Now, as we approach the twenty-first century, it is time to look to the next half. What will it look like? In another hundred years we will see women and men sitting together in equal numbers in Parliament. We will see men carrying their babies in slings to their workplace crèches. We will see as many men as women standing outside the school gates, and their children running towards them with just the same love. We will see women feeling less afraid to walk dark streets at night; we will see women who have been abused finding redress from a justice system in which half the workers are women. We will hear women's laughter and women's anger echoing through every office and every boardroom in the country. We will watch as many films made by women as by men; we will read as many newspapers edited by women as by men; and so we will see women treated with more respect throughout our media. We will see children growing up with dignity even in the poorer parts of Britain.

We won't see that everyone behaves exactly the same, of course. We may never see as many men as women wearing flowers in their hair; we may never see as many women as men at football matches; or as many men as women painting their nails. We may find that women and men still tend to enjoy different books; we may find that more women cry at the end of *Gone with the Wind*; and that more men collect records in alphabetical order. We may find that the pornography business still exists; we may find that the army is still dominated by men; and that nursing is still dominated by women. But we will know that those results have been brought about by choice, not by coercion.

Today, women and men are building a new feminism that is working for ordinary, everyday equality. It isn't a movement that seeks to mould people's desires, but a movement that wants everyone to have the freedom to follow their ambitions and dreams without being stifled by that dead weight of inequality that has moulded our society for too long.

notes

chapter 1 what is the new feminism?

1 *Daily Telegraph*, 17 January 1996.
2 *See* Chapter 9. 76 per cent of working women and 72 per cent of working men say they would work even if there was no financial need.
3 50.3 per cent of solicitors qualified in 1995–6 were women; figures supplied by the Law Society, 1997.
4 *Health and Personal Social Services Statistics for England*, 1996 edition, Department of Health, London, HMSO, 1996.
5 *Social Focus on Women*, Central Statistical Office, London, HMSO, 1995, Table 3.2.
6 Statistics prepared for the author by the Office for National Statistics, August 1997. These figures are based on the New Earnings Survey 1996; they cover gross weekly earnings of employees, full-time and part-time, on all rates, whose pay was not affected by absence. Exact figures are: 39.2 per cent of all women and 9.2 per cent of all men earn under £150 per week.
7 Heather Joshi, Hugh Davies and Hilary Land, *The Tale of Mrs Typical*, London, Family Policy Studies Centre, 1996.
8 Research carried out by the National Group on Homeworking, reported in Ursula Huws, *Home Truths: Key Results from a National Survey of Homeworkers*, Leeds, National Group on Homeworking, 1994.
9 Research carried out by NCH Action for Children, January 1994.
10 Sian Griffiths, ed., *Beyond the Glass Ceiling*, Manchester University Press, 1996.
11 Department of Health, figures published in 1997 for 1995.
12 Institute of Management, 1996.

13 Robin Morgan, 'Theory and Practice: Pornography and Rape', 1974, *The Word of a Woman*, London, Virago, 1993, p88.

14 Dusty Rhodes and Sandra McNeill, eds., *Women Against Violence Against Women*, London, Onlywomen Press, p255.

15 Naomi Wolf, *Fire With Fire*, London, Chatto & Windus, 1993, p9.

16 Caroline Sullivan, 'Girls Just Wanna be Loaded', *Guardian*, 26 July 1996.

17 *Daily Telegraph*, 7 July 1995.

chapter 2 the reality gap

1 Recent books that also examine women's ongoing inequality include: Kate Figes, *Because of Her Sex*, London, Macmillan, 1994; Sue Innes, *Making It Work*, London, Chatto & Windus, 1995; Yvonne Roberts, *Mad About Women*, London, Virago, 1992.

2 Research carried out at Ashridge Management College, reported in *Daily Mail*, 12 October 1995.

3 Broadcasting Standards Council, 'Perspectives of Women in Television', Research Working Paper, 1994, p27.

4 Helen Garner, *Watching Women: Election 1997*, London, Fawcett Society, 1997, p6.

5 Figures for 1995, from the Department of Education. Women make up 23.2% of headteachers in maintained secondary schools.

6 Figures for 1996, from the London Metropolitan Police Force. Women make up 3,951 of 27,205 officers.

7 Figures from 1996, from the Bar Council. Women make up 2,115 of 8,935 barristers.

8 *Health and Personal Social Services Statistics for England*, 1996 edition, Department of Health, London, HMSO, 1996.

9 Frances Tomlinson and Fiona Colgan, *Women in Publishing: Twice as Many, Half as Powerful?*, Polytechnic of North London/Women in Publishing, 1989, p25.

10 Joanna Luke and Diane Stratton, *Investigation into the Representation of Women Authors and Reviewers on the book pages of Quality and Midmarket Newspapers*, West Herts College/Women in Management in Publishing, 1992, p9.

11 Report by the Society of Practitioners of Insolvency, reported in *Evening Standard*, 22 July 1997.

12 S. Carter and T. Cannon, 'Female Entrepreneurs: a Study of Female Business Owners, their Motivations, Experiences and Strategies for Success', Research Paper no. 65, Department of Employment, 1988, cited in Teresa Rees, *Women and the Labour Market*, London, Routledge, 1992, p172.

13 Reported in *MSF at Work*, union magazine, January 1996, p7.

14 Research quoted in *Independent*, leader, 'Cracking the Glass Ceiling', 10 January 1996.

15 Trudy Coe, *The Key to the Men's Club*, London, Institute of Management, 1992.

16 The Hansard Society, *The Report of the Hansard Society Commission on Women at the Top*, HMSO, 1990, p58.

17 *Daily Telegraph*, 21 August 1995.

18 *Independent*, 5 January 1995.

19 *Guardian*, 21 May 1996.

20 *Guardian*, 7 August 1996.

21 Ibid.

22 *Daily Mail*, 30 July 1996.

23 *Daily Telegraph*, 19 October 1996.

24 Samantha Phillips, *Blonde Ambition*, London, Century, 1996, p108.

25 Figures for 1996, from the Bar Council.

26 Institute of Directors, June 1997.

27 *Health and Personal Social Services Statistics for England*, Department of Health, London, HMSO, 1996.

28 Department of Health, figures published in 1997 for 1995.

29 Sian Griffiths, ed., *Beyond the Glass Ceiling*, Manchester University Press, 1996.

30 Ginny Dougary, *The Executive Tart and Other Myths*, London, Virago, p192.

31 Ibid., p117.

32 Ibid., pp19–21.

33 Neil Millward, *Targeting Potential Discrimination*, Manchester, Equal Opportunities Commission, 1995, p6 and p9.

34 *Social Focus on Women*, Central Statistical Office, London, HMSO, 1995, Table 2.27, p34.

35 'Time to be a Game Girl', *Evening Standard*, 22 March 1995.

36 Winter 1996/7, *Labour Force Survey Quarterly Bulletin*, June 1997, Office for National Statistics, London, HMSO, Table 36, p45.

37 Ibid, Table 37, p46.

38 *Social Focus on Women*, Central Statistical Office, London, HMSO, 1995, p25.

39 Winter 1996/7, *Labour Force Survey Quarterly Bulletin*, op. cit.

40 Jean Martin and Ceridwen Roberts, 'Women's Employment: A Lifetime Perspective', Department of Employment 1980, quoted in Kate Figes, *Because of Her Sex*, London, Macmillan, 1994, p133.

41 *Social Focus on Women*, op. cit,. Table 3.2.

42 Heather Joshi, Hugh Davies and Hilary Land, *The Tale of Mrs Typical*, London, Family Policy Studies Centre, 1996, p13.

43 Her name has been changed.

44 Her name has been changed.

45 Rosalind Coward, *Our Treacherous Hearts*, London, Faber, 1992, p20.

46 Ibid, p32.

47 Terri Apter, *Professional Progress: Why Women Still Don't Have Wives*, London, Macmillan, 1993, p120.

48 Helen Simpson, 'Lentils and Lilies', *Mail on Sunday You* magazine, 19 January 1997.

49 Statistics prepared for the author by the Office for National Statistics, August 1997. These figures are based on the New Earnings Survey 1996; they cover gross weekly earnings of employees, full-time and part-time, on all rates, whose pay was not affected by absence. Exact figures are: 4.9 per cent of all men and 23.7 per cent of all women earn under £100 per week. The New Earnings Survey surveys employers and under reports low-paid workers.

50 Winter 1996/7, *Labour Force Survey Quarterly Bulletin*, op. cit., Table 36, p45.

51 Susan Harkness, 'How Would British Women be Affected by the Introduction of a Minimum Wage?', unpublished paper, LSE, June 1995, Table II. These figures are based on the British Household Panel Study.

52 Susan Harkness, Stephen Machin and Jane Waldfogel, 'Evaluating the Pin Money Hypothesis', Discussion Paper no. 108, Welfare State Programme, Centre for Economic Performance, London School of Economics, 1995, p26–27, Table IX. Poverty here, and elsewhere, is defined by the EU definition, of living on less than

half of the national average income. These statistics are based on *Households Below Average Income*, 1990–1991, London, HMSO.

53 Her name has been changed.

54 Her name has been changed.

55 Caroline Glendinning and Jane Millar, 'It All Really Starts in the Family', in Caroline Glendinning and Jane Millar, *Women and Poverty in Britain: the 1990s*, Hemel Hempstead, Harvester Wheatsheaf, 1992, p9.

56 *Social Security Statistics*, London, HMSO, 1995.

57 *Households Below Average Income*, 1979–1993/4, London, HMSO, 1996.

58 *Family Expenditure Survey*, London, HMSO, 1995.

59 Livi Michael, *Under a Thin Moon*, 1992, London, Minerva, 1994, p216.

60 *Health Inequalities*, London, Office for National Statistics, 1997.

61 Jonathan Bradshaw and Hilary Holmes, *Living on the Edge*, London, Tyneside Child Poverty Action Group, 1989, p101.

62 Ibid.

63 Jane Millar, 'Lone Mothers and Poverty', in Glendinning and Millar, op. cit., p155.

64 Ruth Cohen *et al*, *Hardship Britain*, London, Child Poverty Action Group, 1992.

65 Jonathan Bradshaw and Hilary Holmes, op. cit., p64.

66 Statistics prepared by the Labour Party in 1996, reported by *Guardian*, 25 October 1996.

67 Claire Callender, 'Redundancy, Unemployment and Poverty', in Glendinning and Millar, op cit., p145.

68 Research carried out by NCH Action for Children, January 1994.

69 *Observer*, 11 August 1996.

70 Her name has been changed.

71 Quoted in 'The Bad Food Trap', *Observer*, 21 January 1996.

chapter 3 **out of the ghetto**

1 Recent writers who have examined the mainstream nature of feminism today include: Nyta Mann, 'Women on the move', *New Statesman*, 3 March 1995; Suzanne Moore, 'Soft Shoe Shuffle' in *Head Over Heels*, London, Viking, 1996, pp293–298; Helen Wilkinson and Dr Gerda Siann, *Gender, Feminism and the Future*, London, Demos, 1995; Naomi Wolf, *Fire With Fire*, London, Chatto & Windus, 1993.

2 Barbara Deming, 'Remembering Who We Are' (1977), in Mayerding and Smith, eds., *We Are All Part of One Another: a Barbara Deming Reader*, Philadelphia, New Society Publishers, 1984, quoted in Jill Liddington, *The Long Road to Greenham*, London, Virago, 1989, p209.

3 Interview with author.

4 Interview with author.

5 Interview with author.

6 'A Day but not an Era for Women', *Independent*, 8 March 1995.

7 MORI/*Mail on Sunday* survey, *Mail on Sunday*, 25 June 1995.

8 *Guardian*, 7 March 1991.

9 'The Age of the Post-feminist Woman', *Mail on Sunday*, May 1988.

10 Quoted in Ralph M. Wardle, *Mary Wollstonecraft: A Critical Biography*, Bison/University of Nebraska Press, 1951, p318.

11 Marie Corelli, *Woman, or – Suffragette*, 1907, p38, quoted in Lisa Tickner, *The*

Spectacle of Women, London, Chatto & Windus, 1987, p164.

12 *Daily Mirror*, 25 May 1914, reproduced in Lisa Tickner, op. cit., p167.

13 H. G. Wells, *Ann Veronica*, 1909, London, Everyman, 1993, p28.

14 *Guardian*, 24 March 1984.

15 Interview with author.

16 Christabel Pankhurst, *Unshackled*, London, Hutchinson 1959, p30.

17 MORI/*Mail on Sunday* survey on sexual politics, June 1995.

18 Interview with author.

19 *Mail on Sunday*, 3 September 1993.

20 *Guardian*, 16 August 1990.

21 *Evening Standard*, 2 November 1995.

22 Edwina Currie, *What Women Want*, London, Sidgwick & Jackson, 1990, p3.

23 *Sunday Telegraph*, 17 January 1993.

24 Interview with author.

25 Survey canvassing the views of over 1,000 students at Scottish universities, in Dr G Siann, *Gender, Sex and Sexuality: Contemporary Psychological Perspectives*, Taylor and Francis, 1994; cited in Dr Gerda Siann and Helen Wilkinson, *Gender, Feminism and the Future*, London, Demos, 1995, p1.

26 *Daily Mail*, 5 February 1996.

27 British Household Panel Study, cited in Helen Wilkinson and Geoff Mulgan, *Freedom's Children*, London, Demos, 1995, p 46.

28 Interview with author.

29 Interview with author. Her name has been changed.

30 Interview with author.

31 Interview with author.

32 Interview with author.

33 Interview with author.

34 Quoted in Kathy Acker, 'All Girls Together', *Guardian*, 3 May 1997.

35 *See* Olive Banks, *Faces of Feminism*, 1981, Oxford, Blackwell, 1986; Elizabeth Wilson, *Women and the Welfare State*, London, Tavistock, 1977; Eleanor Rathbone, *The Disinherited Family*, with a useful introduction by Suzie Fleming, 1924, Bristol, Falling Wall Press, 1986; Seth Koven and Sonya Michel, eds., *Mothers of a New World*, London, Routledge, 1993, especially the essays by Seth Koven and Pat Thane; Gisela Bock and Pat Thane, eds., *Maternity and Gender Politics: Women and the Rise of European Welfare States, 1880s–1950s*, London, Routledge, 1991, especially the essay by Jane Lewis.

36 For example, Emmeline Pethick-Lawrence, in *My Part in a Changing World*, London, Gollancz, 1938, quoted in Olive Banks, *Faces of Feminism*, 1981, Oxford, Blackwell, 1986, p167.

37 For example, Neil Lyndon, *No More Sex War*, London, Sinclair-Stevenson, 1992, p82. 'The reason why women were enabled, in the mid-sixties, to emerge from the confinements of their domestic ghetto, was that, at precisely that date and for the first time in all of human history, women were provided with a technology which gave them infallible control over their fertility.'

chapter 4 the new feminism is less personal and more political

1 Marianne Grabrucker, *There's a Good Girl*, London, The Women's Press, 1988, p106.

2 Virginia Woolf, *A Room of One's Own* 1929, London, Grafton, 1977, p101 and p103.

3 Christabel Pankhurst, *Unshackled*, London, Hutchinson, 1959, p77.

4 Her name has been changed.

5 Germaine Greer, *The Female Eunuch*, 1971, London, Flamingo, 1993, pp353–371.

6 Dorothy Dinnerstein, *The Mermaid and the Minotaur* (published in Britain by Souvenir Press as *Rocking the Cradle*), 1976, quoted in Miriam Schneir, ed., *The Vintage Book of Feminism*, London, Vintage, 1995, p285.

7 Anna Coote and Beatrix Campbell, *Sweet Freedom*, Oxford, Blackwell, 1982, p14.

8 Lynne Segal, *Straight Sex*, London, Virago, 1994, p57.

9 Leeds Revolutionary Feminist Group, `Political Lesbianism: the Case against Heterosexuality' in *Love Your Enemy?*, London, Onlywomen Press, 1981, p5, cited in Lynne Segal, *Is the Future Female?*, London, Virago, 1987, p96.

10 Lynne Segal, *Straight Sex*, London, Virago, 1994, p58.

11 Radicalesbians, 'The Woman-Identified Woman', 1972, reprinted in Miriam Schneir, ed., *The Vintage Book of Feminism*, London, Vintage, 1995, pp162–7.

12 *Spare Rib*, May 1986.

13 Colette Dowling, *The Cinderella Complex: Women's Hidden Fear of Independence*, London, Michael Joseph, 1981, p28.

14 Ibid, p61.

15 Michelene Wandor, 'Family Ever After', *Spare Rib*, November 1972.

16 Jane Rogers, *Promised Lands*, London, Faber, 1995, p204.

17 Gail Pheterson, 'Alliances Between Women – Overcoming Internalised Oppression and Internalised Domination' in L. Albrecht and R. Brewer, eds., *Bridges of Power: Women's Multicultural Alliances*, Philadelphia, New Society Publishers, 1990, quoted in Nira Yuval-Davis, 'Women, Ethnicity and Empowerment', in Ann Oakley and Juliet Mitchell, eds., *Who's Afraid of Feminism*, London, Hamish Hamilton 1997, p91.

18 Figures quoted to the author by Dame Angela Rumbold, February 1996.

19 Naomi Wolf, *Fire with Fire*, London, Chatto & Windus, 1993, pp249, 251, 267 and 333–4.

20 Interview with author.

21 Interview with author.

22 Interview with author.

23 Lee Bryce, *The Influential Woman*, London, Piatkus, 1989, p33.

24 Kate White, *Why Good Girls Don't Get Ahead But Gutsy Girls Do*, London, Century, 1995.

25 Her name has been changed.

26 MORI/*Mail on Sunday* survey, *Mail on Sunday*, 25 June 1995.

27 Trudy Coe, *The Key to the Men's Club*, London, Institute of Management, 1992.

28 Valerie Hammond and Viki Holton, 'Scenario for Women Managers in Britain', in Nancy J. Adler ed., *Competititve Frontiers: Women Managers in a Global Economy*, Oxford, Blackwell, 1994, p239.

29 Naomi Wolf, op. cit., pp317–337.

30 Maureen Freely, *What About Us?*, London, Bloomsbury, 1995, pp212–213. Other writers who have taken a lead in marking out a pragmatic modern feminism include: Kate Figes, *Because of her Sex*, London, Macmillan, 1994; Sue Innes, *Making It Work*, London, Chatto & Windus, 1995; Suzanne Moore, *Head Over Heels*, London, Viking, 1996; Yvonne Roberts, *Mad About Women*, London, Virago, 1992; Helen

Wilkinson, *No Turning Back*, London, Demos, 1994. Also see Melissa Benn, 'Super-sisters should rap about the struggle', *Guardian*, 8 March 1994; and Nicci Gerrard, 'Damn this raging flood of emotion', *Observer*, 21 September 1997.

31 Interview with author.

32 Helena Kennedy, *Eve Was Framed*, 1992, London, Vintage, 1993, p137.

33 *Independent on Sunday*, 7 November 1993.

34 Geraldine Bedell, *Independent on Sunday*, 29 January 1995.

35 *Guardian*, 5 May 1993.

36 Gloria Steinem, 'Men and Women Talking', in *Outrageous Acts and Everyday Rebellions*, 1983, London, Jonathan Cape, 1984, p179.

chapter 5 let boys wear pink

1 Mary Wollstonecraft, *A Vindication of the Rights of Woman*, 1792, London, Everyman, 1992, p60.

2 Olive Schreiner, *Woman and Labour*, 1911, London, Virago, 1978, p66.

3 Simone de Beauvoir, *The Second Sex*, 1949, London, Jonathan Cape, 1953, p506.

4 Naomi Wolf, *The Beauty Myth*, London, Chatto & Windus, 1990, p2.

5 Winifred Holtby, *Women and a Changing Civilisation*, London, John Lane/Bodley Head, 1934, p119.

6 Dusty Rhodes and Sandra McNeill eds., *Women Against Violence Against Women*, London, Onlywomen Press, 1985, p255.

7 Simone de Beauvoir, *The Second Sex*, 1949, London, Jonathan Cape, 1953, p506.

8 Charlotte Brontë, *Jane Eyre*, 1847, Harmondsworth, Penguin, 1990, p301.

9 Report by Michael Dynes from Afghanistan, *The Times*, 24 October 1996.

10 Anne Frank, *The Diary of a Young Girl*, Otto Frank and Mirjam Pressler, eds., first published 1947, revised edition, London, Viking, 1997, p161.

11 Rebecca West, 'There is no Conversation', in *The Harsh Voice*, 1935, London, Virago, 1982, p99.

12 Doris Lessing, *The Diaries of Jane Somers*, (originally published as Jane Somers, *The Diary of a Good Neighbour*, London, Michael Joseph, 1983), Harmondsworth, Penguin, 1984, p283.

13 Linda Grant, *The Cast Iron Shore*, London, Picador, 1996, p231.

14 Her name has been changed.

15 Linda Grant, *Sexing the Millennium*, London, HarperCollins, 1993, p224.

16 Martha Gellhorn, *The View from the Ground*, London, Granta, 1989, p74.

17 Doris Lessing, *Under My Skin*, London, HarperCollins 1994, p173.

18 Eve MacSweeney, 'Slender girls with Short Careers', *Guardian*, 8 September 1995.

19 'I Love People Watching Me', *Guardian*, 14 September 1995.

20 From Susan Corrigan, 'The Young Pretenders', *Guardian*, 17 July 1996.

21 *Today*, 3 October 1995.

22 *Men's Health* magazine, July 1996, reported in *Independent*, 11 June 1996.

23 1993 study by the University of Texas and Michigan State, quoted in 'You're Beastly about Beauty', *Observer*, 9 June 1996.

24 Andy McNab, *Immediate Action*, London, Bantam, 1995, p65.

25 Alan Clark, *Diaries*, London, Weidenfeld & Nicolson, 1993, p51.

26 *Guardian*, 14 January 1995.

27 *Guardian*, 1 August 1995.

28 Marianne Grabrucker, *There's a Good Girl*, London, The Women's Press, 1988, p81.

chapter 6 **sex without an order of battle**

1 Shulamith Firestone, *The Dialectic of Sex*, 1970, London, The Women's Press, 1979, p121.

2 Andrea Dworkin, *Intercourse*, London, Secker and Warburg, 1987, p194.

3 Demands formulated at the first national Women's Liberation conference in 1970, quoted in Michelene Wandor, ed., *The Body Politic*, London, Stage 1, 1972, p2.

4 Simone de Beauvoir, *The Second Sex*, 1949, London, Jonathan Cape, 1953, p88.

5 Mary McCarthy, *The Group*, 1963, London, Penguin, 1966, p38.

6 Sylvia Plath, *The Bell Jar*, London, Heinemann, 1963 p241.

7 Anne Koedt, 'The Myth of the Vaginal Orgasm', *Notes from the Second Year: Women's Liberation – Major Writings of the Radical Feminists*, April 1970, pp37–41, excerpted in Miriam Schneir, ed., *The Vintage Book of Feminism*, London, Vintage, 1995, pp335–342.

8 Germaine Greer, *The Female Eunuch*, 1970, London, Flamingo, 1993, p48.

9 Quoted in Lynne Segal, *Straight Sex*, London, Virago, 1994, p50.

10 Al Garthwaite, 'Report of Workshop on Male Violence', in Dusty Rhodes and Sandra McNeill, eds., *Women Against Violence Against Women*, London, Onlywomen Press, 1985, p227.

11 Interview with author.

12 Andrea Dworkin, *Pornography: Men Possessing Women*, London, The Women's Press, 1981, p123.

13 Tama Janowitz, *Slaves of New York*, London, Picador, 1987, p1.

14 Catharine MacKinnon, *Only Words*, London, HarperCollins, 1994, p5.

15 Ruth Grinrod and Maria Katyachild, 'Pornography, Theory and Practice' in Sandra McNeill and Dusty Rhodes, op. cit., p265.

16 Susan Brownmiller, *Against Our Will*, London, Secker and Warburg, 1975, p310.

17 Andrea Dworkin, *Woman Hating*, New York, Dutton, 1974 p33.

18 Jack Zipes, *The Trials and Tribulations of Red Riding Hood*, London, Routledge, 1993.

19 Angela Carter, 'The Company of Wolves' in *The Bloody Chamber*, 1979, London, Vintage, 1995, p118.

20 Recent books that support a view of female sexuality in which the woman is not a victim include: Rene Denfield, *The New Victorians*, New York, Warner, 1995; Kate Fillion, *Lip Service*, London, HarperCollins, 1997; Kate Roiphe, *The Morning After*, New York, Little, Brown, 1993; Lynne Segal, *Straight Sex*, London, Virago, 1994; Naomi Wolf, *Fire With Fire*, London, Chatto & Windus, 1993.

21 Olive Banks, *Faces of Feminism*, 1981, Oxford, Blackwell, 1986, p68.

22 Helen Simpson, *Dear George*, London, Heinemann, 1995, p34.

23 Julie Myerson, *Sleepwalking*, London, Picador, 1994, p149.

24 Susan Brownmiller, op. cit., p394.

25 Maureen Freely, *Under the Vulcania*, London, Bloomsbury, 1994.

26 Alina Reyes, *The Butcher*, London, Methuen, 1991.

27 Madonna, *Sex*, London, Secker and Warburg, 1992.

28 *Vogue*, May 1995.

29 *Sun*, 9 October 1995.

30 Spice Girls, *Girlpower*, London, Zone, 1997, p6.

31 Helen Simpson, op. cit., p50.

32 Rachel Swift, *Women's Pleasure, or How to Have an Orgasm as Often as You Want*, London, Pan, 1993.

33 *Cosmopolitan*, August 1995.

34 HEA report, quoted in *Independent*, 20 April 1995.

35 Catharine MacKinnon, op. cit., p5.

36 Sheila Jeffreys, 'Prostitution', in Dusty Rhodes and Sandra McNeill, op. cit., p64.

37 Lynne Segal, op. cit.

38 Naomi Wolf, *Fire with Fire*, London, Chatto & Windus, 1993, p200.

39 Camille Paglia, *Vamps and Tramps*, London, Penguin, 1995, p36.

40 *Nineteen*, August 1995.

41 Robert T. Michael *et al.*, *Sex in America*, London, Little, Brown, 1994, p224 and 227.

42 Diane Russell, *Sexual Exploitation*, Sage 1984, quoted in Sue Lees, *Carnal Knowledge: Rape on Trial*, London, Hamish Hamilton, 1996, p215.

43 Sue Lees, *Carnal Knowledge: Rape on Trial*, London, Hamish Hamilton, 1996, p99. According to Lees' evidence, this is not due to women making deliberately false allegations, but usually because the police believe that the case will not stand up in court (perhaps because of insufficient evidence or because the complainant would not make a good witness); or because the complainant decides not to proceed (perhaps because of intimidation or fear of court procedure).

44 Women Against Rape and Legal Action for Women, *The Crown Prosecution Service and the Crime of Rape*, 1995, p4. See also, A. Godenzi, 'What's the Big Deal? We are Men and They are Women,' in T. Newburn and E Stanko, eds., *Just Boys Doing Business, Men, Masculinites and Crime*, London, Routledge, 1994; and Ruth Hall, *Ask Any Woman*, Bristol, Falling Wall Press, 1985.

45 Diana Scully and Joseph Marolla, 'Convicted Rapists Describe the Rewards', in Pauline B. Bart and Eileen Geil Moran, eds., *Violence Against Women*, London, Sage, 1993, p43.

46 Sue Lees, op. cit.

47 Women Against Rape and Legal Action for Women, *Dossier: The Crown Prosecution Service and the Crime of Rape*, May 1995.

48 Sue Lees, op cit, p32.

49 Women Against Rape and Legal Action for Women, op. cit.

50 *Mail on Sunday*, 2 February 1997.

51 BBC1, *Everyman* documentary, 'No Great Trauma', 14 September 1990, cited in Sue Lees, op. cit., p120.

52 Sue Lees, op. cit., p142

53 *Archbold: Criminal Pleading, Evidence and Practice*, ed., P. J. Richardson, London, Sweet & Maxwell 1997, Section 20–44, p1704.

54 Interview with author.

55 *Observer*, 26 November 1995.

56 Sue Lees, op. cit., p27.

57 Ibid.

58 Sue Lees, op. cit., p30.

59 *Daily Mail*, 7 October 1996.

60 Figures for 1996, from the London Metropolitan Police Force.

61 Figures for 1996, from the Bar Council.

62 Interview with author.

63 The Law Commission, *Consent in the Criminal Law, A Consultation Paper*, London, HMSO, 1995, p97.

64 Report by Maggie O'Kane on findings by Barnardo's, *Guardian*, 21 August 1996.

65 *What Women Want*, compiled by Lesley Abdela, London, The Body Shop, 1994, p75.
66 Katie Roiphe, *The Morning After*, London, Hamish Hamilton, 1993, p44.
67 Betty Friedan, *The Second Stage*, New York, Summit, 1981, p362.
68 Nadine Strossen, *Defending Pornography*, London, Abacus, 1995, p255.
69 Livi Michael, *Their Angel Reach*, London, Secker and Warburg, 1994, p330.
70 Catharine MacKinnon, op. cit., p77.
71 Nancy Friday, *Women on Top*, London, QPD/Hutchinson, 1991, p15.
72 Norman Rush, *Mating*, London, Jonathan Cape, 1992, p307.

chapter 7 **hello, boys!**

1 Richard Littlejohn, *Daily Mail*, 25 July 1996.
2 London Rape Action Group, 'Towards a Revolutionary Feminist Analysis of Rape', first published in Friedman and Sarah, eds., *On the Problem of Men*, London, The Women's Press, 1982, reprinted in Rhodes and McNeill, eds., *Women Against Violence Against Women*, London, Onlywomen Press, 1985, p29.
3 Rachel Adams, 'How All Men Benefit from Rape', in Rhodes and McNeill, eds., op. cit., p33.
4 'Rapists – Castration?', letter in *Spare Rib*, February 1987.
5 Mentioned in Naomi Wolf, *Fire with Fire*, London, Chatto & Windus, 1993, p203.
6 *Against the Grain*, London, Southall Black Sisters, 1990, p35–6.
7 Doris Lessing, *Walking in the Shade*, London, HarperCollins, 1997, p346–7.
8 London Rape Action Group, 'Towards a Revolutionary Feminist Analysis of Rape', in Rhodes and McNeill, eds., op. cit, p29.
9 Naomi Wolf, *Fire With Fire*, London, Chatto & Windus, 1993, p203.
10 Val Walsh, 'Virility Culture', in Evans, Gosling and Seller, eds., *Agenda for Gender, Discussion Papers*, London, Birkbeck College, 1993.
11 Danu, 'Fantasy and Masochism', in Rhodes and McNeill, op. cit., p224.
12 Judith Herman (with Lisa Hirschman), *Father–Daughter Incest*, 1981, quoted in Bart and Moran, eds., *Violence Against Women*, London, Sage 1993.
13 Leeds Revolutionary Feminist Group, 'Incest as an everyday event in the normal family', in Rhodes and McNeill, op. cit., p194.
14 *Daily Mail*, 31 July 1996.
15 NOP poll for Care for the Family, 1995.
16 David Thomas, *Not Guilty: In Defence of the Modern Man*, London, Weidenfeld & Nicolson, 1993, p24.
17 Adrienne Burgess, *Fatherhood Reclaimed*, London, Vermilion/Random House, 1997, p196.
18 H. Parker and S. Parker, 'Father–daughter Sexual Abuse: an Emerging Perspective', *American Journal of Orthopsychiatry*, 56 (4), pp531–549, 1986, quoted in Sebastian Kraemer, *Active Fathering for the Future*, London, Demos, 1995, p12.
19 Adrienne Burgess, op. cit., p179.
20 Matt Seaton, 'How Was It For You?', *Vogue*, August 1996.
21 *Guardian*, 2 October 1995. Other writers who have examined the relationship between men and feminism in a similar light include: Yvonne Roberts, *Mad About Women*, London, Virago, 1992; Helen Wilkinson, *No Turning Back*, London, Demos, 1994; and Naomi Wolf, *Fire With Fire*, op. cit.
22 Interview with author.

23 Vera Brittain, *Testament of Youth*, 1933, London, Virago, 1978, p84.
24 Philip Roth, *Patrimony*, London, Jonathan Cape, 1991, p177.
25 Ibid., p238.
26 Blake Morrison, *And When Did You Last See Your Father?* London, Granta, 1993, pp64–5.
27 Ibid., p219.
28 Nick Hornby, *Fever Pitch*, London, Victor Gollancz, 1992, p80.
29 Ibid., p101.
30 Giles Smith, *Lost in Music*, London, Picador, 1995.
31 Mark Hudson, *Coming Back Brockens*, London, Jonathan Cape, 1994.
32 Ben Watt, *Patient: The True Story of a Rare Illness*, London, Viking, 1996.
33 British Household Panel Study, cited in Helen Wilkinson and Geoff Mulgan, *Freedom's Children*, London, Demos, 1995, p77.
34 MORI Socioconsult survey, cited in Helen Wilkinson and Geoff Mulgan, op. cit., p76.
35 Helen Wilkinson and Ivan Briscoe, *Parental Leave*, Demos, 1996, p9.
36 MORI Socioconsult survey, cited in Helen Wilkinson and Geoff Mulgan, op. cit., p45.
37 *Daily Mail*, 7 April 1995.
38 From 'Not My Type', *Guardian*, 22 January 1996.
39 *Guardian*, 22 January 1996.
40 Adrienne Burgess, op. cit., p144.
41 Adrienne Burgess, op cit, p136.
42 Adrienne Burgess and Sandy Ruxton, *Men and their Children*, London, Institute for Public Policy Research, 1996, p3.
43 Helen Wilkinson and Gerda Siann, *Gender, Feminism and the Future*, London, Demos, 1995, p10.
44 Adrienne Burgess and Sandy Ruxton, op. cit., p3.
45 *The Times*, 1 October 1994.
46 Ibid.
47 Ibid.
48 *Daily Mail*, 22 July 1996.

chapter 8 the new feminism embraces power

1 *Daily Mail*, 5 February 1996.
2 *Independent*, 10 March 1995.
3 *Evening Standard*, 12 April 1995.
4 Survey of 22,000 French businesses carried out by SCRL, reported in *Daily Mail*, 31 October 1996.
5 Ray Strachey, *The Cause*, 1928, London, Virago, 1978, p41.
6 Ibid., p403.
7 Other writers who have examined the new relationship between women and power include: Helen Wilkinson, *No Turning Back: Generations and Genderquake*, London, Demos, 1994; and Naomi Wolf, *Fire With Fire*, London, Chatto & Windus, 1993.
8 Josephine Butler, *Personal Reminiscences of a Great Crusade*, 1896, p189, quoted in Virginia Woolf, *Three Guineas*, 1938, Oxford University Press, 1992, p264.
9 *Independent*, 8 March 1995.
10 Anna Coote and Beatrix Campbell, *Sweet Freedom*, Oxford, Blackwell, 1982, p145.
11 Mary Daly, *Gyn/Ecology*, London, The Women's Press, 1979, p336.

12 'Neither Victim nor Assassin', *Shrew,* summer 1978, p3, issue edited by the Feminism and Nonviolence Study Group, quoted in Jill Liddington, *The Long Road to Greenham*, London, Virago, 1989, p210.

13 Jill Liddington, *The Long Road to Greenham*, London, Virago, 1989, p215.

14 Ibid.

15 *Woman's World*, October 1978.

16 Quoted in *Values and Visions: the What Women Want Social Survey*, London, Women's Communication Centre, 1996, p37.

17 *Sun*, 9 June, 1983.

18 *Guardian*, 6 June 1983, quoted in Marina Warner, *Monuments and Maidens*, 1985, London, Picador, 1987, p43.

19 *News of the World*, 12 June 1983, quoted in Warner, op. cit., p40.

20 Margaret Thatcher, *The Downing Street Years*, London, HarperCollins, 1993, p381.

21 Ibid., p82.

22 *Guardian*, 23 March 1995.

23 *Daily Mail*, 24 May 1996.

24 *Daily Mail*, 25 September 1996.

25 *Daily Mail* 25 October 1996.

26 *Daily Mail*, 6 August 1996.

27 *Newsnight*, 11 July 1996.

28 Told by Maggie O'Kane to author.

29 *Daily Mail*, 22 October 1996.

30 *Mail on Sunday*, 25 June 1995.

31 Katharine Whitehorn, 'Why a Woman Can't be More Like a Man', *Observer*, 4 June 1995.

32 *General Household Survey*, 1993, cited in Susan Harkness, *How Would Women be Affected by the Introduction of a Minimum Wage?*, unpublished paper, LSE, 1995.

33 MORI poll, reported in *Mail on Sunday*, 25 May 1995.

34 Quoted in Jane McLoughlin, *Up and Running: Women in Business*, London, Virago, 1992, p3.

35 Helen Wilkinson and Geoff Mulgan, 'Move Over Baby Doll', *The Sunday Times*, 24 September 1995; and cf Helen Wilkinson and Geoff Mulgan, *Freedom's Children*, London, Demos, 1995; and Helen Wilkinson, *No Turning Back*, London, Demos, 1994.

36 *Daily Mail*, 22 July 1996.

37 Department of Education statistics.

38 Quoted in feature by Linda Grant, *Guardian*, 22 October 1994.

39 British Household Panel Study, quoted in Helen Wilkinson and Geoff Mulgan, *Freedom's Children*, London, Demos, 1995, p26.

40 Mintel, 'Youth Lifestyles 1995', quoted in 'Survey Shows it's a Woman's World', *The Times*, 24 March 1995.

41 MORI/*Mail on Sunday* survey, *Mail on Sunday*, 25 June 1995.

42 Interview with author.

43 British Household Panel Study, quoted in Helen Wilkinson and Geoff Mulgan, *Freedom's Children*, London, Demos, 1995, p46.

44 Colette Dowling, *The Cinderella Complex*, London, Michael Joseph, 1982, p179.

45 Germaine Greer, *The Female Eunuch*, 1971, London, Flamingo, 1993, p161.

46 Mintel, 'Youth Lifestyles 1995', op. cit.

47 *Evening Standard*, 19 April 1996.

48 Ibid.
49 Quoted in Amy Raphael, *Never Mind the Bollocks*, London, Virago, 1995, p87.
50 Interview with author.
51 *Observer*, 16 April 1995.
52 Interview with author.
53 Celia Dodd, 'The Mothers Who Did It Their Way', *Independent*, 24 June 1996.
54 Her name has been changed.
55 Edwina Currie, *What Women Want*, Sidgwick & Jackson, 1990, p31.
56 Broadcasting Standards Council, 'Perspectives of Women in Television', Research Working Paper, May 1994.
57 *Daily Mail*, 10 May 1995.
58 Karren Brady, *United*, Little, Brown, 1996.
59 Louise Bagshawe, *Career Girls*, London, Orion, 1995, p171.
60 Germaine Greer, op. cit., p9.
61 *Independent*, 24 July 1996.
62 *Independent on Sunday*, 20 July 1997.
63 *Guardian*, 6 April 1996.
64 *Daily Mirror*, 15 April 1996.
65 *Guardian*, 17 June 1995.
66 *Independent*, 2 January 1995.
67 *Guardian*, 8 July 1996.
68 *Daily Mail*, 4 July 1996.
69 *Independent*, 15 May 1995.
70 *Daily Mail*, 12 September 1996.

chapter 9 not just for the few

1 *Daily Mail*, 9 March 1995.
2 Christopher Lasch, *Women and the Common Life*, ed. Elizabeth Lasch-Quinn, London, Norton, 1997, p167.
3 MORI/*Mail on Sunday* survey on sexual politics, *Mail on Sunday*, 25 June 1995.
4 Christabel Pankhurst, *Unshackled*, London, Hutchinson, 1959, p57.
5 Ibid., pp66–7.
6 'Humble Petition of the Poor Spinners', 1780, from Sheila Lewenhak, *Women and Trade Unions*, London, Ernest Benn, 1977, p17.
7 *Leeds Mercury*, 4 May 1833, from Sheila Lewenhak, op. cit., p33.
8 Sheila Lewenhak, op. cit., p32.
9 Hansard 1844, vol. 73, 1096, in Sheila Lewenhak, op. cit., pp 54–5.
10 *Daily Chronicle*, August 1911, from Michelene Wandor, ed., *The Body Politic*, London, Stage 1, 1972, p217. *See also* Sheila Rowbotham, *Hidden from History*, London, Pluto Press, 1973; and Sally Alexander, *Becoming a Woman and other Essays in 19th and 20th Century Feminist History*, London, Virago, 1994.
11 Margaret Llewelyn Davies, ed., *Life As We Have Known It*, by Co-operative Working Women, 1931, London, Virago, 1977, p132. *See also* Jean Gaffin and David Thoms, *Caring and Sharing: The Centenary History of the Co-operative Women's Guild*, Manchester, Co-operative Union, 1983.
12 Sheila Lewenhak, op. cit., p247.
13 Sheila Lewenhak, op. cit., p284.
14 Olive Banks, *Faces of Feminism*, 1981, Oxford, Blackwell, 1988, p222.

15 Ibid.
16 *Daily Telegraph*, 7 July 1995.
17 *Daily Mail*, 17 September 1997.
18 Robert Taylor, *The Future of the Trade Unions*, London, TUC, 1994, pp58–9.
19 Northern News Report on Equal Opportunities, November 1993.
20 *Guardian*, 4 December 1994.
21 Interview with author.
22 Interview with author.
23 Alice Russell, interviewed by Marina Cantacuzino in 'The Young Ones', *Guardian*, 23 July 1996.
24 Kate Atkinson, *Behind the Scenes at the Museum*, London, Doubleday, 1995.
25 Catherine Cookson, *The Golden Straw*, London, Bantam, 1993.
26 Pat Barker, *Blow Your House Down*, Virago 1984, p99.
27 Catherine Hakim, 'The Myth of Rising Female Employment', *Work Employment and Society* 7, 1993, pp97–120.
28 Catherine Hakim, 'Explaining Trends in Occupational Segregation: the Measurement, Causes and Consequences of the Sexual Division of Labour', *European Sociological Review* 8, 1992, pp127–52.
29 MORI poll, 'Sex in the Professions,' carried out for Hays Personnel Services, November 1994, reported in *Guardian*, 14 November 1994.
30 'Housewives Endure Slow Torture', *Guardian*, 28 January 1994.
31 Susan Harkness, Stephen Machin and Jane Waldfogel, 'Evaluating the Pin Money Hypothesis', Discussion Paper no. 108, Welfare State Programme, Centre for Economic Performance, London School of Economics, 1995.
32 'Families and Work', 1994, Factsheet 3, quoted in Helen Wilkinson and Ivan Briscoe, *Parental Leave*, London, Demos, 1996.
33 Susan McRae, *Maternity Rights in Britain*, Policy Studies Institute, 1991, pp6–7.
34 Patricia Hewitt, *About Time*, London, Institute of Public Policy Research, 1993, p12.
35 Survey carried out by the Grey advertising agency, reported in *Evening Standard*, 27 November 1996.
36 *Guardian*, 27 March 1996.
37 *Daily Mail*, 27 March 1996.
38 *Guardian*, 29 March 1996.
39 *Daily Telegraph*, 17 January 1996.
40 *Guardian*, 19 September 1995.
41 From Helen Wilkinson, *Through the Eyes of Shopfloor Workers*, London, Demos, 1995, p5.
42 1991 Census figures; the proportion of single-parent families is thought to be much higher now.

chapter 10 **where do we go from here?**

1 Heather Joshi, Hugh Davies and Hilary Land, *The Tale of Mrs Typical*, London, Family Policy Studies Centre, 1996.
2 *Low Income Statistics: Low Income Families 1989–1992*, London, HMSO, 1995.
3 Eleanor Rathbone, *The Disinherited Family*, 1924, new edition, Bristol, Falling Wall Press, 1986, p52.
4 Quoted in Sheila Rowbotham, *The Past is Before Us*, 1989, London, Penguin, 1990, p45.

5 Survey by Professional Personnel Consultants, reported in *Daily Mail*, 7 October 1996.

6 *Common Cause*, 27 February 1914, quoted in Jill Liddington and Jill Norris, *One Hand Tied Behind Us*, London, Virago, 1978, p260.

7 Shulamith Firestone, *The Dialectic of Sex*, 1970, London, The Women's Press, 1979, p193.

8 Virginia Woolf, *To the Lighthouse*, 1927, London, Everyman, 1991, p39.

9 Doris Lessing, *The Golden Notebook*, 1962, London, Flamingo, 1993, p303.

10 J. A. Seltzer, 'Relationships Between Fathers and Children who Live Apart: the Father's Role after Separation', *Journal of Marriage and the Family*, 1991, cited in Adrienne Burgess and Sandy Ruxton, *Men and Their Children*, London, Institute for Public Policy Research, 1996, p39.

11 MORI Socioconsult survey, cited in Helen Wilkinson and Geoff Mulgan, *Freedom's Children*, London, Demos, 1995, p45.

12 Amitai Etzioni, *The Spirit of Community*, 1993, London, Fontana/HarperCollins, 1995, p70.

13 Charles Handy, *The Empty Raincoat*, London, Hutchinson, 1994, p170.

14 Ibid., p185.

15 Robert Reich, *The Work of Nations*, New York, Knopf, 1991, cited in Handy, op. cit., p202.

16 Charles Leadbeater and Geoff Mulgan, 'The End of Unemployment', *Demos Quarterly* Issue 2, 1994.

17 Helen Wilkinson and Geoff Mulgan, op. cit., p43.

18 Isabel Boyer, 'Flexible Working for Managers', Chartered Institute of Management Accountants, 1993, quoted in Helen Wilkinson, *No Turning Back: Generations and the Genderquake*, London, Demos, 1994, p14.

19 S. Burgess and H. Rees, *Lifetime Jobs and Transient Jobs: Job Tenure in Britain*, 1994, cited in Helen Wilkinson and Geoff Mulgan, *Freedom's Children*, London, Demos, 1995, p40.

20 Charles Handy, op. cit., p73.

21 *Daily Mail*, 17 August 1995.

22 Heather Joshi, Hugh Davies and Hilary Land, op. cit., p18.

23 Helen Wilkinson and Geoff Mulgan, op. cit., pp55–56.

24 Adrienne Burgess, *Fatherhood Reclaimed*, London, Vermilion/Random House, 1997, p57.

25 Heather Joshi, Hugh Davies and Hilary Land, op. cit., pp18–19.

26 *Independent*, 29 January 1997.

27 *Daily Mail*, 28 November 1995.

epilogue the future is feminist

1 Winifred Holtby, 'Ladies in Restaurants', *Guardian*, 28 March 1930, in Vera Brittain and Winifred Holtby, *Testament of a Generation*, ed. Paul Berry and Alan Bishop, London, Virago, 1985, p.68.

2 Rebecca West, *The Fountain Overflows*, 1957, London, Virago, 1984, p277.

3 H. G. Wells, *Ann Veronica*, 1909, London, Everyman, 1993, pp94–5.

4 Jane Austen, *Pride and Prejudice*, 1813, Harmondsworth, Penguin, 1981, pp294, 305 and 312.

index